MW01056176

HIGH-RISE
BUILDING
STRUCTURES

N T8875NT

HIGH-RISE BUILDING STRUCTURES

WOLFGANG SCHUELLER
SCHOOL OF ARCHITECTURE
SYRACUSE UNIVERSITY

A WILEY-INTERSCIENCE PUBLICATION
JOHN WILEY & SONS
NEW YORK • LONDON • SYDNEY • TORONTO

Copyright © 1977 by John Wiley & Sons, Inc.

All rights reserved.   Published simultaneously in Canada.

Reproduction or translation of any part of this work beyond
that permitted by Sections 107 or 108 of the 1976 United States
Copyright Act without the permission of the copyright owner
is unlawful. Requests for permission or further information
should be addressed to the Permissions Department, John
Wiley & Sons, Inc.

Library of Congress Cataloging in Publication Data:

Schueller, Wolfgang, 1934–
     High-rise building structures.

     "A Wiley-Interscience publication."
     Bibliography: p.
     Includes index.
     1. Tall buildings.   2. Structural engineering.
I. Title.

TH845.S37   690   76-28734
ISBN 0-471-01530-X

Printed in the United States of America

10 9 8 7 6 5 4 3

To My Parents

Preface

The aim of this book is to present an orderly survey of high-rise building structures. The organization of various building skeletons is derived from the anatomy of their structural components. Actually built or proposed tall structure systems are compared in plan, elevation, and three-dimensional view. The geometrical order of the building structure is interpreted in terms of its response to external force action, which is rather complex as the related literature indicates. This book translates this complex field of structural engineering into simplified language understandable by anyone concerned with the construction of buildings.

Since the behavior of tall structures is highly indeterminate, primary emphasis is given to visual and descriptive analysis. The quantitative analytical approach is used as an important analogue for approximating the qualitative behavior of the building structure. The mathematics (slide rule accuracy) and the engineering mechanics are kept to a basic level. Different types of building components are designed approximately based on simple considerations of current American Concrete Institute (ACI), American Institute of Steel Construction (AISC), and Structural Clay Products Institute (SCPI) Specifications, whose respective sections are briefly reviewed.

The complexity of load action on the building is described in Chapter 2. The reader not familiar with the basic principles of high-rise building structures, however, may first want to study the common high-rise building structures in Chapter 3, which introduces tall buildings as related to geometrical principles, historical context, and other design considerations. Chapters 4 and 8 investigate the primary subsystems of the building support structure: the vertical building planes (i.e., frames and walls) and the horizontal planes (i.e., floor structures). Common building structures are discussed from a conceptual point of view in Chapter 5. In Chapter 7 several typical building structures are designed approximately. Chapters 6 and 10 investigate the building forms and structural principles different from the ones commonly used. The prefab element in the context of the building assemblage and as part of the process of construction is briefly dealt with in Chapter 9.

In the analytical portion of the book the structural element is considered in the context of the entire building. This approach should further strengthen the student's understanding of structural behavior, since college courses in structures are often concerned with the analysis and design of component and linkage only and do not consider the actual building context or the building structure as part of an overall structural order.

This book addresses primarily the architect, the principal form giver of the building, who must develop the self-confidence to express the strength and inherent beauty of structure and materials. To gain this sensitivity he must understand the laws of nature as reflected by the play of forces in the building assemblage. That is, he needs a reasonable knowledge of the physical sciences as one very important form determinant and as the necessary basis for constructive collaboration with the structural engineer.

This book is intended as a text for a structure course for college students of architecture or building science; a background in statics and design of concrete and steel elements is required. The many examples of building structures should make the book a helpful reference to studio courses dealing with the design of tall buildings. Furthermore, the book may assist the young engineer, faced for the first time with the design of a building, in developing an intuitive feeling for the structural behavior of the building as a whole. The presentation of actual buildings on a comparative basis (i.e., like a catalog), together with references, should be an asset to the structural engineer and to the architectural designer in practice.

Our treatment of the skyscraper structure is no more than introductory. However it is hoped that through the process of establishing order by discussing performance criteria, the reader will gain an appreciation for high-rise building structures and, as such, will lay the basis for future adaptibility and creative design.

WOLFGANG SCHUELLER

Syracuse, New York
November 1976

Acknowledgments

This book is the outgrowth of a seminar on high-rise building structures conducted by me at the School of Architecture, Syracuse University, during the academic year 1973–1974. I am indebted to the following student participants for their thorough investigation of the different topics and the preparation of many of the drawings under my direction: Nicholas Baldo, Ansar Burney, Brian Buttner, Fred Lorenc, Joseph Peckelis, David Petty, Andrew Quient, Samuel Rashkin, Leslie Reiss, Michael Stellato, Lori Vallario, and David Wildnauer.

My sincere gratitude to Prof. Siegfried Snyder of the School of Architecture at Syracuse University for reading the manuscript and offering criticism and constructive suggestions.

Greatly appreciated is the help of my assistants Pete Blewett, Richard Correll, and Joe Lomonaco, who prepared and corrected many of the illustrations.

I am grateful to the publisher's editorial and production staff for their sincere support.

I acknowledge the contribution of the many individuals whose research or design of buildings has formed the basis for this book. Their names appear in the references and list of illustrations sections; they are too numerous to repeat here.

I thank Sue Merriett for her patience in typing the manuscript of this book, mostly from a first draft typed by Martha Gerwitz, whose help is also very much appreciated.

W.S.

Contents

CHAPTER ONE

Introduction

High-rise buildings are closely related to the city; they are a natural response to dense population concentration, scarcity of land, and high land costs. The massing of the high-rise building evolves out of the designer's interpretation of the environmental context and his response to the purpose of the building. A high-rise building may be free standing—that is, vertical and slender or horizontal and bulky—or it may be placed directly adjacent to other tall buildings, thus forming a solid building block. In both approaches the building is basically an isolated object. However the tall building of the future may very well be an integral part of one large building organism, the city, where the buildings or activity cells are interconnected by multilevel movement systems.

High-rise buildings range in height from below 10 to more than 100 stories. A rather complex planning process is necessary to determine the height or the massing of a building. Some of the factors to be considered are the client's needs versus the land available and the location of the land as related to facets of the environmental context, for example necessary services to support the building and its inhabitants or the ecological impact of the building or the scenic character of the landscape.

THE TALL BUILDING IN THE URBAN CONTEXT

The development of the high-rise building follows closely the growth of the city. The process of urbanization, which started with the age of industrialization, is still in progress in many parts of the world. In the United States this process began in the nineteenth century; people migrated from rural to urban areas, thereby forcing an increase in the density of cities. Technology responded to this pressure with the lightweight steel cage structure, the elevator, and the energy supply systems necessitated by the high density vertical city.

At the beginning of this century building blocks about 20 stories high were set opposite each other, separated only by dark narrow streets, forming urban canyons. Primary concern was the placement of a maximum number of people on a minimum area of land. The resulting congestion and its impact on people and the city as an organic interaction system was hardly a design consideration. The needs for light, air, and open ground level for public activity spaces led to the evolution of the free-standing skyscraper. It is much taller, since it must provide a density at least equivalent to the building block it is replacing. Present technology is far enough advanced to allow construction of the single skyscraper at an economically feasible cost.

From a technological or material space point of view, the design of tall buildings is relatively well understood, however consideration of the behavioral space, that is, identification of human needs and space adaptibility, is still in an early developmental stage. The isolation and lack of contact between people within the building, and the loss of contact with street life, are some of the problems designers are trying to overcome.

Although to some degree the density of tall buildings in cities is now controlled by zoning regulations, this design is not based on the context of the total, dynamic urban fabrics. The consequences to the urban environment of close grouping of tall buildings are of utmost importance. The impact of scale of some of the superskyscrapers on the city, such as the 109-story Sears Tower in Chicago, more than a quarter-mile high, is apparent. The building's electrical system can serve a city of 147,000 people and its air conditioning complex can cool 6000 one-family houses. A total of 102 elevators are needed to distribute about 16,500 daily users to the different parts of the building. Visualize the many elevators as equivalent to a dead-end street system and the sky lobbies as plazas where people pass from one part of the building to another either by nonstop, double-deck, express elevators to the next sky lobby or by local, low speed shuttle elevators. Since the building contains all necessary services and amenities, theoretically the people have never to leave it. The support facilities, such as shopping, entertainment, recreation, health, education, security, transportation, parking, utilities, waste, and sewage services, are equivalent to the services needed for a small city. A building of this scale forms a city within a city. The design of such an intricate interaction system requires systematic programming of social, ecological, economical, and political implications exerted not just on the surrounding urban context but also on its own environment.

For many metropolitan areas, the tall building is the only answer to continuous growth of population concentration. It should not be rejected because of its dehumanizing effects or put aside as a symbol of technological achievement. To the contrary, educational and other research institutions should take much more initiative to systematically investigate the high-rise building environment and its context to improve its living conditions.

THE TALL BUILDING AND ITS SUPPORT STRUCTURE

The design of the tall building, whether for such single uses as apartments, offices, schools, and hospitals or for the larger scale multiple uses just outlined, requires a team approach between the various disciplines of design, material fabrication, and building construction. The architect coordinates the team effort so that the different material, service, and activity components act as a whole. No longer can the architect speak of freedom of design. Not only is he limited by the generally closed form of the skyscraper and the necessity for efficient usage of materials, he must also observe many more specifications related to complex security, fire, and health requirements.

The architect must approach the design of a building as a total system in which the physical support structure as an organic part grows with the design of the building; structure cannot be considered separately as an unrelated addition to be plugged into the functional space later by the engineer. Though this total design approach should apply to the design of any architectural building, it is essential with respect to the scale of a high-rise, which requires rather complex structural support systems where the physical, environmental forces are among the primary design determinants. The building must cope with the vertical forces of gravity and the horizontal forces of wind above ground and the seismic forces below ground. The building envelope has to accommodate the differences in temperature, air pressure, and humidity between the exterior and interior environments. The structural elements of the building must respond to all these forces. The members must be arranged and connected to one another in such a manner as to absorb the forces and guide them safely with a minimum effort to the ground.

The architect who is sensitive to these forces and their sources, and is aware of the nature of structural order, can respond with a reasonable layout in the early design stage. He can communicate with the structural engineer because he talks his language. That is, an architect having a basic understanding of engineering principles can truly collaborate with the structural specialist to achieve the optimum solution.

The structural elements are the necessary bones for the building body, and it is the architect who can manipulate these structural elements and expose them to express clearly the spirit of the building, thus identify and reflect its purpose as an enclosure for the interaction of different activity systems.

CHAPTER TWO

Load Action on High–Rise Buildings

Loads acting on a structure are generated either directly by the forces of nature or by man himself; that is, there are two basic sources for building loads: geophysical and man-made (Fig. 2.1).

The geophysical forces, being the result of continuous changes in nature, may be further subdivided into gravitational, meteorological, and seismological forces. As a result of gravity, the weight of a building itself produces on the structure forces called dead load, and this load remains constant throughout the building's life span. The ever-changing occupancy of a building is also subject to gravitational effects producing a variation of loads over a period of time. Meteorological loads vary with time and location and appear in the form of wind, temperature, humidity, rain, snow, and ice. Seismological forces result from the erratic motion of the ground (i.e., earthquakes).

The man-made sources of loading may be the variations of shocks generated by cars, elevators, machines, and so on, or they may be the movement of people and equipment or the result of blast and impact. Furthermore, forces may be locked into the structure during the manufacturing and construction processes. The stability of the building may require prestressing, which induces forces.

Geophysical and man-made sources for building loads are often mutually dependent. The mass, size, shape, and materials of a building influence the geophysical force action. For instance, if building elements are restrained from responding to temperature and humidity changes, forces are induced into the building.

Careful studies of the building's theoretical response to load actions must be made, to ensure that future problems are eliminated and structural efficiency is achieved. The designer must understand forces and their respective load actions so that the building will be safe and serviceable. The following sections survey forces and their load actions on buildings.

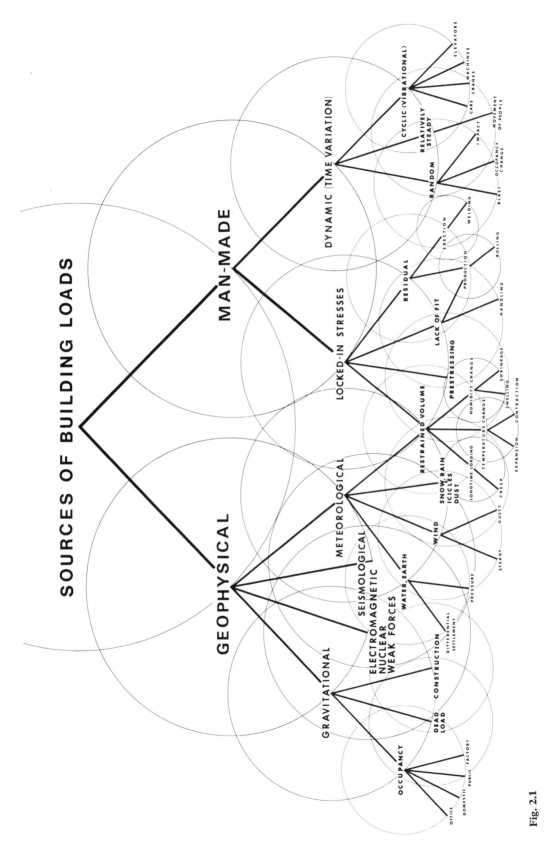

Fig. 2.1

DEAD LOADS

Relative to the gravitational forces to which a building is subjected, loads can be classified into two distinct categories: static and dynamic. Static loads are always a permanent part of the structure. Dynamic loads are all temporary: they change as time and season change, or as a function of spaces within or on a structure.

Dead loads may be defined as the static forces caused by the weight of every element within the structure. The forces resulting in dead load consist of the weights of the load-bearing elements of the building, floor, and ceiling finishes, permanent partitioning walls, facade cladding, storage tanks, mechanical distribution systems, and so on. The combined weights of all these elements make up the dead load of a building.

It appears to be a simple matter to determine the weights of materials, thus the dead load of a structure. However the estimate of dead loads may be in error by 15 to 20% or more because of various problems in making an accurate analysis of the loads (Reference 2.1a). At an early design stage it is impossible for the structural analyst to predict accurately the weight of building materials not yet selected. Specific nonstructural materials to be chosen include prefabricated facade panels, light fixtures, ceiling systems, pipes, ducts, electrical lines, and components of special interior requirements. The weight of stiffening elements and joinery systems for steel structures is estimated only on a percentage basis. The unit weights of materials given by the producers or codes are not always consistent with those of the manufactured product. The nominal sizes of building elements may differ from the actual sizes; the formwork for poured-in-place concrete may have inaccuracies of $\frac{1}{2}$ in.

These few examples indicate that in the absence of precise information, dead loads cannot be accurately predicted.

LIVE LOADS

Live loads differ from dead loads in their character: they are variable and unpredictable. Change in live loads occurs not only over time but also as a function of location. The change may be a short- or long-term one, thus making it almost impossible to predict live loads in statical terms.

Loads caused by the contents of objects within or on a building are called occupancy loads. These loads include allowance for the weights of people, furniture, movable partitions, safes, books, filing cabinets, fixtures, mechanical equipment (e.g., computers, business machines), automobiles, industrial equipment, and all other semipermanent or temporary loads that act on a building system but are not part of the structure and are not considered under dead loads.

Given the potential versatility of high-rise structures, it is nearly impossible to predict the possible live load conditions to which a structure will be subjected. Through experience, survey analysis, and practice, however, recommended load values for various occupanices have been developed. The results are in the form of load table listings given in building codes and featuring built-in empirical safety factors to account for maximum possible loading conditions.

The load values take the form of equivalent uniform loads and prescribed concentration loads. Equivalent uniform loads reflect the varying, actual occupancy loading conditions. The values, established by approximation of actual loads, appear to be rather conservative. A survey taken on the actual occupancy load in various office buildings showed a maximum load of 40 psf versus a recommended design value of 80 psf. A load survey on apartments noted that the maximum load intensity measured in a 10 year period was about 26 psf; the usual value for design, however, is 40 psf (Reference 2.1a).

Concentrated loads indicate possible single load action at critical locations such as on stair treads, accessible ceilings, parking garages (e.g., jack for changing a tire), and other vulnerable areas that are subject to high concentrated stresses.

Although it may appear that the regulations are too conservative, there is always the unpredictable element to consider. The minimum regulated safety factors are warranted by such uncontrollable, extraordinary situations as people crowding because of ceremonies, parties, and fire drills, or overloading of parts of the building due to change of occupancy or furniture and wall rearrangements that will exert more load on a specific area.

The likelihood of having a full occupancy load simultaneously on every square foot of every floor supported by a column is very slim. The actual loading consists of different areas with different loading conditions. Generally, the smaller the area, the larger the potential load intensity. The occupancy loads on floors are never uniform. Building codes take this into account by allowing the use of live load reduction factors. For example, the New York State Building Construction Code (Reference 2.17), excerpted below, allows an 80% occupancy load on the top three floors of a building and a 5% decrease per floor to at least 50% of assumed load. Notice that the 0.08% check permits an increase in the percentage of reduction with a corresponding increase in the amount of contributory area.

C 304-2 **Live Loads**

C 304-2.1 General

b—Where such unusual concentrations do not occur, structural members, and flooring spanning between the supporting structural members, shall be designed to support the uniformly distributed loads or the concentrated loads set forth in Table C 304-2.2, whichever produces the greater stress.

c—Uniformly distributed live loads on beams or girders supporting other than storage areas and motor vehicle parking areas, when such structural member supports 150 square feet or more of roof area or floor area per floor, may be reduced as follows:

When the dead load is not more than 25 psf, the reduction R shall be not more than 20%. When the dead load exceeds 25 psf and the live load does not exceed 100 psf, the reduction shall be not more than the least of the following three criteria:

60%
0.08% for each square foot of area supported
100% times (dead load, DL, psf plus
   live load, LL, psf) divided by (4.33 times live load psf).

$$R = 100 \frac{DL + LL}{4.33 \, LL} = 23.1 \left(1 + \frac{DL}{LL}\right)$$

d—For columns, girders, supporting columns, bearing walls, and foundation walls, supporting 150 square feet or more of roof area or floor area per floor other than storage areas and motor vehicle parking areas, the uniformly distributed live loads on these members shall be not less than the following percentages of the total live loads on the following levels:

80% on the roof
80% on the floor immediately below the roof
80% on the second floor below the roof
5% decrease for every floor (75% from the third floor to
   55% to the seventh floor below the roof)
50% on the eighth, ninth, tenth, and subsequent floors
   below the roof.

Codes do not take into account that live load action on a building element is reduced because of the ability of the continuous building structure to redistribute loading as it deforms. On the other hand, the load capacity of buildings is reduced, since they are subject to fatigue brought about by years of combating wind loads, vibrations, temperature changes, settlement, and the continuous change of environmental forces. However the concrete and masonry materials have the advantage of gaining strength with age, therefore increasing their loading capacity.

From a structural standpoint, the choice of an appropriate structural system depends on the knowledge of three factors:

• The loads to be carried.

• The property of the construction materials.

• The structural action by which the load forces are transferred through the members into the ground.

Bearing in mind these three elements, the structural designer uses realistic models to predict material and structural behavior; however empirical code values are used to predict loading intensities. This seems to be contradictory, since the economy of construction and materials is considered in one case and neglected in the other. Future research will make possible more accurate prediction of actual loading conditions.

CONSTRUCTION LOADS

Structural members are generally designed for dead and live loads; however a member may be subject to loads larger by far than the design loads during erection of a building. These loads, called construction loads, constitute an important consideration in the design of structural elements.

Every contractor has developed a construction process proved to him to be economical. Although an architect may design a building to suit a particular construction system, he may not know the individual practices of the contractor. Contractors commonly stockpile heavy equipment and materials on a small area of the structure. This causes concentrated loads that are much larger than the assumed live loads for which the structure was designed. Structural failures have resulted from such conditions.

A major problem in concrete construction results when the contractor fails to allow sufficient curing time before removal of shoring and formwork. Concrete increases its strength with time; but since time is money to the contractor, he may remove the forms before the concrete has reached its minimum design strength, whereupon the structural element may be subject to loads it is unable to support, and failure may result.

Construction loads also must be considered for a beam designed to act compositely with a concrete slab, assuming that no temporary shoring is used during the construction process. In this case, the beam has to be checked with respect to carrying construction loads in noncomposite action.

For precast concrete, the most critical period is at the lifting of a heavy panel element from its form. The number of lifting points and their placement must be known. Also, since the element has to be designed for any possible position it may encounter during handling and erection, impact and stress at that time must be considered.

SNOW, RAIN, AND ICE LOADS

Observation of the depth and density of snowfalls over many years has resulted in a reasonable prediction of maximum snow

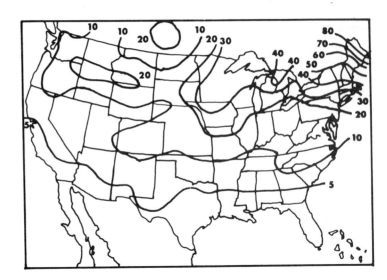

Fig. 2.2. Minimum snow loads (psf).

loads. The U.S. Weather Bureau (Fig. 2.2) indicates the minimum snow loads for various regions, in pounds per square foot, ranging from 5 psf in the South to 80 psf in the northeastern United States. One inch of snow weighs approximately 0.5 to 0.7 psf, depending on its density. Refer to local codes for information on snow characteristics of a particular area.

Snow loads need be considered only for roofs and other areas of a building that may gather snow, such as elevated courtyards, balconies, and sun decks. The snow loads, as established by codes, are based on the maximum snow on the ground. In general these loads tend to be higher than the snow loads acting on a roof, since the wind blows the loose snow off the roof or the snow melts and evaporates because of heat loss through the roof skin. Codes generally allow a percentage reduction of the load value on pitched roofs, since the snow can easily slide off the roof. However certain roof conditions may influence the behavior of the wind, resulting in high snow load accumulations locally.

Water, though not often thought of when calculating live load, should certainly be kept in mind when designing. Rain loads in general are less than snow loads, but it should be remembered that the accumulation of water, weighing 62.4 lb/ft³, will result in appreciable loads. Heavy loads can occur on flat roofs because of clogged drains. As water accumulates, the roof deflects, allowing more water to collect, and resulting in more deflection. This process is called ponding and may cause the eventual collapse of the roof.

Ice will collect on protruding elements, especially on exterior ornamental elements that otherwise receive no load other than their own. It is therefore necessary to design and secure such elements to withstand heavy loads of icicles. Furthermore, the ice formation on open-trussed structures will increase the area as well as the weight, resulting in larger wind pressure.

WIND LOADS

The first skyscrapers were not vulnerable to the complex consequences of lateral action caused by wind. The enormous weight of the masonry bearing wall building was such that wind action could not overcome the locked-in-gravity forces. Even when the bearing wall system was replaced by the rigid frame structure in the late 1800s, gravity remained the prime determining factor. Heavy stone facades with small openings, closely spaced columns, massive built-up frame members, and heavy partition walls still generated so much weight that wind action was not a major problem.

The glass-walled skyscraper of the 1950s with its optimum interior open space and relatively small weight was first to respond to the complexity of wind forces. With the introduction of the lightweight steel frame, weight was no longer a factor limiting the potential height of buildings. The era of the high-rise building, however, has brought with it new problems. To reduce dead weight and create larger, more flexible spaces, longer spanning beams, movable non-load-bearing interior partitions, and non-load-carrying curtain walls have been developed. All these innovations have taken away from the overall rigidity of the structure; now the lateral stiffness (i.e., lateral sway) of a building may be a more important consideration than its strength. Wind action has become a major problem for the designer of high-rise buildings.

To understand the wind and predict its behavior in precise scientific terms may be impossible. Wind action on a building is dynamic and is influenced by such environmental factors as large-scale roughness and form of terrain, the shape, slenderness and facade texture of the structure itself, and the arrangement of adjacent buildings. How do all these elements influence the speed, direction, and behavior of the wind as it acts on a building?

Wind Velocity

The dynamic character of the wind is illustrated in Fig. 2.3. Wind velocity readings were recorded at a specific height on a building, indicating two phenomena: a generally constant mean wind velocity and a varying gust velocity. Hence the wind has two components, one static and one dynamic.

The mean wind velocity in general increases with height, as Fig. 2.4 reveals. The rate of increase in the mean velocity is a function of the ground roughness, however, since wind is retarded near the ground by friction. The greater the interference by surrounding objects (i.e., trees, land forms, buildings), the higher the altitude at which maximum velocity V_{max} will occur (Reference 2.7).

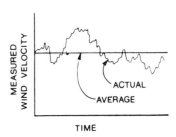

Fig. 2.3

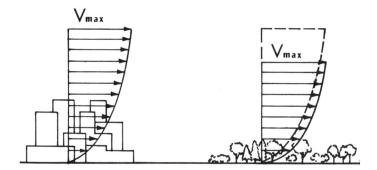

Fig. 2.4

Wind Loading as Related to Building Codes

Extensive research into the prediction of wind action on high-rise buildings is now being conducted. Building codes, however, still reflect a static approach to the dynamic action of the wind. Wind pressure values are given as functions of maximum annual mean wind velocities, in miles per hour, 30 ft above ground, for a 50 year recurrence interval. The maximum regional wind values (Fig. 2.5) are published by the U.S. Weather Bureau.

The pressure generated by the wind on a building is calculated from the formula

$$p = 0.002558(C_D)(V)^2 \qquad (2.1)$$

where p = pressure (psf) on a building face
$\quad\quad\ C_D$ = shape coefficient
$\quad\quad\ V$ = maximum mean velocity (mph)

The shape coefficient C_D depends on the form of the building and the roof slope. For rectangular buildings $C_D = 1.3$, which includes the pressure effect acting on the windward face (0.8) and the suction effect present on the leeward side (0.5) of the structure. The New York State Building Construction Code

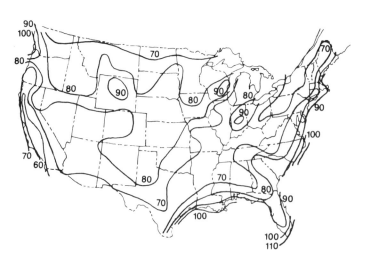

Fig. 2.5. Maximum wind velocities
30 ft above ground (mph).

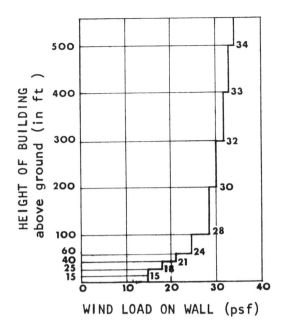

Fig. 2.6. New York State Code, Minimum Wind Loads for Rectangular Buildings.

gives minimum required wind loads as a function of the height of the building. The code values (Fig. 2.6) are for rectangular buildings and are based on the mean wind velocity of 75 mph at 30 ft above the ground.

The preceding formula gives the wind pressure on a rectangular building 30 ft above ground with a wind velocity $V = 75$ mph as

$$p = 0.002558(1.3)(75)^2 = 18.7 \text{ psf}$$

This pressure value compares with the code requirements given above.

For buildings hexagonal or octagonal in plan, tabular values may be reduced by 20%. For buildings that are round or elliptical in plan, values may be reduced by 40%.

The code approach is insufficient in predicting the true complexity of wind action because it fails to consider the dynamic nature of gust effects or the impact of the physical context on wind behavior.

Designers must develop a better conceptual understanding of the dynamic character of wind behavior. The main types of wind action affecting high-rise buildings are discussed in the following sections.

Topography as a Wind Pressure Determinant

A study conducted on the Earth Sciences Building at the Massachusetts Institute of Technology demonstrates several types of wind action and provides special insight into topographical elements affecting air movement (Reference 2.15).

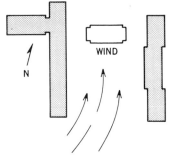

Fig. 2.7. M.I.T. Center (Reference 2.15, p. 262).

The M.I.T. Center is located in the center of a large court-yard north of the Charles River. To the east and west are rows of lower four- or five-story buildings. It was observed that high pressure airflow repeatedly blew off the river and moved north-ward through the courtyard even before the tower was con-structed (Fig. 2.7).

Since construction, the M.I.T. Center has experienced unusu-ally large wind velocities around and through the building. Especially critical is the wind action prevalent in the 21 ft high arcade at the base of the structure. At times wind velocities reach such proportions that pedestrians find it difficult to walk by the building or open doors to it. In an attempt to explain these occurrences, wind tunnel studies were made, using scale models. The following results were recorded.

As a positive high pressure air mass moved from the Charles River, across the courtyard, it encountered the M.I.T. Center, creating a high pressure zone on the windward face. Wind tunnel studies (Fig. 2.8) demonstrated that wind pressure was highest at the center of the windward face where wind motion almost stopped, lessening as the wind velocity increased toward the edge of the surface (Fig. 2.8b).

The location of the arcade was significant in that the opening was placed on the windward surface at a point where maximum wind pressure was normally observed (Fig. 2.8a). In addition, the opening created an exit for a high pressure air mass to an area normally characterized by low pressure because of its location on the leeward side of the building (Fig. 2.8c). In combining these findings it is easy to see why wind velocities recorded in and around the building's arcade were at times twice the normal wind velocity of the area.

Fig. 2.8. Wind pressure readings recorded as isobars on M.I.T. Center (Reference 2.15 p. 262).

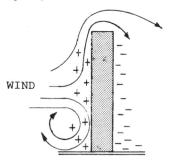

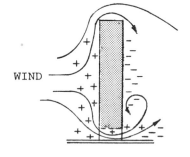

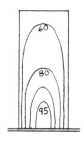

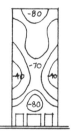

One may conclude that wind velocity—that is, wind pressure—does not necessarily increase with height as is assumed by building codes. Pressure is greatest at midheight of the building (Fig. 2.8b) with the arcade, or at the base (Fig. 2.8a) if there is no opening.

Wind Direction

All building movement is in response to wind direction. When an air mass moving in a given direction contacts a building surface, an overturning force is created. This overturning force is wind pressure, and it can become greater either by an increase in wind velocity or by an increase in the area of the obstructing surface.

Substantial wind action on more than one building face may cause double flexure in the building (Fig. 2.9b). The primary wind direction can be separated into two components showing the resulting wind action on each building face.

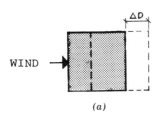
(a)

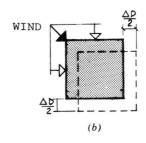
(b)

Fig. 2.9. (a) Unidirectional displacement. (b) Double flexure.

Double flexure may have either positive or negative effects on building motion. The multidirectional displacement may be less than it would have been if the same airflow had encountered the building on only one face.

The aerodynamic design of the building may also help to alleviate building displacement in double flexure. Wind pressure is always greatest when the wind direction is perpendicular to the building face. Hence when the airflow strikes the building surface at other than 90° to the face, much of the wind force is naturally dissipated.

Wind loads induced by double flexure, however, also place additional shear and torsional stresses on the structural members that do not develop in unidirectional displacement.

Wind Pressure

The wind pressure originates from two components previously defined: mean velocity and gust velocity. Since static mean velocities are averaged over longer periods of time, the resulting wind pressures are also average pressures and exert a steady

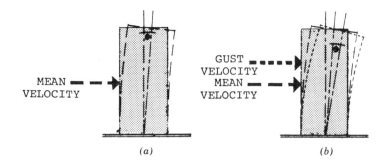

MEAN —— —→
VELOCITY

GUST ▪▪▪▪▪▪→
VELOCITY
MEAN —— —→
VELOCITY

Fig. 2.10. (*a*) Steady (Static) deflections. (*b*) Dynamic movement.

(*a*)

(*b*)

deflection on the building (Fig. 2.10). The dynamic gust velocities produce correspondingly dynamic wind pressures that create additional displacement possibly equal to the steady deflection of the building; for slender buildings they may become dominant! Such dynamic movement is called gust buffeting. The random forces created by gust action induce building oscillation generally parallel to the wind direction.

Turbulence

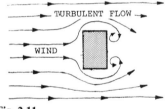

Fig. 2.11

When any moving air mass meets an obstruction, such as a building, it responds like any fluids by moving to each side, then rejoining the major airflow. Wind velocity increases as the larger air mass moves through a constant area at the same given time, and turbulent air currents develop (Fig. 2.11).

The Venturi effect, illustrated in Fig. 2.12, is one type of turbulent wind action. Turbulence develops as the moving air mass is funneled through the narrow space between two tall buildings. The corresponding wind velocity in this space exceeds the wind velocity of the major airflow.

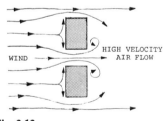

Fig. 2.12

In any turbulent airflow positive air pressures are recorded as long as the air is in contact with the building's surface. When the building face is too sharply convex or the airflow is too rapid, however, the air mass will leave the surface of the building, creating dead air zones of negative pressure. Vortices and eddies are circular air currents generated by turbulent winds in these low pressure areas. Such currents are shown in Fig. 2.13 on the leeward side of the building; the chamfered corners on the windward side allow a much smoother transition of the wind.

Vortices are high velocity air currents that create circular updrafts and suction streams adjacent to the building. As the periodic shedding of vortices about the building approaches the natural frequency of the structure, oscillation occurs. The resulting motion is generally transverse to the direction of the wind (Fig. 2.14).

The shedding frequency is a function of the shape and size of the building and often can be reduced by the use of rough textured walls and/or irregular building shapes.

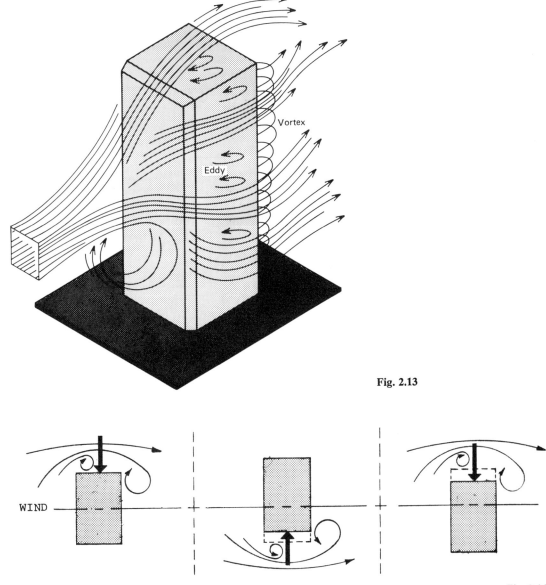

Fig. 2.13

Fig. 2.14

Eddies, though formed much the same as vortices, are slow moving circular air currents creating little perceivable building motion.

Human Tolerance to Wind Action

Human tolerance to wind action both inside and outside buildings has become an increasingly important factor in the design of high-rise buildings.

Excessive lateral sway that a building's structural system may be able to withstand still must be reduced to the acceptable limits for human use. Some inhabitants in existing buildings have experienced motion sickness caused by building sway; people feel the movement and sense the twisting of the building. In some restaurants atop tall buildings wines are not clear when served because wind action has caused sediment to be stirred up. At times minor damage to furniture and equipment has occurred, strange creaking sounds from shaking elevator shafts and air leakage around windows were noticed, and unpleasant whistling of wind around the sides of the building itself was heard.

In several buildings in the 40- to 50-story range in New York City, excessive lateral sway and noise have made it impossible for people to work at their desks. Employees are regularly excused from work during high wind storms.

Strange occurrences observed outside high-rise buildings also cause discomfort and annoyance to both inhabitants and neighbors. Changes in the local wind character such as vortex currents formed in the wake of tall buildings have torn wash from clotheslines, damaged gardens, wrenched opened doors off automobiles, and scattered debris through the air. Some building occupants find it impossible to use balconies except on totally calm days because of constantly turbulent winds on the building face. Worse yet, windows can be smashed or sucked from buildings, causing serious injury or death to people walking below.

The list of examples can go on and on. What is important, however, is the need to recognize that a concern for human tolerance and the activities to be performed in and around the building must be a major factor in the design of today's high-rise buildings.

Conclusion

The true complexity of wind action on tall buildings is just beginning to be investigated. To find acceptable answers to the problems that are now apparent, designers must attempt to overcome the present limitations through the following avenues of investigation:

- Wind tunnel studies using general models to establish a data bank of information for wind behavior and wind loading.

- The derivation of scientific formulas and theory models tested against the wind tunnel data.

- Modification of existing building concepts through material or structural damping, flexural control, facade treatment, and building form.

SEISMIC LOADING

The earth's crust is not static; it is subject to constant motion. According to the geological theory of plate tectonics, the surface of the earth consists of several thick rock plates that float on the earth's molten mantle. New tectonic plates are continuously formed along the deep rift valleys of the ocean floor, where molten material from the earth's interior is pushed upward, thus building up the edges of the oceanic plates to cause the so-called continental drift; that is, the ocean plates are pushed against the continental plates. Where the plates collide they may be locked in place, thus being temporarily prevented from moving by the frictional resistance along the plate boundaries. Stresses are built up along the plate edges until sudden slippage due to elastic rebound or fracture of the rock occurs, resulting in a sudden release of strain energy that may cause the upper crust of the earth to fracture along a certain direction and form a fault (Fig. 2.15). Some of that energy is propagated in the form of shock waves in all directions. It is this wave motion that is known as earthquake. It is apparent that a fault which has suffered from earthquakes in the past is most likely subject to future disturbances.

The regions in the United States having a history of earthquakes are identified in Fig. 2.18. Across the more critical areas, a network of automated sensing stations equipped with instruments such as seismographs and tiltmeters is distributed to record any seismic motion. This monitoring grid can locate the focus of an earthquake—that is, its location deep in the earth's crust where the rupture originated, and the epicenter that lies on the earth's surface directly above the focus. The network also records the point of highest wave intensity, which is generally centered around the fault and thus can be far away from the epicenter. The ground motion is measured by the strong-motion accelerograph, a device specifically sensitive to the intensities of

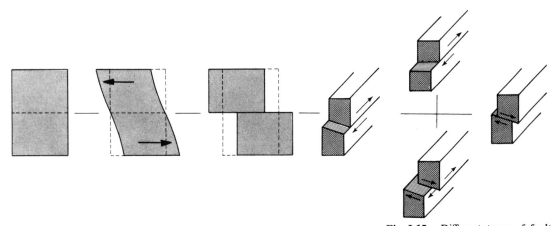

Fig. 2.15. Different types of faulting.

ground movement most likely to affect structures. It records three components of ground acceleration, two horizontal (such as north–south and east–west) and one vertical. Acceleration is measured as a percentage of the acceleration of gravity G.

These measurements are the basis for earthquake-resistant building design; to ensure the protection of human life, a building must survive earthquakes without collapsing. The probability of seismic hazard in any given region is accounted for by provisions of the Uniform Building Code, which is discussed later in this chapter.

Building Behavior During Earthquakes

Since the foundation is the point of contact between the building and the earth, seismic motion acts on the building by shaking the foundation back and forth. The mass of the building resists this motion, setting up inertia forces throughout the structure; the action is similar to the lateral inertia experienced by a person in a car that stops suddenly. This is obviously an oversimplification, since seismic motion also acts to distort the foundation and to shake it back and forth. Vertical inertia forces are ignored, however, since buildings are already designed for static vertical loading. Thus we consider only horizontal forces that may exceed the wind forces acting on a structure. The practice of neglecting vertical forces, especially at a building location close to the surface rupture of a fault, is currently being reexamined.

The magnitude of the horizontal inertia force F (Fig. 2.16) depends on the building's mass M, ground acceleration A, and the nature of the structure (Reference 2.9). If a building and its foundation were rigid, it would have the same acceleration as the ground; that is, by Newton's law, $F = MA$.

In reality, this is never the case, since all buildings are flexible to some degree. For a structure that deforms only slightly, thereby absorbing some energy, the force may be less than the product of mass and acceleration (Fig. 2.16b). But a very flexible structure, having a natural period near that of the ground waves, may be subject to a much larger force under repetitive ground

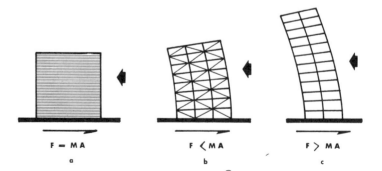

Fig. 2.16

motion (Fig. 2.16c). Thus the magnitude of lateral force action on a building is not caused by the acceleration of the ground alone but by the type of response of the building structure and its foundation, as well. This interrelationship of building and ground motion is expressed in the so-called response spectrum.

Visualize different building types to be represented by single degree of freedom oscillators of various periods, that is, cantilever pendulums of various heights (Fig. 2.17a). These oscillators are mounted to a movable base that is shaken back and forth in a cyclic motion similar to actual recorded seismic waves (Reference 2.9). The maximum response of each oscillator is plotted as a function of the natural period of vibration, yielding a curve as shown in Fig. 2.17b. The maximum response of the oscillators may be represented in terms of acceleration, velocity, deflection, or force action. Since all structural systems by their very nature contain damping mechanisms, the response of the oscillators is largely reduced, especially for continuing repetitive motion.

The application of the response spectrum to actual building structures depends on how closely the behavior of a simple oscillator simulates the complex action of a building. Because

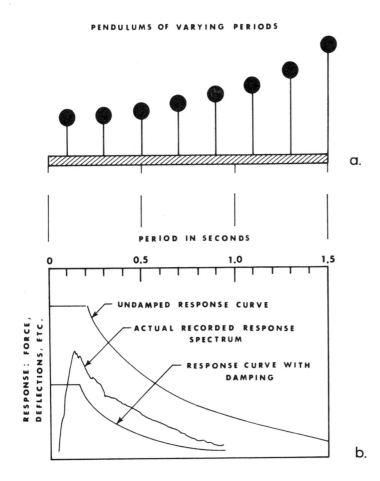

Fig. 2.17

of lack of more information, present codes use the response spectrum as a simple way to predict the maximum building response as caused by earthquake motion. The Uniform Building Code makes use of the seismic coefficient, which responds roughly in shape to the response spectra of some recorded earthquakes and reflects the fact that taller buildings, like taller pendulums, have a longer period of vibration, thus are subject to smaller inertia forces than stiff, short buildings having short periods.

Provisions of the Uniform Building Code (Reference 2.13)

The code uses equivalent horizontal static forces to design a building for maximum earthquake motion.

Total Lateral Force

According to the Uniform Building Code using Newton's second law of motion,

$$\text{force} = \text{mass} \times \text{acceleration} = M(A) = \left(\frac{W}{g}\right) A = W(C)$$

Hence

total lateral force
   = seismic coefficient × total dead weight of the building

where seismic coefficient $C = \dfrac{\text{acceleration due to earthquake } A}{\text{acceleration of gravity } g}$

This basic formula is modified by two other factors taking into account seismic region and type of construction to yield the total base shear V:

$$V = ZKCW \tag{2.2}$$

where Z = seismic probability zone factor
   K = horizontal force factor
   C = seismic coefficient
   W = total dead load (plus 25% floor live load for warehouses)

The seismic coefficient is taken as

$$C = \frac{0.05}{(T)^{1/3}} \tag{2.3}$$

and C is taken as 0.1 for all one- and two-story buildings. The shape of the seismic coefficient appears in Fig. 2.17b.

   In equation 2.3, T is the fundamental period of vibration of the structure, in seconds, in the direction under consideration. The value of T can be computed or measured by sophisticated methods; at the stage of preliminary design, however, T cannot be known. On the basis of measurements made on many existing structures, an approximation of T has been formulated:

$$T = \frac{0.05h_n}{(D)^{1/2}} \qquad (2.4)$$

where h_n = building height (ft) above base
D = dimension of the building (ft) in a direction parallel to the applied force

In the case of a moment-resisting space frame that resists 100% of lateral forces and is not connected to more rigid elements,

$$T = 0.10N \qquad (2.4a)$$

where N is the total number of stories above grade in the main portion of the structure.

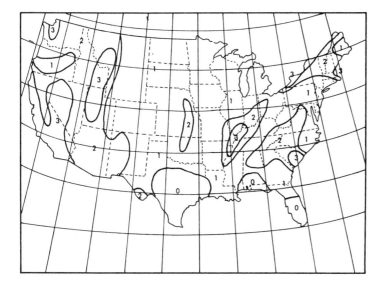

Fig. 2.18. Seismic risk map.

The seismic probability zone factor Z is based on the Uniform Building Code seismic probability map (Fig. 2.18). Values of Z are as follows:

$Z = 0$ in zone 0 (no damage)
$Z = \frac{1}{4}$ in zone 1 (minor damage)
$Z = \frac{1}{2}$ in zone 2 (moderate damage)
$Z = 1$ in zone 3 (major damage)

The horizontal force factor K depends on the type of structural system employed; it ranges from 0.67 to 1.33 as based on the past performance of the structure evaluated empirically rather than on a quantitative basis. The high energy absorbing, ductile, moment-resisting frame responded quite well and thus has the low factor, whereas the rigid shear wall structure was assigned the high factor because it experiences a higher degree of damage (Table 2.1).

Table 2.1

Structural Type	K-Value
1. All systems not otherwise classified.	1.00
2. Buildings with a box system: lateral forces resisted by shear walls.	1.33
3. Buildings with a dual bracing system of ductile moment-resisting space frame plus shear walls, meeting these criteria:	0.80
a. The frame and shear walls shall resist lateral force in accordance with their relative rigidities.	
b. Shear walls acting alone shall be able to resist total lateral force.	
c. The frame acting alone shall be able to resist 25 % of total lateral force.	
4. Ductile moment-resisting space-frame, capable of resisting total lateral force.	0.67

Lateral Distribution of Base Shear

The formula $V = ZKCW$ does not indicate how the shear force is distributed throughout the height of the structure. The shear force at any level depends on how the structure deforms, that is, on the mass at that level and the amplitude of oscillation, which may be assumed to vary linearly with height of the building. That is, earthquake forces deflect a structure into certain shapes known as the natural modes of vibration. Related to the shape of each mode is a certain distribution of lateral forces. As long as there is no large inelastic deformation, instantaneous lateral forces are found by superposition of the forces resulting from each mode (Reference 2.9). Sometimes the forces add and sometimes they cancel one another. The resulting maximum shear envelope is shown in Fig. 2.19*b*. The Uniform Building

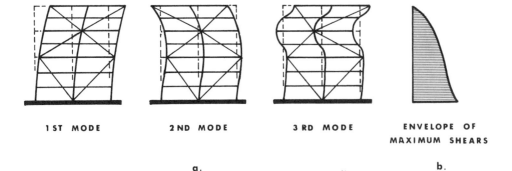

1 ST MODE   2 ND MODE   3 RD MODE   ENVELOPE OF
MAXIMUM SHEARS

a.   b.

Fig. 2.19. Vibration mode shapes of a building.

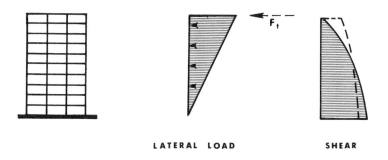

LATERAL LOAD   SHEAR

Fig. 2.20. Lateral seismic force distribution according to Uniform Building Code.

Code uses a triangular lateral load distribution for symmetrical building structures with equal floor weights and heights (Fig. 2.20). Notice the similarity of the maximum shear envelope (Fig. 2.19b) to the shear diagram due to triangular loading (Fig. 2.20).

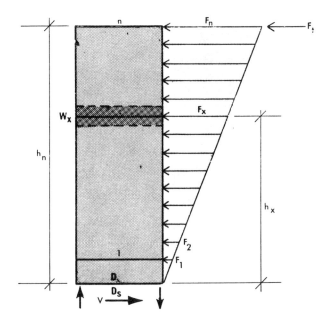

Fig. 2.21

The formula given by the Uniform Building Code for distribution of the base shear may be developed as follows (Fig. 2.21):

let $V = ZKCW$ = base shear
$\quad F_x$ = force at level x
$\quad h_x$ = height (ft) above base to level x
$\quad w_x$ = load assigned to level x

If w is taken to be constant for every floor, then the force F is proportional to height h:

$$\frac{F_1}{h_1} = \frac{F_2}{h_2} = \frac{F_3}{h_3} = \cdots = \frac{F_x}{h_x}$$

Horizontal equilibrium yields

$$V = F_1 + F_2 + \cdots + F_n$$

However, $F_1 = h_1(F_x/h_x)$, $F_2 = h_2(F_x/h_x)$, and so forth, so that

$$V = \frac{F_x}{h_x}(h_1 + h_2 + \cdots + h_n)$$

Solving for F_x yields

$$F_x = \frac{Vh_x}{h_1 + h_2 + \cdots + h_n}$$

or

$$F_x = V \frac{h_x}{\sum_{i=1}^n h_i}$$

Taking into account that weight is not constant for every floor, the final formula for shear at level x becomes

$$F_x = V \frac{h_x w_x}{\sum_{i=1}^n h_i w_i} \qquad (2.5)$$

Recognizing the whiplash effect of slender buildings, the code places part of the base shear as an extra concentrated force at the top of the building.

If h_n/D_s is greater than 3, where D_s is the width of the lateral force-resisting system (ft), the extra force at top of the building is

$$F_t = 0.004V \left(\frac{h_n}{D_s}\right)^2 \le 0.15V \qquad (2.6)$$

In this case the formula for F_x becomes

$$F_x = \frac{h_x w_x}{\sum_{i=1}^n h_i w_i}(V - F_t) \qquad (2.7)$$

Exception: One- and two-story buildings are assumed to have uniform lateral force distribution.

Lateral Forces on Parts of Buildings

The Uniform Building Code specifies that parts of buildings and their anchorages are to be designed on the basis of the formula

$$F_p = ZC_p W_p \qquad (2.8)$$

where F_p = lateral force on the part being considered
Z = zonal probability factor
W_p = weight of the part being considered
C_p = coefficient as determined from Table 2.2

Table 2.2

Part of Structure	Value of C_p
1. Interior and exterior bearing and nonbearing walls	0.20 (force normal to surface)
2. Cantilever parapet walls	1.00 (force normal to surface)
3. Ornamentations, appendages	1.00 (force in any direction)
4. Floors and roofs acting as diaphragms	0.10 (any direction)
5. Connections for exterior panels	2.00 (any direction)
6. Connections for prefabricated structural elements, other than walls	0.30 (any horizontal direction)

Additional Code Requirements

Pile Foundations

Individual pile or caisson footings shall be interconnected by ties, each capable of carrying in tension or compression a horizontal force equal to 10% of the larger pile cap loading.

Distribution of Horizontal Shear

Total shear in any horizontal plane shall be distributed to the elements of the lateral force resisting system in proportion to the rigidities of those elements.

Horizontal Torsional Moments

Provisions shall be made for the increase in shear resulting from the horizontal torsion due to eccentricity between the center of mass and the center of rigidity. Negative torsional shears are to be neglected. Shear resisting elements shall be able to resist a torsional moment equal to the story shear acting with an eccentricity of 5% of the maximum building dimension at that level.

Overturning

Every building shall be designed to resist overturning caused by wind or earthquake, whichever governs. Moments can be calculated from the triangular load distribution formula. However the loading is based on an envelope of maximum shears and may be less at any moment in time. Thus earthquake overturning moments may be reduced by the coefficient

$$J = \frac{0.5}{(T)^{2/3}} \leq 1 \qquad (2.9)$$

The overturning moment at the base of the buildings is

$$M = J\left(F_t h_n + \sum_{i=1}^{n} F_i h_i\right) \qquad (2.10)$$

Buildings Taller than 160 ft

Such buildings shall have a ductile moment-resisting space frame capable of resisting at least 25% of the required seismic force of the total structure. All buildings designed with a K-factor of 0.67 or 0.80 shall have a ductile moment-resisting space frame of structural steel or cast-in-place reinforced concrete. Reinforced concrete frames must meet certain special code requirements.

Other Design Requirements

* All portions of structures shall be designed and constructed to act as a unit in resisting horizontal forces, unless separated structurally by a distance sufficient to avoid contact under deflection from seismic or wind forces.

* Masonry or concrete elements resisting seismic forces shall be reinforced.

* Only roof live load may be neglected when considering the effect of seismic forces in combination with vertical loads.

* Concrete or masonry walls shall be anchored to all floors and roofs providing lateral support for the wall, for a minimum force of 200 lb per linear foot of wall.

* Interior partitions shall be designed for a minimum force of 10 psf applied perpendicular to the partitions.

The following points may be added to the requirements of the Uniform Building Code just outlined:

* A structure designed to have ductility, or the ability to undergo inelastic deformation, will have increased seismic resistance.

- Since earthquake motion causes rapid stress reversals in structural members, the structure must be able to withstand the effects of fatigue.

- Structural continuity of the entire building is essential, in case individual members fail.

- Consider use of special damping devices.

- The mass of the building should be uniformly distributed; any discontinuous structural parts should be avoided. Building plans should be simple to prevent complicated torsional vibrations and stress concentrations at intersection of different building parts (Fig. 2.22).

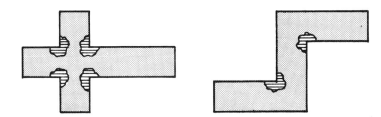

Fig. 2.22

- Since a structure with significant flexibility has a longer period of vibration than a stiffer building, it may be subject to less force. However a building that is too flexible may deflect noticeably from wind and moderate earthquakes, causing nonstructural damage and psychological discomfort to the occupants.

Seismic design is still based largely on trial and error. Researchers are constantly trying to find more accurate ways of prediction and new ways to respond to earthquakes. Some of the shortcomings of the current code approach are as follows:

- Most records of earthquakes are measurements taken far away from the location of high intensity waves.

- The values for the periods of buildings are independent of the geology of the site; certain soil conditions can amplify the period of vibration of the structure.

- The response spectrum neglects the duration of the force action. The seismic coefficient attempts to consider dynamic effects but often does not reflect actual motion records; it has largely underestimated spectrum values of several earthquakes.

- The structure is assumed to behave elastically under dynamic loading. Under strong earthquakes, however, a building will deform partially inelastically, dissipating part of the seismic force action. In consequence, buildings are often observed to resist forces far greater than their rated capacity on the basis of elastic analysis. The reserve strength provided by inelastic deformation should allow the designer to lower the seismic coefficient. However the role of inelastic deformation is not yet well enough understood to enable an accurate reduction of the coefficient.

- The damping factor is not constant: it changes with the age of the building and the amplitude of vibration.

- Code formulas apply methods of static analysis to dynamic conditions. This does not account for the different behavior of materials under static and dynamic loadings.

- The frequence of building vibration is affected by "non-structural" elements, such as nonbearing partitions that increase a building's stiffness.

Following, several earthquake problems are solved to exemplify the application of the Uniform Building Code.

PROBLEM 2.1 (FIG. 2.23)

Determine the critical lateral loads for a rigid frame building 120 ft long with the frames spaced at 30 ft on center. Story heights are 10 ft. The weight of each floor is assumed to be constant, $w_1 = w_2 = w_3 = 1600$ k. The building is located in seismic zone 3. Consider only the lateral forces acting against the long facade.

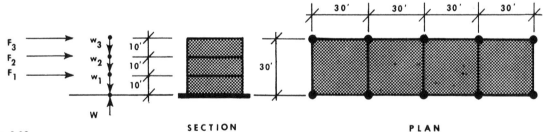

SECTION   PLAN

Fig. 2.23

A. Lateral Loads Due to Earthquake

Zone coefficient: $Z = 1$ (zone 3)
Horizontal force factor (moment-resisting steel frame): $K = 0.67$
Total building weight: $W = 3 \times 1600 = 4800$ k

Fundamental period: $T = 0.05 h_n / (D)^{1/2}$
$$= 0.05(30)/(30)^{1/2} = 0.274 \text{ sec}$$
$$\leq 0.1N = 0.1(3) = 0.30 \text{ sec} \qquad (2.4)$$

Seismic coefficient: $C = 0.05/(T)^{1/3}$
$$= 0.05/(0.274)^{1/3} = 0.077 \qquad (2.3)$$

Total base shear: $V = ZKCW$
$$= (1)(0.67)(0.077)(4800) = 248 \text{ k} \qquad (2.2)$$

Distribution of base shear along building height:

$$F_x = V \frac{h_x w_x}{\sum_1^n h_i w_i} \qquad (2.5)$$

In equation 2.5

$$F_x = V \frac{h_x w_x}{h_1 w_1 + h_2 w_2 + h_3 w_3} = V \frac{h_x}{h_1 + h_2 + h_3}$$

since $w_1 = w_2 = w_3 = w_x$

$$F_x = 248 \frac{h_x}{10 + 20 + 30} = 4.13 h_x$$

The lateral forces are

at 10 ft above base: $F_1 = 4.13 h_1 = 4.13(10) = 41.3 \text{ k}$
at 20 ft above base: $F_2 = 4.13 h_2 = 4.13(20) = 82.6 \text{ k}$
at 30 ft above base: $F_3 = 4.13 h_3 = 4.13(30) = 123.9 \text{ k}$

Check: $\sum H = 0$: $V = F_1 + F_2 + F_3$
$248 = 41.3 + 82.6 + 123.9$
$248 = 247.8$ OK

Note that F_x is proportional to height h_x because of uniformity of loads (Fig. 2.25).

B. Lateral Loads Due to Wind

According to the New York State Building Code (Fig. 2.6), wind loads are

15 psf for 0–25 ft above grade
18 psf for 26–40 ft above grade

The wind pressure is distributed as shown in Fig. 2.24.

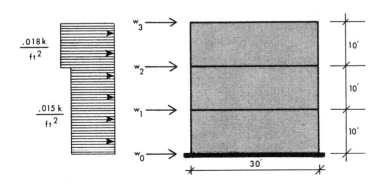

Fig. 2.24

The wind forces at different floor levels for a contributing building width of 30 ft are

$$w_0 = 0.015(10/2)\,(30) = \qquad\qquad\qquad\qquad 2.25\text{ k}$$
$$w_1 = 0.015(10)\,(30) \quad = \qquad\qquad\qquad\qquad 4.50\text{ k}$$
$$w_2 = 0.015(10/2)\,(30) + 0.018(10/2)\,(30) = \quad 4.95\text{ k}$$
$$w_3 = 0.018(10/2)\,(30) = \qquad\qquad\qquad\qquad 2.70\text{ k}$$

$$\text{total wind load per bay} \qquad\qquad 14.40\text{ k}$$

The wind force acting on the whole building is

$$W_T = 4(14.40) = 57.60\text{ k}$$

The seismic loads are greatly in excess of wind loads:

$$V = 248\text{ k} > W_T = 57.6\text{ k}$$

Check overturning moments as based on controlling earthquake loads. Consider the base shear as the resultant of a triangular lateral load distribution (Fig. 2.25).

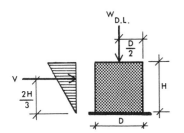

Fig. 2.25

The reduction factor J to be applied to earthquake moments is

$$J = \frac{0.5}{(T)^{2/3}} = \frac{0.5}{(0.274)^{2/3}} = \frac{0.5}{0.42} = 1.2 > 1.0 \qquad (2.9)$$

Take $J = 1$.

The acting moment due to earthquake forces is

$$M_{\text{rot}} = V\left(\frac{2H}{3}\right)J = 248\left(\frac{2}{3}\right)(30)\,(1) = 4960\text{ ft-k}$$

The counteracting moment generated by the weight of the building is

$$M_{\text{res}} = W_{DL}\left(\frac{D}{2}\right) = 4800\left(\frac{30}{2}\right) = 72{,}000\text{ ft-k}$$

The safety factor against overturning is

$$\text{S.F.} = \frac{M_{\text{res}}}{M_{\text{rot}}} = \frac{72{,}000}{4960} = 14.5 > 1.5 \qquad\qquad \text{OK}$$

PROBLEM 2.2

Determine the critical lateral loads for the four-story building shown in Fig. 2.26. The structure is of the box type, meaning that lateral forces are distributed by roof and slab diaphragms and resisted by exterior shear walls. The building is located in seismic zone 2. Assume following dead loads:

roof and floors: 0.1 ksf
8-in. masonry wall (120 lb/ft³): 0.08 ksf

The walls are assumed to be of constant thickness.

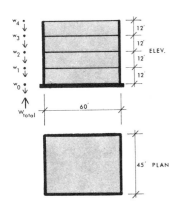

Fig. 2.26

The dead load for each level is equal to the weight of floor or roof plus the weight of walls from midstory to midstory.

A. Lateral Loads Due to Earthquake

Plan area $= (45)(60) = 2700 \text{ ft}^2$
Total building perimeter $= 2(60) + 2(45) = 210 \text{ ft}$
Contributory wall areas

  roof: $A_{wr} = 210(6) = 1260 \text{ ft}^2$
  floors: $A_{wf} = 210(12) = 2520 \text{ ft}^2$

Dead loads

  roof: $w_4 = 2700(0.1) + 1260(0.08) = 371 \text{ k}$
  floors 1, 2, 3: $w_1 = w_2 = w_3 = 2700(0.1) + 2520(0.08) = 472 \text{ k}$
  ground floor: $w_0 = 1260(0.08) = 101 \text{ k}$

The ground floor weight must be included in the total building weight, although no seismic load is assigned to the base of the ground level.

$$W_{total} = w_0 + w_1 + w_2 + w_3 + w_4 = 101 + 3(472) + 371$$
$$= 1888 \text{ k}$$

Zone coefficient: $Z = 0.5$ (zone 2)
Horizontal force factor (box-type shear wall structure): $K = 1.33$
Fundamental period
  in longitudinal direction

$$T_L = \frac{0.05 h_n}{(D)^{1/2}} = \frac{0.05(48)}{(60)^{1/2}} = 0.31 \text{ sec} \qquad (2.4)$$

  in transverse direction

$$T_T = \frac{0.05 h_n}{(D)^{1/2}} = \frac{0.05(48)}{(45)^{1/2}} = 0.357 \text{ sec}$$

Seismic coefficient C

$$C_L = \frac{0.05}{(T_L)^{1/3}} = \frac{0.05}{(0.31)^{1/3}} = 0.0737$$

$$C_T = \frac{0.05}{(T_T)^{1/3}} = \frac{0.05}{(0.357)^{1/3}} = 0.0704 \qquad (2.3)$$

To be conservative, use the greater value for C

$$C_L = 0.0737$$

Total base shear: $V = ZKCW$
$$= (0.5)(1.33)(0.0737)(1888) = 92.4 \text{ k} \quad (2.2)$$

Check: $\dfrac{h}{D} = \dfrac{48}{45} < 3$

No extra lateral force is assigned to the top level:

$$F_{top} = 0$$

Distribution of base shear along building height:

$$F_x = V \frac{h_x w_x}{\sum_1^n h_i w_i} \tag{2.5}$$

Here $\sum hw = 12(472) + 24(472) + 36(472) + 48(371) = 51{,}784$
The lateral forces are

at 12 ft above base: $F_1 = \dfrac{92.4(12)(472)}{51{,}784} = 10.2$ k

at 24 ft above base: $F_2 = \dfrac{92.4(24)(472)}{51{,}784} = 20.3$ k

at 36 ft above base: $F_3 = \dfrac{92.4(36)(472)}{51{,}784} = 30.4$ k

at 48 ft above base: $F_4 = \dfrac{92.4(48)(371)}{51{,}784} = 31.9$ k

Check: $\sum H = 0$: $V = F_1 + F_2 + F_3 + F_4$

$92.4 = 92.8$ OK

B. Lateral Loads Due to Wind

According to the New York State Building Code (Fig. 2.6) wind loads are:

15 psf for 0–25 ft above grade
18 psf for 26–40 ft above grade
21 psf for 41–60 ft above grade

The distribution of wind forces is shown in Fig. 2.27.

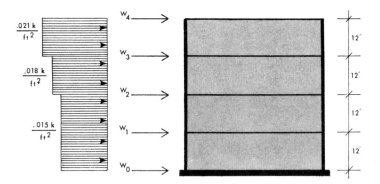

Fig. 2.27

The wind forces at different floor levels for a contributing building width of 60 ft are as follows:

$w_0 = 15(60)(6)/1000 =$	5.4 k
$w_1 = 15(60)(12)/1000 =$	10.8 k
$w_2 = [18(60)(6) + 15(60)(6)]/1000 =$	11.9 k
$w_3 = [21(60)(6) + 18(60)(6)]/1000 =$	14.0 k
$w_4 = 21(60)(6)/1000 =$	7.6 k

The wind force on the whole building is: 49.7 k

$$W_T = 49.7 \text{ k} < V = 92.4 \text{ k}$$

The total seismic load exceeds total wind load, even when comparing the higher earthquake pressure acting against the 45 ft facade with the higher wind pressure against the 60 ft facade.

Check overturning moments.

reduction factor J to be applied to earthquake moments

$$J = \frac{0.5}{(T)^{2/3}} = \frac{0.5}{(0.31)^{2/3}} = 1.09 > 1.0 \qquad (2.9)$$

Take $J = 1$

The acting moment due to earthquake forces as caused by triangular load distribution is

$$M_{\text{rot}} = V\left(\frac{2H}{3}\right) = 92.4\left[2\left(\frac{48}{3}\right)\right]1 = 2960 \text{ ft-k}$$

The overturning moment due to wind forces is

$$M_{\text{rot}} = w_4(48) + w_3(36) + w_2(24) + w_1(12) + w_0(0)$$

$$= 7.6(48) + 14.0(36) + 11.9(24) + 10.8(12)$$

$$= 1283 \text{ ft-k} < 2960 \text{ ft-k}$$

The overturning moment due to seismic forces is critical.
The counteracting moment generated by the weight of the building is

$$M_{\text{res}} = W_{DL}\left(\frac{D}{2}\right) = 1888\left(\frac{60}{2}\right) = 56.640 \text{ ft-k}$$

The safety factor against overturning is

$$\text{S.F.} = \frac{M_{\text{res}}}{M_{\text{rot}}} = \frac{56,640}{2960} = 19.15 > 1.5 \qquad \text{OK}$$

PROBLEM 2.3 (FIG. 2.28)

Determine the critical lateral loads for a 25-story rigid frame building. For reasons of simplicity assume average story height as 12 ft and average dead load as 0.195 ksf. The building is located in seismic zone 3.

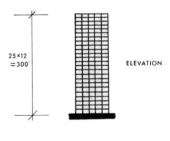

A. Lateral Loads Due to Earthquake

Zone coefficient: $Z = 1$ (zone 3)
Horizontal force factor (moment-resisting steel frame): $K = 0.67$
Total building weight: $W = 25(0.195)(100)(175) = 85,400 \text{ k}$

Fundamental period: $T = 0.1(N) = 0.1(25) = 2.5 \text{ sec}$ (2.4a)

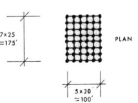

Seismic coefficient: $C = \dfrac{0.05}{(T)^{1/3}} = \dfrac{0.05}{(2.5)^{1/3}} = 0.0369$ (2.3)

Fig. 2.28

Problem 2.3 (Fig. 2.28)   35

Total base shear:

$$V = ZKCW \qquad (2.2)$$

$$= (1)\,(0.67)\,(0.0369)\,(85,400) = 2120 \text{ k}$$

$$\frac{h}{D} = \frac{300}{100} = 3 \leq 3$$

No whip effect on top of building, $F_{top} = 0$; therefore use equation 2.5.

The distribution of base shear along building height is

$$F_x = V\frac{h_x w_x}{\sum_1^n h_i w_i} = V\frac{h_x}{\sum_1^n h_i} \qquad \text{because of constant floor weight}$$

Here

$$\sum h = 1(12) + 2(12) + \cdots + 25(12)$$

$$= 12(1 + 2 + 3 + \cdots + 25)$$

$$= 3900 \text{ ft}$$

$$F_x = \frac{2120 h_x}{3900} = 0.543\, h_x$$

The lateral forces at 25th and 24th floor levels are

$$F_{25} = 0.543(300) = 163 \text{ k}$$

$$F_{24} = 0.543(288) = 156.5 \text{ k}$$

The forces at the following floor levels may be obtained by subtracting 6.5 k per floor.

Check at base of first floor level: $F_0 = 163 - 6.5(25) = 0 \quad$ OK

B. Lateral Loads Due to Wind

According to New York State Building Code, wind loads are as follows:

15 psf for 0–25 ft above grade
18 psf for 26–40 ft above grade
21 psf for 41–60 ft above grade
24 psf for 61–100 ft above grade
28 psf for 101–200 ft above grade
30 psf for 201–300 ft above grade

The wind pressure is distributed as shown in Fig. 2.29.

$$\begin{aligned}
w_1 &= (0.015)\,(24)\,(175) &= &\quad 63.0 \text{ k}\\
w_2 &= (0.018)\,(12)\,(175) &= &\quad 37.8 \text{ k}\\
w_3 &= (0.021)\,(24)\,(175) &= &\quad 88.2 \text{ k}\\
w_4 &= (0.024)\,(36)\,(175) &= &\quad 151.2 \text{ k}\\
w_5 &= (0.028)\,(96)\,(175) &= &\quad 470.0 \text{ k}\\
w_6 &= (0.030)\,(108)\,(175) &= &\quad 566.0 \text{ k}
\end{aligned}$$

total wind load $\quad W_T = 1376.2$ k

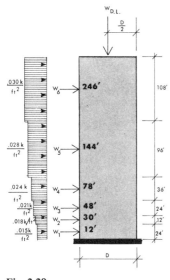

Fig. 2.29

$$V = 2120 \text{ k} > W_T = 1376.2 \text{ k}$$

The seismic load is in excess of wind load.

Check overturning moments.

Overturning moment due to seismic forces may be reduced by factor

$$J = \frac{0.5}{(T)^{2/3}} \tag{2.9}$$

$$= \frac{0.5}{(2.5)^{2/3}} = 0.272$$

The acting moment due to earthquake forces as based on triangular load distribution is

$$M_{rot} = V\left(\frac{2H}{3}\right)(J) = 2120(200)\,(0.272) = 115{,}000 \text{ ft-k}$$

The counteracting moment generated by the weight of the building is

$$M_{res} = W_{DL}\left(\frac{D}{2}\right) = 85{,}400\left(\frac{100}{2}\right) = 4{,}270{,}000 \text{ ft-k}$$

The overturning moment due to wind forces is

$$M_{rot} = 63(12) + 37.8(30) + 88.2(48) + 151.2(78)$$
$$+ 470(144) + 566(246)$$

$$= 226{,}040 \text{ ft-k} > 115{,}000 \text{ ft-k}$$

The overturning moment due to wind forces is critical.

Safety factor against overturning:

$$\text{S.F.} = \frac{M_{res}}{M_{rot}} = \frac{4{,}270{,}000}{226{,}040} = 18.89 > 1.5 \qquad \text{OK}$$

WATER AND EARTH PRESSURE LOADS

Structures below ground are subject to loads that differ from those encountered above ground. The substructure of a building must support lateral pressures caused by earth and ground water. These forces act perpendicularly to the substructure walls and floors.

The water pressure at any point on a foundation structure is equal to the unit weight of the liquid (62.4 lb/ft³) multiplied by the distance from the water level to the depth in question. In Fig. 2.30 with a ground water table 15 ft below grade, the maximum water pressure at the intersection of wall and foundation is

$$P_{max} = \gamma H = 62.4(39) = 2433.60 \text{ psf/ft of wall}$$

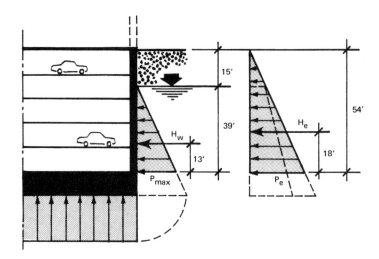

Fig. 2.30. Lateral earth and water pressure on building substructure.

The total lateral water pressure is

$$H_w = \frac{2433.60(39/2)}{1000} = 47.46 \text{ k/ft of wall}$$

The maximum lateral water pressure at the base of the foundation is equal to the buoyancy pressure attempting to lift the building. In the early stages of construction the upward lift is of major concern. The basement floor slab has to be designed for the uplift force.

The lateral pressure exerted by the earth on the wall may be considered to act similarly to water pressure: an equivalent liquid pressure is assumed. The magnitude of lateral earth pressure is dependent on the type of soil. For dry soils, an equivalent liquid pressure of 30 psf/ft of depth may be used as a rough first approximation.

The maximum lateral earth pressure acting on the wall in Fig. 2.30 is

$$P_E = 30(54) = 1620 \text{ psf/ft of wall}$$

The resultant maximum force is

$$H_E = 1.62 \left(\frac{54}{2}\right) = 43.74 \text{ k/ft of wall}$$

This oversimplified approach does not consider the buoyant weight of the earth below the ground water level, which is equal to the weight of the soil minus the weight of the water displaced by the soil.

Additional lateral wall pressure may be caused by surcharge loads on the ground surface (e.g., street) or by the swelling (creeping) of certain soils (e.g., clays), or it may be generated by the thrust caused by ice if the ground water table is above the frost line. Lateral forces will be increased during an earthquake, which vibrates and accelerates the ground.

LOADS DUE TO RESTRAINED
VOLUME CHANGES OF MATERIAL

Material volume changes are generated by shrinkage, creep, and temperature effects. When the natural response of building members at their boundaries is prevented, loads result. Axial and rotational stresses are then induced in the building where these volume changes are restrained. Volume change is a function of the form and size of the building, the material, the stiffness of the structural members, and the mode of connection. Volume changes can be controlled by applying restraint at building locations where axial and rotational stresses may develop, that means, the members are designed to resist these stresses. Volume changes, obviously, can be controlled by allowing free movement through the use of expansion joints.

Temperature Loads

Until the 1940s the structure in skyscrapers was concealed behind a facade within a temperature controlled environment and not susceptible to temperature change. Following World War II, a new design aesthetic developed, exposing the structural frame in order to decrease building weight and cost. With this trend, high-rise buildings are less rigid and are highly vulnerable to temperature-induced loading and movement; the structural facade is exposed now to the controlled temperature of the interior building environment and the daily and seasonal changes of the weather. This temperature differential causes vertical movement in the building envelope, that is, contraction for temperature drop and expansion for temperature increase. Horizontal movement of floor structures is caused by the roof structure exposed to the temperature differential of exterior and interior environment and by the difference in temperatures of opposing facades, one being exposed to the sun and the other protected from the sun.

Types of Column Exposure

The degree of exposure on any exterior column is critical to the potential thermal movement caused by temperature effects. Interior temperatures remain generally constant, whereas the exterior temperatures often respond in a dynamic manner. Hence as column exposure to the outside air becomes greater, the possibility for critical thermal movement also increases. Fig. 2.31 shows the four basic types of column exposure in order of increasing thermal response to ambient temperatures.

The degree of exposure of the column, thus its behavior, is related both to the location of the column and to the type of cladding material used. That is, the ambient temperature of a

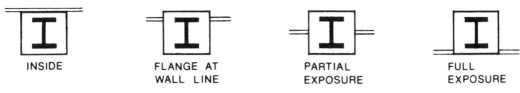

INSIDE   FLANGE AT   PARTIAL   FULL
          WALL LINE   EXPOSURE   EXPOSURE

Fig. 2.31. Column exposures.

steel column in response to air temperature is directly related to the thermal resistance of any material surrounding the column. Various types of column insulation have been devised to control the temperature differential across a column.

The greatest temperature changes in a steel column exist in the web where heat from the warm inside flange is rapidly conducted to the cold outside flange, thus producing bending. The ideal solution when insulating an exterior column is to create a uniform temperature across the column so that differential stresses do not develop. Three basic types of cladding details for a partially exposed column are discussed below (Reference 2.19a).

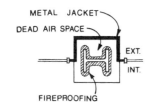

Fig. 2.32

Simple Cladding (Fig. 2.32)

Column insulation of this type is least effective because the air surrounding the column responds readily to the temperature of the metal cladding, which is highly susceptible to the effects of exterior temperatures. Insulation of this type should not be used in buildings more than 10 stories high.

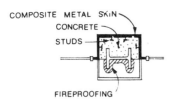

Fig. 2.33

Columns Encased in Concrete with Exterior Cladding (Fig. 2.33)

A seamless composite skin is created, offering effective insulation as well as increased structural rigidity.

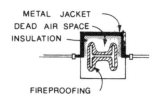

Fig. 2.34

Insulated Cladding (Fig. 2.34)

The insulation of the cladding controls the transition of outside temperature to the column. Furthermore, a nonventilated air space is created between the cladding and column providing good insulation for the column.

The differential movement of columns, independent of their location, can be influenced by the use of mechanical or physical control mechanisms. This aspect is discussed later in this section.

Types and Effects of Temperature-Induced Movement

Many types of building movement are related to temperature effects. A building's response to any temperature-induced movement is proportional to the number of floors in the structure. Critical response to temperature loads will lessen as structural rigidity is increased. Vertical and horizontal temperature action must always be considered in buildings taller than 30 stories. Some of the effects of temperature induced movements are as follows:

Column Bending (Fig. 2.35)

The interior to exterior temperature differential, called temperature gradient, causes unequal stresses in exterior columns which cause bending.

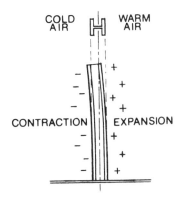

Fig. 2.35

Differential Movement Between Interior and Exterior Columns (Fig. 2.36)

A vertical displacement occurs between the interior and exterior columns as changes in the gradient temperature create either expansion or contraction along the exterior column line. Interior column temperatures generally remain constant (72°F), whereas exterior column temperatures may vary from −20°F to 120°F depending on the locality.

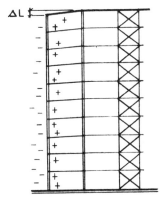

Fig. 2.36

Differential Movement Between Exterior Columns (Fig. 2.37)

Differential vertical movement may appear between columns having different external surface exposures such as for corner columns.

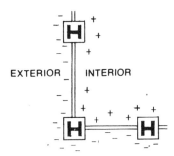

Fig. 2.37

Floor Wracking (Fig. 2.38)

Floor wracking is caused in a rigid frame structure by any vertical change in the exterior columns. This differential movement is cumulative and always greatest at the uppermost exterior bay. As differential movement in a structure occurs, windows, curtain walls, and partitions are particularly sensitive to load action and material separation. The use of flexible partition material and/or slip joints can control possible damage caused by temperature movement.

Differential Movement Between Roof and Lower Floors (Fig. 2.39)

The differential expansion and contraction between the exposed roof plane and lower floors may cause shear cracks in a masonry bearing wall structure or column bending in a rigid frame building.

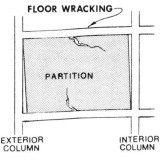

Fig. 2.38

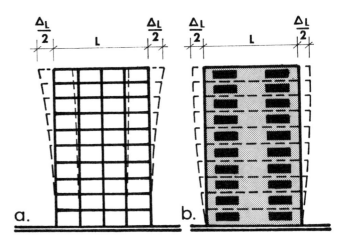

Fig. 2.39

Designing for Temperature Loads

When any material of a specified shape is allowed to respond to the ambient temperature, the internal stresses generated are a function of the change in length permitted.

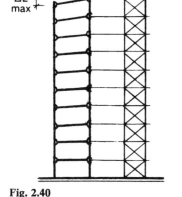

Fig. 2.40

A. When totally unrestricted expansion or contraction is allowed, the internal stresses are equal to zero. The hinging of top floors allows unrestricted movement to occur, but this may not be possible in high-rise buildings because of the considerable reduction in stiffness (Fig. 2.40).
B. When total restraint is maintained and material change is prohibited, the internal stresses are at a maximum.
C. When partial restraint is applied, but not so as to produce a rigid condition, internal stresses are greater than zero but less than maximum. This system is most widely used because it takes into account the relative displacement that can be tolerated by partitions and building finishes.

It is recommended by Faslur R. Khan and Anthony F. Nassetta (Reference 2.19a) that the thermal movement between exterior steel columns and interior columns be limited to

$$\Delta L_{\text{ALLOW}} = \Delta L_{\text{EXT}} - \Delta L_{\text{INT}} \leq \frac{L_{\text{BM}}}{300} \quad \text{or } 0.75 \text{ in.} \quad (2.11)$$

where ΔL_{EXT} = exterior column displacement
ΔL_{INT} = interior column displacement
L_{BM} = distance between columns

PROBLEM 2.4

A 50-story building has a height of $H = 650$ ft. The temperature change of the steel column $\Delta_t = 40°F$ is equal to the difference between the inside temperature and the average steel column temperature which, in turn, is a function of the exterior temperature and the exposure conditions of the column. The thermal coefficient of expansion for steel is

$$\alpha = 6.5 \times 10^{-6} \text{ per } °F$$

The free movement in the upper story is

$$\Delta L_1 = \alpha H \, \Delta_t$$

$$= (6.5 \times 10^{-6})(650)12(40) = 2.03 \text{ in.} \qquad (2.12)$$

Assuming a tolerable deformation of $\Delta L = 0.75$ in. yields

$$(100)\frac{0.75}{2.03} = 37\% \text{ of the totally unrestrained movement.}$$

Hence 63% of the total movement must be taken by the restraint of the structure. The effects of temperature loads must be superimposed with other loads to determine the ultimate building response.

The effect of column shortening on the exterior bay girders of a rigid frame is represented in Fig. 2.41 in an oversimplified manner. The moments in the beams are

$$M_{BM} = \frac{6EI_{BM}}{L_{BM}^2}(\Delta L) \qquad (2.13)$$

The beam moment is equivalent to

$$M_{BM} = V_{BM}\left(\frac{L}{2}\right)$$

Hence the constant beam shear is

$$V_{BM} = \frac{12EI_{BM}}{L_{BM}^3}(\Delta L) \qquad (2.14)$$

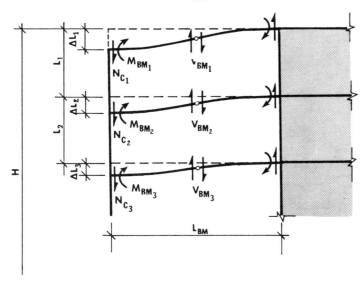

Fig. 2.41

The preliminary beam inertia I_{BM} can be obtained from the gravity case.

The axial force in the exterior column at the top floor is obtained from $\Delta L = NL/AE$ and thus is

$$N_{c_1} = \frac{A_{c_1}E}{L_1}(\Delta L_1 - \Delta L_2)$$

Vertical equilibrium at top floor level yields the additional column area to cover temperature stresses.

$$N_{c_1} = V_{BM_1}$$

$$A_{c_1} = \frac{12L_1I_{BM_1}}{L_{BM}^3}\left(\frac{\Delta L_1}{\Delta L_1 - \Delta L_2}\right)$$

Substituting equation 2.12 yields

$$A_{c_1} = \frac{12HI_{BM_1}}{L_{BM}^3}$$

A similar approach can be used for finding the column forces at the other floor levels.

Critical in any restrained volume change is differential movement; there are several means of controlling such action by physical and mechanical restraint.

Physical Restraint

It is possible to obtain physical restraint in the following ways (Reference 2.16).

• COMPENSATING ROOF TRUSS. The rigid truss at the top of a building eliminates differential movement between interior and exterior columns by providing compressive restraint for exterior columns in expansion, and tension restraint when columns are in contraction (Fig 2.42).

• THERMAL BREAK. A compensating truss is placed at central points in the structural frame, ensuring that the total thermal movement along the exterior column line is greatly decreased (Fig. 2.43).

• RESTRAINING FLOOR SYSTEM. Structural rigidity can be increased by applying restraint at each floor level. Restraint of this nature requires deep floor systems (Fig. 2.44).

• RIGID BEAM-TO-COLUMN CONNECTIONS. When rigidly connected beams span between exterior and interior columns, resistance to the free movement of the exterior columns is provided (Fig. 2.45). The amount of counteraction offered by these beams is dependent on their relative stiffness (Problem 2.4).

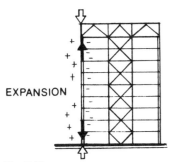

EXPANSION

Fig. 2.42

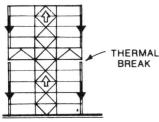

THERMAL BREAK

Fig. 2.43

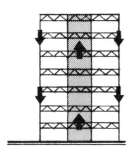

Fig. 2.44

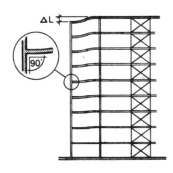

ΔL

$90°$

Fig. 2.45

Except for column insulation, mechanical restraint can be obtained in the following ways (Reference 2.19a):

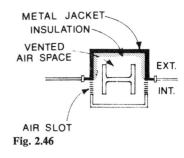

METAL JACKET
INSULATION
VENTED
AIR SPACE
EXT.
INT.
AIR SLOT
Fig. 2.46

• FORCED MECHANICAL VENTILATION. Exterior columns can be mechanically heated by either forced air ventilation or radiant electric elements, to create a constant, uniform temperature around the column, thus eliminating column movement due to temperature changes. The structural system must be designed, however, to supply sufficient natural restraint if mechanical malfunction should occur.

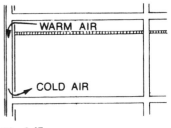

WARM AIR
COLD AIR
Fig. 2.47

• GRAVITY-TYPE VERTICAL AIR CIRCULATION. In buildings exceeding 50 stories, temperature effects on exterior columns are not significantly reduced by any insulation methods using non-ventilated air spaces. Gravity-type air circulation through the column air spaces provides a uniform air temperature corresponding to the controlled interior environment. Openings at the top and bottom of the column shaft at each floor permit a natural circulation of air through the ventilated air space; warm air enters the column at ceiling level, as it cools it drops and leaves the column space at floor level (Figs. 2.46, 2.47).

Creep and Shrinkage

The effects of creep and shrinkage on a structure often are similar to those caused by temperature.

The time-dependent deformation that occurs in concrete for years after the initial loading deformation is creep. The effects of creep are generally confined to concrete but can also occur in steel tendons used in the prestressing of building elements. Under a constant stress, the steel tendons elastically stretch, thereby gradually decreasing the unit stress in the structural element.

Creep in concrete members is dependent on the magnitude of the stress, the length of time that the stress has been applied, and the age and strength of the concrete when the stress is applied. The quality of the concrete and exposure are also significant factors in the amount of creep that will occur.

Material shrinkage is a major cause for volume change in concrete and is generally characterized by a gradual loss of moisture within the concrete members. As shrinkage stresses appear, additional restraint is required which, in turn, places additional loads on the structure.

Material shrinkage may be reduced up to 40%, however, by decreasing the amount of water used in the original mix, by use of high plasticizing admixtures allowing for further reductions in the amount of water required, and by curing the concrete at lower temperatures, so that less water is absorbed into the surrounding air as the concrete hardens.

IMPACT AND DYNAMIC LOADS

A building is subjected to a variety of nonstatic loads. Actually all loads except dead load are variable. However the question is not only how fast a load fluctuates but how much time it takes for the structure to go through one cycle of free vibration (i.e., natural period of the structure).

A load can be considered static if it varies slowly relative to the natural period of the structure (e.g., occupancy loads). Certain building loads have to be considered dynamic relative to the natural period of typical buildings. These vibrational loads may come from within the building or outside it. Internal sources are elevators, escalators, oscillating machinery, mechanical equipment, cars, and cranes. These forces may not be merely cyclic but may be due to sudden acceleration or deceleration of cars or elevators, for instance; considerable impact forces may be imposed on the structure at a given instant. Outdoor sources of vibrational loads are wind and seismic forces, noise (e.g., sonic booms), and nearby traffic systems (e.g., streets, railways, subways, and building bridges). In addition, the skyscraper of today is rather susceptible to these loads, since designers strive for minimum weight. This results in reduced mass and stiffness, that is, in an increase of the natural period of the structure approaching the period of the load. Resonance occurs when the natural period is equal to the period of the source, yielding forces infinitely large.

Notice that in addition to the static element of stiffness, dynamic analysis introduces the dynamic aspect of mass.

The building designer has to control vibrational forces not just by providing the necessary member strength but by isolating the source or damping the movement. The source of vibration can be isolated by separating the source from the structure. Vibrational movement can be damped by controlling the transmission of vibration from one element to another. The continuity of members can be interrupted by resilient isolators (e.g., neopreme pads, lead plates, spring supports, rubber pads, viscoelastic sandwich systems).

Dynamic analysis basically consists of finding the time variation of deflection and the directly related stresses. Instead of performing an accurate dynamic analysis, it is the usual practice for typical cases to provide for these loads by increasing the assumed live load in the area where impact loads are expected to occur. According to the American Institute of Steel Construction Specification for the Design, Fabrication, and

Erection of Structural Steel for Buildings (1969), the increase of the live loads to cover dynamic effects is

For supports of elevators	100%
For traveling crane support girders and their connections	25%
For supports of light machinery, shaft motor driven, not less than	20%
For supports of reciprocating machinery or power driven units, not less than	50%
For hangers supporting floors and balconies	33%

In areas receiving heavy impact and dynamic loads, the structural elements may experience fatigue. Codes take into account the resulting reduction in strength due to stress reversal.

BLAST LOADS

A building may have to withstand not only external but also internal pressure forces caused by blasts. The partial collapse of an apartment building in London, England, due to an internal gas explosion, brought major attention to that type of loading in 1968. Most buildings will never encounter such forces; however the chance of detonation of explosives due to sabotage or the accidental ignition of flammable gases due to leakage or fire is always present. Blasts cause high pressures in the area of the explosion, putting extreme loads on building elements, resulting in the blowing out of windows, walls, and floors. This internal pressure should be contained locally and should not generate progressive collapse of the structure.

The possible causes for external blast loads range from sonic booms to nuclear explosions. The damage attributable to sonic booms is relatively minor (i.e., broken windows and cracked plaster walls). Extensive research is being conducted on the response of structures to the effects of nuclear weapons to design buildings capable of resisting nuclear attack.

COMBINATION OF LOADS

Tall buildings are subject to many loads during their lifetime, and many of the loads act simultaneously on the structure. The effects of loads should be combined if they act along the same line of action and are superimposable. This condition makes it necessary to design a structure considering all possible load combinations.

The probability of occurrence of combined loads has to be

statistically evaluated and its effect predicted. The more accurate determination of the load action reduces the need for larger safety factors to cover the unknown.

The effective load combinations are specified in the codes. It is recognized that the maximum meteorological loads probably will never occur simultaneously with the full value of other live loads. Thus codes permit a 33 % increase in allowable stresses if full live loads are used concurrently with the maximum wind or earthquake loads.

CHAPTER THREE

Introduction to High–Rise Building Structures

A general basis of understanding should be established before we begin a detailed treatment of high-rise buildings. Thus the following discussion first traces the development of the sky-scrapper structure in its historical context; then typical structural building systems are introduced from the point of view of geometrical layout. The chapter concludes by relating the building structure to other design determinants.

DEVELOPMENT OF HIGH–RISE BUILDINGS

The first high-rise buildings date back to antiquity. Load-bearing wall structures 10 stories high were already used in the Roman cities. Western cities expanded rapidly in the nineteenth century, and the high density of population forced the revival of the tall building that had disappeared with the fall of the Roman Empire. The principle of the masonry bearing wall structure was again utilized. However this type of structural system has the disadvantage that with increase of height, the wall thickness (i.e., building weight) must increase responding directly to the nature of gravity flow.

The limits of this construction became apparent with the 16-story Monadnock Building (1891) in Chicago, which required the lower walls to be more than 6 ft thick.

The usage of lightweight frame systems seemed to be the natural answer, since iron and later steel framing allowed greater heights and more and larger openings. The development of the steel skeleton took more than 100 years. Not only did iron have to be recognized as a building material, but production methods had to be developed. This required research into the behavior of the new material to generate the best member shapes and assemblage forms, and also necessitated the development of precision detail and craftmanship.

The engineer of the nineteenth century made the architect recognize the potential of the frame element. He advanced its usage in bridges, factories, warehouses, and exhibition spaces. This influence can be seen as far back as 1801 in a seven-story iron framed English cotton mill in Manchester, in which iron columns and beams served as interior framework. The I-beam shape was used in this building, probably for the first time. The designer intuitively recognized the efficiency of the shape to resist bending. In fact, the mill established the base for the development of the steel frame eventually to appear in Chicago around 1890.

The Crystal Palace, built for the London International Exhibition of 1851, revealed the first autonomous iron frame. The gravity construction of solid walls, the basis for architectural standards at that time, was challenged by the antigravity effects of the glass planes and wood-iron framework. The building amplifies the first large-scale approach towards mass production. The division of space was planned around the largest standard sheet of glass (4 ft long), and the construction process became part of the design.

The Lighthouse at Black Harbor, Long Island, built in 1843, was the first wrought iron frame structure in the United States. About 10 years later several buildings employed an interior skeleton together with load-bearing masonry facade walls. The interior frame consisted of cast iron columns supporting wrought iron beams.

Before high-rise buildings could respond to the new potential of metal framing, vertical transportation had to be developed. The first elevator appeared in 1851 in a hotel on New York's Fifth Avenue. This vertical railway system was improved to the suspended system in 1866, but the possibilities of the elevator in high-rise buildings were for the first time realized in the Equitable Life Insurance Company Building in New York in 1870.

William Jenny carried framing systems further with his 11-story Home Insurance Building in Chicago in 1883. This was the first example of a high-rise building totally supported by the metal framework; while the masonry facade walls were only self-supporting. Jenny's building was also the first to employ steel beams in the upper portion of the building. In 1889 Jenny's second Leiter Building, became the first true skeleton building not using any single self-supporting walls.

The nine-story second Rand McNally Building (1889, Chicago) by Burnham and Root used an all-steel frame for the first time. The same architects developed the concept of vertical shear wall in the 20-story Masonic Temple (1891, Chicago). At that height, wind forces became an important design consideration. To increase the lateral stiffness of the steel skeleton, the architects introduced diagonal bracing in the facade frame, thus creating a vertical truss or the shear wall principle.

Improved steel design methods allowed buildings to grow steadily upward: in 1905 the 50-story Metropolitan Tower Building was constructed in New York, followed in 1931 by the 102-story Empire State Building. Further improvements have concentrated on the development of new framing layouts, improved material qualities, and better construction techniques rather than on significant increases in height.

In the 1890s concrete started to establish itself as a common structural material. Designers like Auguste Perret, François Hennebique, and Tony Garnier in France, and Robert Maillart in Switzerland, were among the designers who explored the potential of reinforced concrete. Perret was the first to employ the reinforced concrete skeleton in high-rise construction and to express it architecturally in his rue Franklin Apartment Building (Paris, 1903). At the same time the 16-story Ingall Building in Cincinnati was the world's first reinforced concrete frame skyscraper. During the first half of this century, however, concrete buildings appeared only sporadically. There was no real search for the true personality of the material; concrete systems generally imitated the steel skeleton approach. This attitude, however, changed after World War II. Sophisticated construction techniques together with development of high quality materials began to yield such new design concepts as the flat slab and the load-bearing facade grid wall. Both systems were challenging the traditional one-way slab and curtain wall typical for rigid frame structures. Skyscrapers such as the 65-story Marina City Towers (Chicago, 1963) truly express the monolithic sculptural nature of the material concrete.

COMMON HIGH–RISE BUILDING STRUCTURES

The purpose of this section is to introduce the most common load-bearing high-rise building systems. The basic structural elements of a building are the following:

Linear elements.

•• Column and beam.   Capable of resisting axial and rotational forces.

• Surface elements.

•• Wall.   Either solid with perforations or trussed, capable of carrying axial and rotational forces.

•• Slab.   Solid or ribbed, supported on floor framing, capable of supporting forces in and perpendicular to the plane.

- Spatial elements.

  •• Facade envelope or core, for example, tying the building together to act as a unit.

The combination of these basic elements generates the bone structure of the building. One can visualize an infinite number of possible solutions. Only the most common building types are discussed in Fig. 3.1.

Parallel Bearing Walls (Fig. 3.1a)

This system is comprised of planar vertical elements that are prestressed by their own weight, thus efficiently absorb lateral force action. The parallel wall system is used mostly for apartment buildings where large free spaces are not needed and mechanical systems do not necessitate core structures.

Cores and Facade Bearing Walls (Fig. 3.1b)

Planar vertical elements form exterior walls around a core structure. This allows for open interior spaces, which depend on the spanning capacities of the floor structure. The core houses mechanical and vertical transportation systems and adds to the stiffness of the building.

Self-Supporting Boxes (Fig. 3.1c)

Boxes are prefabricated three-dimensional units that resemble the bearing wall building of Fig. 3.1a when they are in place and joined together. In the case shown, the boxes are stacked like bricks in the "English pattern bond," resulting in a criss-crossed wall beam system.

Cantilevered Slab (Fig. 3.1d)

Supporting the floor system from a central core allows for a column-free space with the strength of the slab as the limit of the building size. Large quantities of steel are required, especially with large slab projections. Slab stiffness can be increased by taking advantage of prestressing techniques.

Flat Slab (Fig. 3.1e)

This horizontal planar system generally consists of uniformly thick concrete floor slabs supported on columns. If there are no

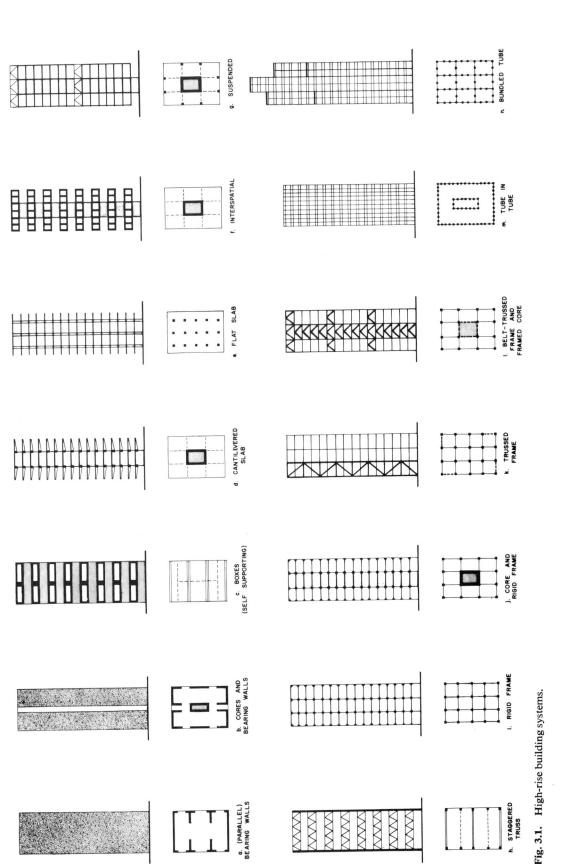

a. (PARALLEL) BEARING WALLS
b. CORES AND BEARING WALLS
c. BOXES (SELF SUPPORTING)
d. CANTILEVERED SLAB
e. FLAT SLAB
f. INTERSPATIAL
g. SUSPENDED
h. STAGGERED TRUSS
i. RIGID FRAME
j. CORE AND RIGID FRAME
k. TRUSSED FRAME
l. BELT-TRUSSED FRAME AND FRAMED CORE
m. TUBE IN TUBE
n. BUNDLED TUBE

Fig. 3.1. High-rise building systems.

drop panels and/or capitals on top of the columns, it is referred to as a flat plate system. With either form, the system has no deep beams allowing for a minimum story height.

Interspatial (Fig. 3.1f)

Cantilevered story-high framed structures are employed on every other floor to create usable space within and above the frame. The space within the framed floor is used for fixed operations, and the totally free space above the frame can adapt to any type of activity.

Suspension (Fig. 3.1g)

This system offers the efficient usage of material by employing hangers instead of columns to carry the floor loads. The strength of a compression member has to be reduced because of buckling, which is not the case for a tensile element, capable of utilizing its full capacity. The cables carry the gravity loads to trusses cantilevering from a central core.

Staggered Truss (Fig. 3.1h)

Story-high trusses are arranged so that each building floor rests alternatively on the top chord of one truss and the bottom of the next. Besides carrying the vertical loads, this truss arrangement minimizes wind bracing requirements by transferring wind loads to the base through web members and floor slab.

Rigid Frame (Fig. 3.1i)

Rigid joints are used between an assemblage of linear elements to form vertical and horizontal planes. The vertical planes consist of columns and girders mostly on a rectangular grid; a similar organizational grid is used for the horizontal planes consisting of beams and girders. With the integrity of the spatial skeleton depending on the strength and rigidity of the individual columns and beams, story height and column spacing become controlling design considerations.

Rigid Frame and Core (Fig. 3.1j)

The rigid frame responds to lateral loads primarily through flexure of the beams and columns. This type of behavior results in large lateral drift for buildings of a certain height. However introducing a core structure will significantly increase the lateral resistance of the building as a result of the core and frame interaction. Such core systems house the mechanical and vertical transportation systems.

Trussed Frame (Fig. 3.1k)

Combining a rigid (or hinged) frame with vertical shear trusses provides an increase in strength and stiffness of the structure. The design of the structure may be based on using the frame for the resistance of gravity loads and the vertical truss for wind loads similar to the rigid frame and core case.

Belt-Trussed Frame and Core (Fig. 3.1l)

Belt trusses tie the facade columns to the core, thus eliminating the individual action of frame and core. The bracing is called cap trussing when it is on the top of the building and belt trussing when around lower sections.

Tube in Tube (Fig. 3.1m)

The exterior columns and beams are spaced so closely that the facade has the appearance of a wall with perforated window openings. The entire building acts as a hollow tube cantilevering out of the ground. The interior core (tube) increases the stiffness of the building by sharing the loads with the facade tube.

Bundled Tube (Fig. 3.1n)

The bundled tube system can be visualized as an assemblage of individual tubes resulting in a multiple-cell tube. The increase in stiffness is apparent. The system allows for the greatest height and the most floor area.

GENERAL PLANNING CONSIDERATIONS

The selection of a high-rise building structure is not based merely on understanding the structure in its own context. The selection may be more function of factors related to cultural, social, economical, and technological needs. One should keep in mind that structure is just one important consideration among many. Some of the factors related primarily to the technological planning of high-rise buildings are discussed next.

General Economic Considerations

The architect is usually obliged to respond to the purpose of many building types: to make money. As he forms a better understanding of the economic aspects of the design process, he may improve his chance of creating better architecture.

The important point to realize is that a building system should not just be a preconceived preference; rather, it should incorporate careful consideration of economic factors. Thus two or more different methods of construction may hold up a particular building and may even look very similar, but one system usually is more economical to build.

A designer must think not only about how much the project costs to build but also about how much the finished project costs to operate (e.g., expenses associated with utilities, maintenance, insurance, taxes, interest on borrowed money); he has to deal with the building economy. As the height of the building increases, more and more space is needed for structure, mechanical systems, and elevators, leaving less rental space. In addition, the costs of elevators and mechanical systems increase with height. The same reasoning applies to contractor costs, since more sophisticated construction equipment is necessary as buildings get taller. However all these cost increases may be offset by the high land costs and the need for the building at a specific location. As the building height increases, the land costs per square foot of floor area obviously decrease. Similarly, management costs are reduced, since it costs less per square foot to operate one large building than several small structures.

Accurate evaluation of all the complex economic considerations for high-rise buildings has come to depend on the computer. It is beyond human calculation to decipher all the factors along with all the ramifications of each factor concerned with the skyscrapers of today.

The coordination of architect, engineer, and contractor during a project's planning and drawing stage will improve the potential of achieving an economical solution. Such team efforts may allow building construction to start before all final drawings are completed. When construction begins earlier, buildings save money on inflating construction prices and earn profits sooner.

Soil Conditions

The performance of a building is dependent on the strength of the soil on which it is founded. The foundation or substructure binds the superstructure to the soil. It receives its loads and distributes them so that the soil is capable of carrying them. The selection of the building type is very much a function of the geology of the site. The soil conditions must be explored before any structural system can be decided on, so that its behavior can be predicted. If, for instance, the bearing capacity of the soil is rather low at a specific site, piles or caissons may be required to reach the proper foundation support. In this type of situation a building of heavy materials such as concrete may be much more expensive than lightweight steel construction. In any case, the three building structure variables—superstructure, substructure, and soil—leave some combinational freedom with respect to choice of the structural system.

Height-to-Width Ratio of a Building

As the minimum height-to-width ratio increases, so should the building's inherent stiffness. The stiffness of the building structure is dependent on size and number of bays, structural system, and rigidity of members and connections. The general height-to-width ratio for a plane frame structure seems to be in the range of 5 to 7.

Very often in high-rise building designs for cities, the given site dictates a maximum height-to-width ratio, and the designer must select a system that can economically accommodate the lateral drift and desired bay sizes.

Fabrication and Erection Considerations

The planning of fabrication and erection procedures may indicate important factors concerning structural system selection. Indeed, these may be the governing considerations when choosing a prefabricated construction method. Such systems are used because they may reduce labor costs and time required for erection of buildings. There should be a minimum number of structural pieces to shorten construction time; complicated closed-form shapes should be avoided, and field welding should be minimized. Thus before choosing a construction method, the fabrication and erection procedures must be known.

Mechanical Systems Considerations

Mechanical systems, consisting of HVAC (heating, ventilating, and air conditioning), elevator, electric, plumbing, and waste disposal systems, average more than one-third of total high-rise building costs. This significant cost factor exemplies clearly that the structural system selection must respond to these building services. Energy supply systems may be concentrated in mechanical cores integrated with a general core area, sometimes separate duct spaces are provided in the exterior facade, or interspatial systems with mechanical levels for heavy service requirements are used. All these approaches have definite effects on the overall building appearance and economic selection of a structural system.

Fire Rating Considerations

In tall buildings fire becomes an important consideration for two major reasons. First, since almost all floors are beyond the reach of firetruck ladders, fire fighting and rescue action are possible only from the inside of a building. Second, total emergency evacuation is impossible within a reasonably short period of time.

The danger of fire is less the burning heat than the effects of smoke and toxic gases, which cause most of the casualties. Therefore, in accordance with required fire rating considerations, a building construction system must be able to ensure the following:

- Structural integrity for a certain period of time through use of noncombustible materials that will not burn or produce smoke.

- Confinement of the fire, to prevent it from spreading to certain building areas.

- Adequate exit systems.

- Effective smoke and fire detection systems.

- Sprinklers and necessary smoke and heat venting.

These rating requirements vary with the characteristics of the building and its use, such as for buildings with special occupancies for physically disabled persons or buildings housing vitally important equipment.

Local Considerations

Every community has unique specific considerations. Zoning regulations and codes may have requirements that affect the construction and system selection. For example, if there is a height limitation when a maximum number of floors are needed, the floor-to-floor heights must be kept to a minimum, suggesting the use of the flat slab concrete system or the application of the prestress principle.

Situations involving air rights are encountered with buildings over roads, railways or over other buildings. Such buildings usually have constricted column dimensions and need minimum sized girders for proper clearances.

Similarly, local labor rates and union regulations may make one method of construction more economical than others. For example, the low cost of labor in certain countries may suggest masonry construction or concrete as more economical even if intricate formwork is required.

Availability and Cost of Main Construction Materials

Certain building locations may be near sources of specific construction materials. This can reduce shipping costs and may make a normally expensive material cheaper. Where proximity to material sources is not a factor, availability should be considered. If a desired material is hard to acquire, it may delay the building schedule and add significantly to building costs. Such considerations must be checked along with costs of the possible material choices.

CHAPTER FOUR

The Vertical
Structural Plane

A building structure consists of vertical planes such as walls and/or frames and the horizontal planes that are the floor structures.

Gravity and lateral forces are dispersed through the floor structure to the vertical building planes and from there to the ground. The intensity, direction, and type of action of the force flow depend on the geometry of the vertical planes and on their arrangement within the building volume.

DISPERSION OF VERTICAL FORCES

The gravity loads acting on a building have to be transferred through continuous vertical or inclined planes to the ground. Those vertical planes may be either post-beam type skeletons or wall systems, which may be solid or trussed (Fig. 4.1).

The flow of the gravity forces is obviously dependent on the arrangement of the vertical structural planes within the building. In Fig. 4.2 a five-bay organizational space grid has been selected and a process developed to indicate the large variety of possible juxtapositions. The vertical structural planes may be either staggered (Figs. 4.2h, i) or continuous (Figs. 4.2a–g). The two staggered systems give some idea of potential geometrical arrangements. The examples using continuous vertical planes are subdivided according to the number and location of the planes within the given space grid.

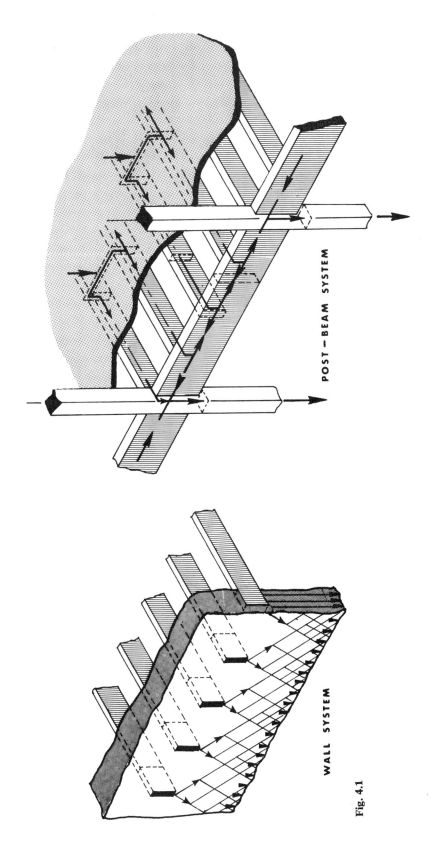

POST–BEAM SYSTEM

WALL SYSTEM

Fig. 4.1

Dispersion of Vertical Forces   61

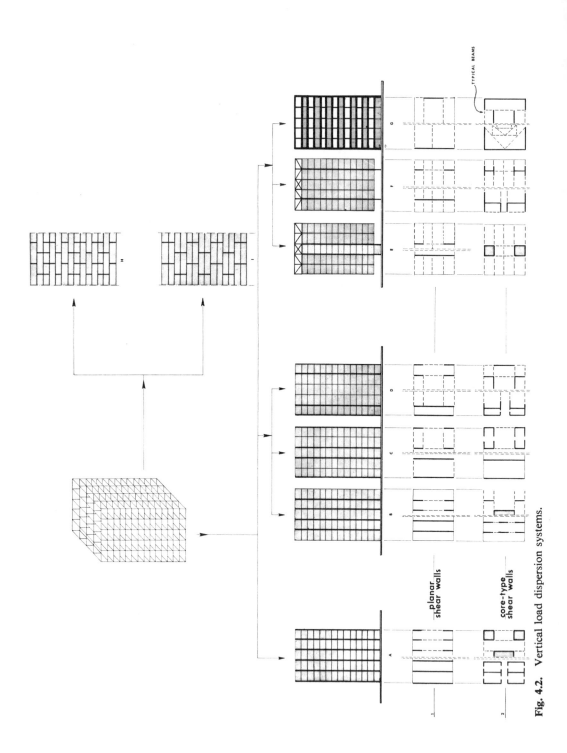

Fig. 4.2. Vertical load dispersion systems.

- The planes are evenly distributed across the building or concentrated at center and facade (Figs. 4.2*a, c*) or as exemplified in Fig. 4.3.

- The planes form the exterior envelope of the building (Figs. 4.2*d, g*) or as exemplified in Fig. 4.4.

- The planes are concentrated at the center of the building (Figs. 4.2*b, e*) or as exemplified in Fig. 4.5.

Possible locations of the vertical structural systems in the building plan are shown on the bottom of Fig. 4.2. These systems are identified as shear walls (see discussion of lateral load dispersion systems), which can be visualized as post-beam, trusses, or solid wall systems. The walls may be either linear surface systems (line 1) or closed or staggered, three-dimensional core systems (line 2). The planar wall systems are further subdivided into continuous planes, passing through the entire building (left half of each plan on line 1), or wall assemblages, interconnected by beams (right half of each plan on line 1).

From a purely geometrical point of view, a rather large number of different wall arrangements can be generated within the given space grid. This discussion primarily provides for flexibility of thought in terms of establishing structural order and allows us to visualize the flow of gravity from slab to beam to wall.

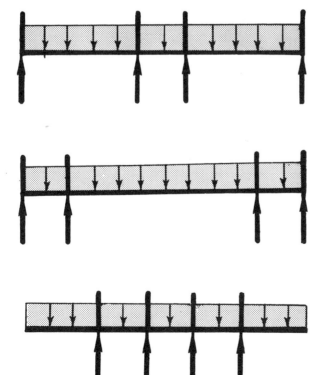

Fig. 4.3

Fig. 4.4

Fig. 4.5

DISPERSION OF LATERAL FORCES

Building structures have to be capable of resisting different types of lateral forces, such as those created by wind or earthquakes. Hence some type of bracing must be provided in the longitudinal and cross direction of the building. The lateral forces are dispersed through the floors, acting as deep horizontal beams, to the braced vertical building planes. These in turn direct the forces into the foundations (Fig. 4.6). Only shear connections between horizontal planes (floors) and vertical planes can transmit the lateral forces. Hinged (roller) connections between the planes transfer only gravity loads. The number and types of lateral dispersion systems determine the amount of stress imposed on the ground. It is obvious that overstressing the soil should be avoided.

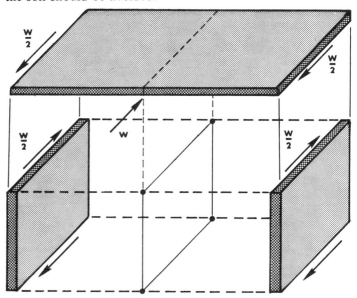

Fig. 4.6

Basic Lateral Dispersion Systems

The discussion of lateral load dispersion systems is closely related to Fig. 4.7, and a general organizational building grid appears at the center of the illustration. Different structural systems, as indicated in the outer circle, may be plugged into this grid. The relationship of these systems to the overall building is dealt with later in this chapter and in other parts of the book.

The transmission of lateral forces across the short direction of the building may be accomplished by the structural systems represented in the outer circle of Fig. 4.7. They are arranged in terms of stiffness, starting with the least stiff, the rigid frame (Fig. 4.7a) and ending with the stiffest system, the closed solid core (Fig. 4.7m). Stiffness is measured by the spring constant K which is a function of the lateral deformation Δ generated by a force P: $K = P/\Delta$.

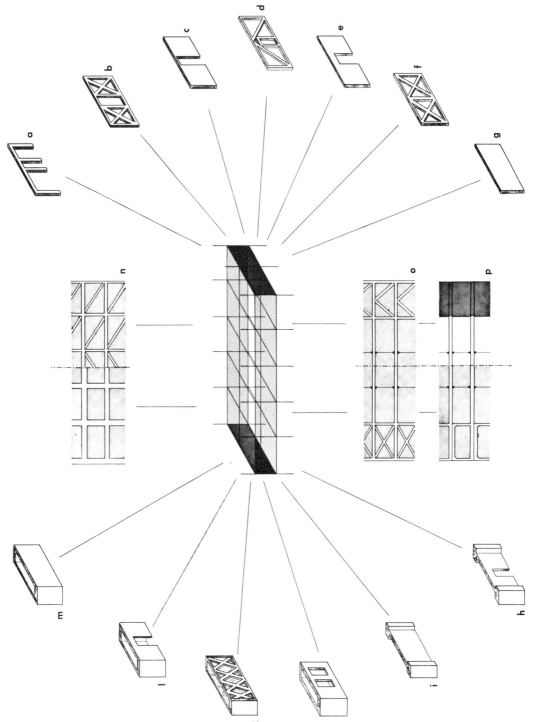

Fig. 4.7. Lateral force dispersion systems.

Lateral dispersion of forces may be achieved by planar systems, such as solid walls (Figs. 4.7c, e, g) trussed walls (b, d, f) or just a rigid frame (a). The solid walls and trussed walls (Figs. 4.7g and f, respectively) have approximately the same stiffness. This comparison is clearly relative, approximate, and based on dimensional and material relationships.

The dispersion of lateral forces along the longitudinal axis of the building may be accomplished in different ways:

• Continuous resistance through rigid frame or truss action (Fig. 4.7n).

• Stiffening certain building bays either with rigid frames or with solid walls or trusses (Figs. 4.7p and o, respectively).

It is assumed that no shear core systems are used in the short direction of the building. Depending on their shape, cores may resist lateral forces from any direction (Fig. 4.8), as indicated later in this chapter.

Possible applications of the basic, vertical structural systems (Fig. 4.7) to high-rise buildings are approached first by discussing typical, vertical interior building planes, then exterior facade structures.

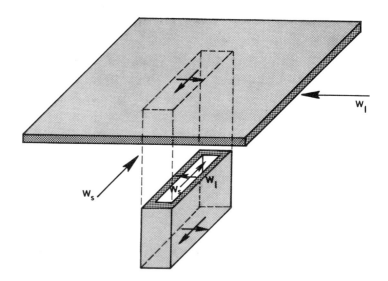

Fig. 4.8

Typical Vertical Interior Building Planes

Common vertical building planes (Fig. 4.9) may be single planar systems or part of a three-dimensional core system. Their possible location within the building is indicated in Fig. 4.5 and is discussed in more detail in the section dealing with the shear wall arrangement.

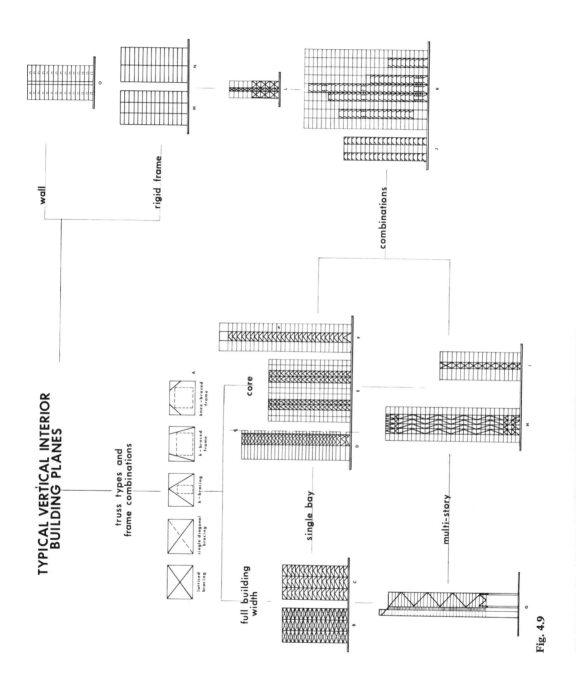

TYPICAL VERTICAL INTERIOR
BUILDING PLANES

Fig. 4.9

The vertical structural building planes may be organized as follows:

- The solid wall (Fig. 4.9*o*).

- The rigid frame (Figs. 4.9*m*, *n*).

- The trussed wall (Figs. 4.9*b–i*).

- Mixed frames (Figs. 4.9*j–l*).

This section primarily emphasizes the geometry of trussed systems and mixed frames. Rigid frames and solid walls are discussed in other parts of the book.

The basic bracing types for frames are indicated in Fig. 4.9*a*, starting with the stiffest case, the latticed truss at the left side, and ends with the least stiff case, the knee-braced frame at the right. The selection of the bracing type is a function not only of the required stiffness but also of the size of the wall openings needed for circulation.

The vertical building plane may be trussed across the full width of the building (Figs. 4.9*b*, *c*) or orly certain bays (*d–f*) or portions of the building may be braced (*k*, *l*).

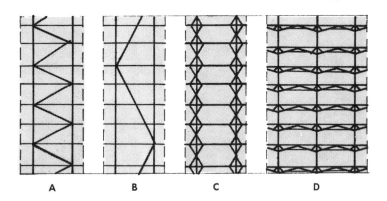

Fig. 4.10   A   B   C   D

Figure 4.10 illustrates the principle of bracing as related to a typical continuous vertical building bay. The basic solutions are as follows:

- Each story may be fully braced (Fig. 4.10*a*).

- The bracing may run across several stories (Fig. 4.10*b*).

- Vertical K-bracing may be used along the columns (Fig. 4.10*c*).

- Horizontal portal bracing may be applied along the beams (Fig. 4.10*d*).

The typical examples discussed are only suggestions for the application of the principles of bracing to interior vertical building planes.

Structural Facades

Lateral bracing for high-rise buildings need not be restricted to internal cores, shear walls, and braced frames to resist wind and earthquake forces. All these systems may be expressed on the exterior facade, serving aesthetic as well as structural functions.

For tall buildings, frame bracing proves to be more easily accommodated on the exterior. Interior braced frames restrict the free flow of the activity space. The columns of these frames have to be spaced relatively close to reduce the depth of the floor structure.

Structural facade systems may be subdivided into two groups: basic uniform facade grids repetitive throughout the building elevation (Fig. 4.11 and part of Fig. 4.12) and structural patterns such as diagonals extending over the whole facade structure (Fig. 4.12).

The systems in Fig. 4.11 incorporate some form of flexural rigidity—girders continuously connected to columns (rigid frames), trussed systems, or perforated walls. The illustrations indicate various structural methods according to decreasing spandrel spans (from top to bottom and left to right) and increasing density of triangulation (from top to bottom). The longest spanning systems, such as plate girders and Vierendeel and Warren trusses, allow more natural light to enter the building; however the shortest spanning systems (i.e., perforated tubes) are stiffer, hence permit much taller buildings.

The long span plate girders or truss spandrels extend over the full depth between the windows; their flanges provide window heads and sills. To the Warren spandrel (Fig. 4.11k), tension cables are added between trusses to improve wind resistance of the facade structure. The perforated wall system made of concrete or steel plates is devoid of slender columns or beams; the wall envelope acts structurally like a bearing wall.

Facade structures need not be uniform over an entire facade; they are concentrated where they most efficiently resist forces. Belt and cap perimeter trussing, for instance, are located at levels where they tie building units most efficiently together into a cohesive entity (4.12c).

The principles displayed in the overall facade structures (Fig. 4.12) range from facade triangulation and perimeter trussing to exterior cores and multistory framing. All these and other structural facade methods clearly express a particular building's response to imposed loads, generating a natural architectural aesthetic.

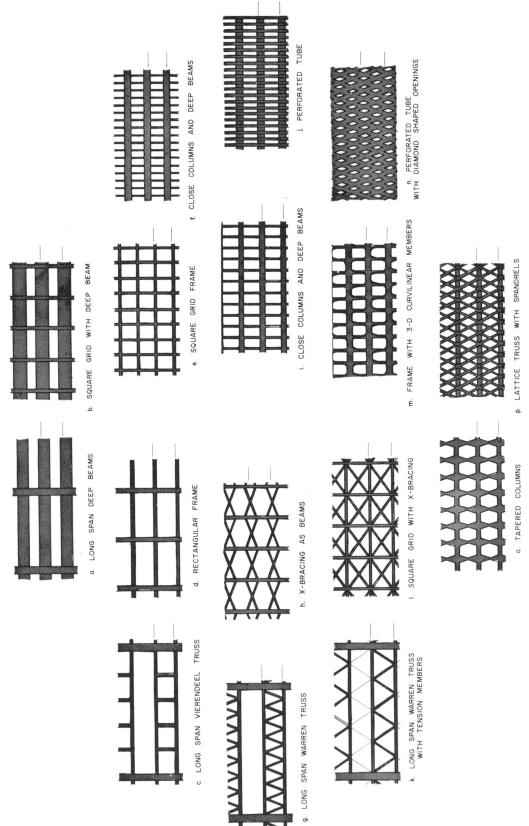

Fig. 4.11. Repetitive structural facade grids.

a. LONG SPAN DEEP BEAMS

b. SQUARE GRID WITH DEEP BEAM

c. LONG SPAN VIERENDEEL TRUSS

d. RECTANGULAR FRAME

e. SQUARE GRID FRAME

f. CLOSE COLUMNS AND DEEP BEAMS

g. LONG SPAN WARREN TRUSS

h. X-BRACING AS BEAMS

i. CLOSE COLUMNS AND DEEP BEAMS

j. PERFORATED TUBE

k. LONG SPAN WARREN TRUSS WITH TENSION MEMBERS

l. SQUARE GRID WITH X-BRACING

m. FRAME WITH 3-D CURVILINEAR MEMBERS

n. PERFORATED TUBE WITH DIAMOND SHAPED OPENINGS

o. TAPERED COLUMNS

p. LATTICE TRUSS WITH SPANDRELS

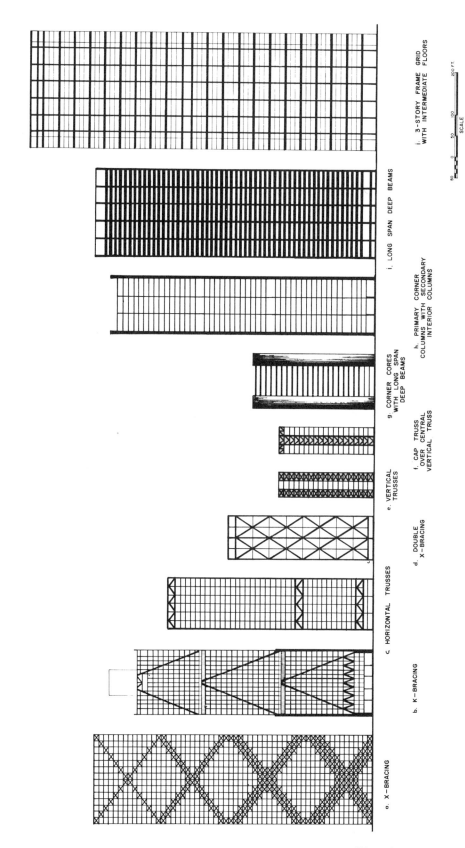

Fig. 4.12. Total facade structures.

a. X-BRACING

b. K-BRACING

c. HORIZONTAL TRUSSES

d. DOUBLE X-BRACING

e. VERTICAL TRUSSES

f. CAP TRUSS OVER CENTRAL VERTICAL TRUSS

g. CORNER CORES WITH LONG SPAN DEEP BEAMS

h. PRIMARY CORNER COLUMNS WITH SECONDARY INTERIOR COLUMNS

i. LONG SPAN DEEP BEAMS

j. 3-STORY FRAME GRID WITH INTERMEDIATE FLOORS

SCALE

0   50   100   200 FT.

Optimum Ground Level Space

Free space at ground level is very desirable for many buildings. Functionally, the open space below a building may become part of an urban plaza, a lobby, or a parking garage. From a psychological point of view, this free space tends to make the building's mass more tolerable by creating an environment of a more human scale. In most cases openings at ground level are created by elimination of some of the building's bearing elements or addition of a structural system supporting the building above.

Some common solutions for the opening of the building's ground level appear in Figs. 4.13 and 4.14.

There seem to be two basic approaches to the achievement of free space at the street level:

- To support the bearing elements of the building by individual structural elements such as the following.

  •• Portal frames along the width of the building (Figs. 4.13*d*, *e*).
  •• Two- and three-forked columns collecting the building compression members (Figs. 4.13*a*–*c*). This method responds quite well to vertical symmetrical loads; however, it is less well suited for torsional and lateral loads perpendicular to the columns, since high bending moments will be generated by the individual action of the columns.

- To eliminate or correct certain structural facade elements at ground level by using the following features of Fig. 4.14.

  •• Transfer girders (*a*), transfer trusses (*b*), transfer wall beams (*c*), indirect arch action (*d*), column collection (*e*), or true arches (*f*).

SHEAR WALL ARRANGEMENT

Shear walls are vertical stiffening elements designed to resist lateral forces exerted on a building by wind or earthquakes. Figure 4.15 indicates that they may be expressed as exterior or interior walls or cores enclosing elevator shafts or stairways.

There does not seem to be any limitation to the geometrical configuration of shear wall systems. The most common basic shapes are given in the central ring of Fig. 4.15. The triangle, rectangle, angle, channel, and wide flange are examples of forms familiar in the architectural language.

The basic shear wall systems may be subdivided into open and closed systems. Open systems are made up of single linear elements or a combination of such elements that do not completely enclose a geometric space. Such shapes are L, X, V, Y,

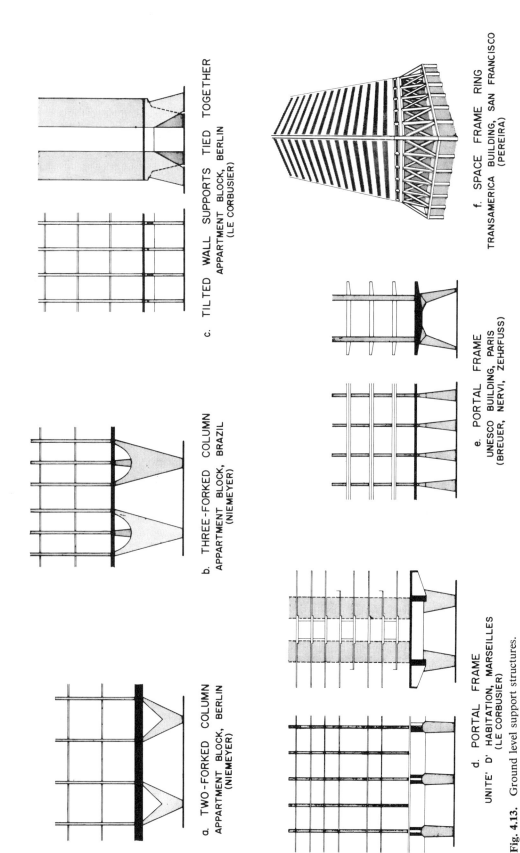

a. TWO-FORKED COLUMN
APPARTMENT BLOCK, BERLIN
(NIEMEYER)

b. THREE-FORKED COLUMN
APPARTMENT BLOCK, BRAZIL
(NIEMEYER)

c. TILTED WALL SUPPORTS TIED TOGETHER
APPARTMENT BLOCK, BERLIN
(LE CORBUSIER)

d. PORTAL FRAME
UNITE' D' HABITATION, MARSEILLES
(LE CORBUSIER)

e. PORTAL FRAME
UNESCO BUILDING, PARIS
(BREUER, NERVI, ZEHRFUSS)

f. SPACE FRAME RING
TRANSAMERICA BUILDING, SAN FRANCISCO
(PEREIRA)

Fig. 4.13. Ground level support structures.

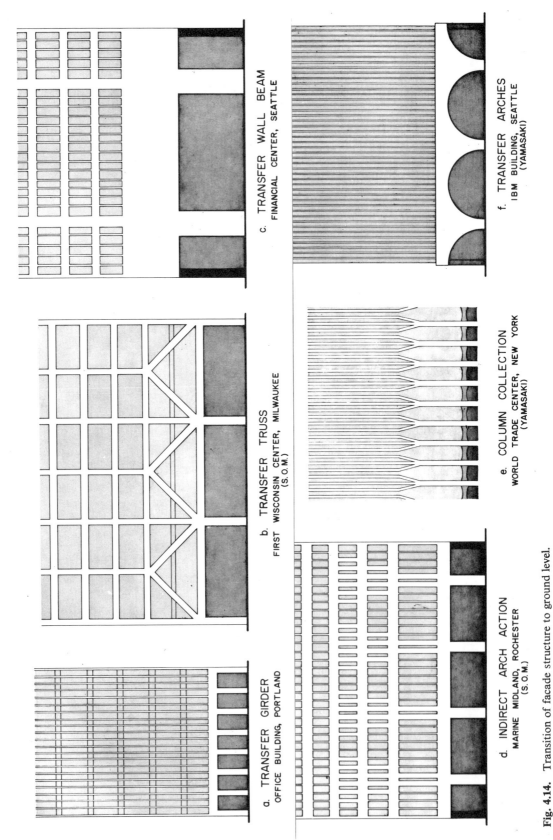

a. TRANSFER GIRDER
OFFICE BUILDING, PORTLAND

b. TRANSFER TRUSS
FIRST WISCONSIN CENTER, MILWAUKEE
(S.O.M.)

c. TRANSFER WALL BEAM
FINANCIAL CENTER, SEATTLE

d. INDIRECT ARCH ACTION
MARINE MIDLAND, ROCHESTER
(S.O.M.)

e. COLUMN COLLECTION
WORLD TRADE CENTER, NEW YORK
(YAMASAKI)

f. TRANSFER ARCHES
IBM BUILDING, SEATTLE
(YAMASAKI)

Fig. 4.14. Transition of facade structure to ground level.

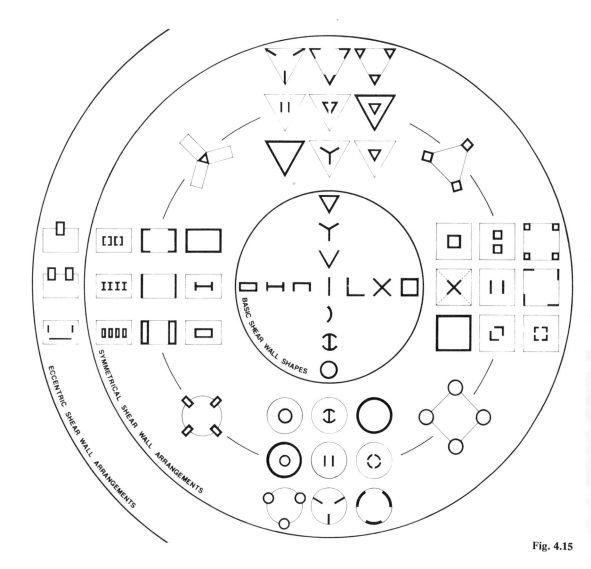

Fig. 4.15

T, and H. In contrast, closed systems enclose a geometrical space; common forms are square, triangular, rectangular, and circular cores.

Shear wall systems, whether inside or outside a building, may be arranged symmetrically or asymmetrically. The middle ring of Fig. 4.15 presents possible symmetrical arrangements for simple building forms by using one, two, three, or four basic shear wall elements at different building locations. The outer ring of the same figure touches a few cases of the infinite number of possible asymmetrical wall arrangements.

The shape and location of the shear walls have significant effects on their structural behavior under lateral loads. A core eccentrically located with respect to building shape has to carry torsion as well as bending and direct shear. However torsion may also develop in buildings featuring symmetrical shear wall arrangements when wind acts on facades of different surface

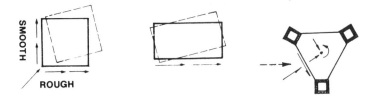

Fig. 4.16

textures (i.e., roughness) or when the wind does not act through the centroid of the building's mass (Fig. 4.16).

Optimal torsional resistance is obtained with closed core sections. When evaluating section resistance, however, the torsional rigidity must be reduced for door, window, and other openings, because the stiffness of the resisting walls decreases as the walls are perforated. In fact, walls having large openings to accommodate mechanical and electrical systems might not be able to carry such loads.

BEHAVIOR OF SHEAR WALLS UNDER LATERAL LOADING

Floors acting as horizontal diaphragms transmit lateral loads equally to the shear walls. It is assumed that the floors are relatively deep and have no major openings; in other words, the floors are infinitely stiff and do not distort. The distribution of lateral forces to the shear walls is a function of the geometrical arrangement of the resisting wall systems.

If the resultant of the lateral forces acts through the centroid of a building's relative stiffness, only translational reaction will be generated. The most obvious case is the symmetrical pure shear wall building. In a rigid frame shear wall building, the shear may be assumed to be resisted completely by the core as a first approximation. This is because its stiffness is so much greater than the lateral stiffness of the frame.

If the shear wall arrangement is asymmetrical, the resultant lateral force does not act through the centroid of the building's stiffness. Rotation of the shear walls in addition to translation will be generated. The distribution of the stresses is dependent on the shape of the shear wall system. In the following examples, three basic shapes are investigated.

PROBLEM 4.1. THE LINEAR SHEAR WALL SYSTEM (FIG. 4.17)

Check the shearing stresses due to seismic loading for 8 in. brick walls of a one-story building. Allowable shear stresses are 50 psi. The building is located in seismic zone 3. Assume the building weight to be 200 k.

The center of the shear wall arrangement is found by summing the moments of wall areas A and B about wall C and setting them equal to the moments generated by the total area (Fig. 4.17a).

$$A_a(40) + A_b(15) = (A_a + A_b + A_c)\, X$$

but

$$A_a = A_b = A_c = A$$

then

$$40 + 15 = 3X$$

Hence the center of mass is located at

$$X = 18.33 \text{ ft}$$

The total seismic shear according to equation 2.2 is

$$V = KCWZ = 1.33(0.1)200(1) = 26.6 \text{ k}$$

Although the wall arrangement (mass) is asymmetrical, it is safely assumed that the base shear is equally distributed across the building width. The walls must resist in direct shear 26.6k and in rotational shear the moment 26.6 (1.67) = 44.4 ft-k. Each wall carries an equal amount of direct shear (Fig. 4.17b), and

$$P = \frac{26.6}{3} = 8.87 \text{ k}$$

Rotational equilibrium about wall C yields (Fig. 4.17a).

$$\sum M_c = 0 = P_a(40) - P_b(15) - 44.4$$

$$P_b = 2.66P_a - 2.96 \qquad (a)$$

Assuming rigid diaphragm action (i.e., linear rotation of slab, Fig. 4.17c), we can write

$$\frac{P_a}{21.67} = \frac{P_b}{3.33} = \frac{P_c}{18.33}$$

$$P_a = 6.51P_b$$

$$P_c = 5.51P_b \qquad (b)$$

Substituting equation (b) in equation (a) gives

$$P_b = 2.66(6.51P_b) - 2.96$$

$$P_b = 0.18 \text{ k}$$

$$P_a = 6.51(0.18) = 1.17 \text{ k}$$

$$P_c = 5.51(0.18) = 0.99 \text{ k}$$

Direct and rotational shear for each wall are summarized as follows (Fig. 4.17d):

wall A: $P_{at} = 8.87 + 1.17 = 10.04$ k
wall B: $P_{bt} = 8.87 - 0.18 = 8.69$ k
wall C: $P_{ct} = 8.87 - 0.99 = 7.86$ k

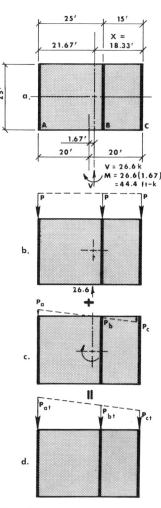

Fig. 4.17

The shear stress in the critical wall A is

$$v = \frac{P}{A} = \frac{10,040}{8(12)25}$$

$v = 4.19$ psi, which is less than $v_{all} = 50$ psi

The walls are more than satisfactory with respect to seismic shear.

PROBLEM 4.2. THE CLOSED CORE STRUCTURE (FIG. 4.18)

Assume that the rigid frame building in Problem 2.3 has an eccentric concrete service core. What is the required wall thickness of the core as based on translational and rotational shear? Neglect the shear resistance of the columns for this approximate analysis (in general, columns may take from 10 to 30% of the load). Use 4000 psi concrete. The core has to resist in translation

$$F = 2120 \text{ k}$$

and in rotation, the moment

$$M = 2120(22.5) = 47,700 \text{ ft-k}$$

The translational forces are assumed to be carried by the shear walls parallel to the load as based on the much higher stiffness of these walls (Fig. 4.18c).

$$P'_1 = \frac{F}{2} = \frac{2120}{2} = 1060 \text{ k}$$

or in terms of direct shear stresses

$$v_d = \frac{P'_1}{ta} = \frac{1060}{t(30 \times 12)}$$

where $t = $ thickness of wall.

The torsion is resisted by the closed core. It is assumed that each wall represents a constant shear force, and the assumption is reasonable because closed sections develop approximately uniform torsional stresses.

Fig. 4.18

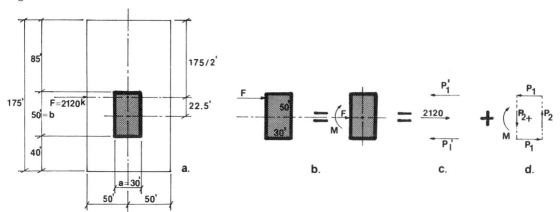

a.   b.   c.   d.

The external moment is balanced by the two wall couples (Fig. 4.18d).

$$M = P_1(b) + P_2(a)$$

The forces expressed in terms of stresses are

$$P_1 = vta \qquad P_2 = vtb$$

Replacing the forces in the moment equation yields

$$M = vta(b) + vtb(a) = 2vtba$$

Hence the rotational shear stress is

$$v_r = \frac{M}{2tba}$$

The total shear stress due to translation and rotation is

$$v_{t\,otal} = \frac{F}{2ta} + \frac{M}{2tba} \qquad (4.1)$$

If shear reinforcing is used and the increase of the shear capacity of concrete due to the compression forces in the wall is neglected, the allowable shear stress is

$$v_c = 3.3 \sqrt{f_c'} = 3.3 \sqrt{4000} = 208.7 \text{ psi}$$

Substituting the allowable shear stress yields the required wall thickness

$$208.7 = \frac{2,120,000}{2(t)30(12)} + \frac{47,700,000(12)}{2(t)30(50)12^2}$$

$$t = 14.11 + 6.35 = 20.46 \text{ in.}$$

The selected wall thickness as based on shear only is 1.75 ft.

PROBLEM 4.3.   THE OPEN CORE STRUCTURE

Rotation on open cores produces nonuniform torsional stresses. The twisting of the system generates warped surfaces, and the warping is accompanied by an increase in shearing stress in some parts and a decrease in other parts.

Figure 4.19 is a very rough approximation for the channel core, assuming constant shear stresses.

It is also assumed that the lateral shear is resisted directly by the wall parallel to the force action and the rotation by the walls perpendicular to the force action.

Fig. 4.19

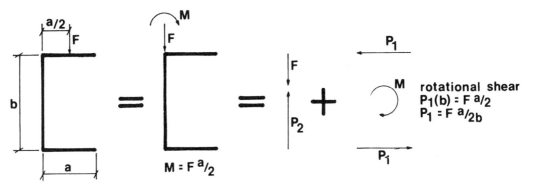

CHAPTER FIVE

Common High–Rise Building Structures and Their Behavior Under Load

As building heights increase, the importance of lateral force action rises at an accelerating rate. At a certain height the lateral sway of a building becomes so great that considerations of stiffness, rather than strength of structural material, control the design. The degree of stiffness depends primarily on the type of structural system. Furthermore, the efficiency of a particular system is directly related to the quantity of materials used. Thus optimization of a structure for certain spatial requirements should yield the maximum stiffness with the least weight; this results in innovative structural systems applicable to certain height ranges. Some of the factors responsible for the development of these new systems are as follows:

• High strength structural materials (e.g., 9000 psi concrete and high strength, low alloy steels).

• Composite action between structural elements.

• New fastening techniques (e.g., welding and bolting).

• Prediction of complex structural behavior by computer.

• Use of lighter construction materials.

• New construction techniques.

The most common structural framing systems are introduced in the following sections. The discussion emphasizes typical geometrical layouts, behavior under loading, and efficiency of the system.

THE BEARING WALL STRUCTURE

Historically, bearing wall structures have been of thick, heavy masonry wall construction. Their high weight and inflexibility in plan layout made them rather inefficient for multistory application. However the development of new technologies in the use of engineered masonry and prefabricated concrete panels has made the bearing wall concept economical in the medium high-rise range. Building types requiring frequent subdivision of space, such as apartments and hotels, lend themselves to this approach. The bearing wall principle is adaptable to a variety of building layouts and forms. Several applications to high-rise buildings in the range of 10 to 20 stories are illustrated in Fig. 5.1. Plan forms vary from simple rectangular shapes to circular and skewed triangular forms.

Bearing wall structures generally consist of an assemblage of linear walls. Depending on how these walls are arranged within the building, one may subdivide them into three basic groups.

- The *cross wall system* consists of parallel linear walls running perpendicular to the length of the building (Fig. 5.1a), thus does not interfere with the treatment of the main facade.

- The *long wall system* consists of linear walls running parallel to the length of the building (Fig. 5.1e), thus forming the main facade wall.

- The *two-way system* consists of walls running in both directions (Fig. 5.1f).

Also, a building may be subdivided into distinctly different structural parts, each using its own wall system (Fig. 5.1h).

The organization just described may be clearly expressed in rectangular buildings, but it may be rather difficult to classify buildings with more complex plan forms.

The response of a bearing wall structure to loading depends on the materials used and the type of interaction between the horizontal floor plane and the vertical wall plane. That is the behavior is a function of the degree of continuity within the walls and between the walls and floor slabs. In masonry construction and most prefabricated concrete systems one must visualize the floor structure as hinged to the continuous walls (assuming no special connection systems are used), whereas in the cast-in-place concrete building the slabs and walls are

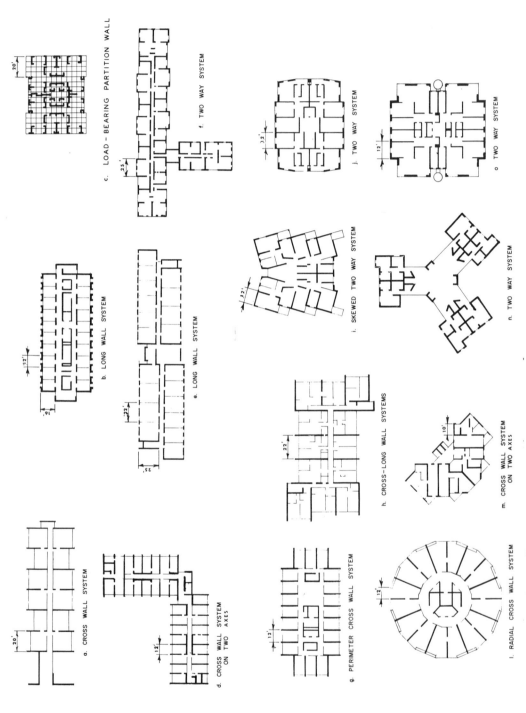

Fig. 5.1. Linear shear wall systems.

truly continuous. It is obvious that the concrete building, given its truly three-dimensional response, is much stiffer than the hinged masonry or prefab building; this makes concrete economical for taller structures.

Vertical loads are transferred in bending through the floor structure (Chapter 8) directly to the walls. Common floor spans (i.e., wall spacings) are in the range of 12 to 25 ft depending, among other factors, on the carrying capacity and lateral rigidity of the floor system. Since the wall resists the loads much like a wide narrow column, it must be checked for stability against buckling.

The compressive stresses in the wall are a function of the floor span, the height and type of building, and the size and arrangement of wall openings. The wall openings should be placed on the same vertical axis to avoid compounding of bearing stresses caused by staggered window arrangement. Also, the wall must resist bending moments caused by the floors eccentrically linked to the walls (Problem 7.2).

Horizontal forces are distributed through the floor structure, acting as a horizontal diaphragm, to the shear walls, parallel to the force action. These shear walls respond because of their high rigidity as deep beams, reacting to shear (Fig. 5.2) and flexure against overturning.

Figure 5.3 reveals that for wind action parallel to the short direction of the building, the walls in the cross wall system not only carry gravity loads but also resist the wind in shear. On the other hand, the long wall system separates the two tasks of the walls. The longitudinal walls carry the gravity loads and transfer the wind forces in local bending to the floor diaphragm or directly to the shear walls located at the center and ends of the building.

For the less critical wind action against the short side of the building, the bearing walls in the long wall system now also act as shear walls. In the cross wall system, shear walls may be provided along the central corridor (Fig. 5.3b). In a cast-in-place concrete building, stability is provided by portal action of the monolithic floor-wall system reacting as a cage unit in bending (Fig. 5.4).

The walls in Fig. 5.3b are arranged in a symmetrical manner; thus they resist wind loads directly according to their relative stiffness, assuming infinitely rigid floor diaphragms (Problem

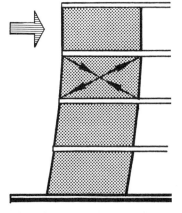

Fig. 5.2

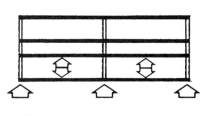

a. LONG WALL

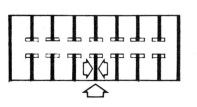

b. CROSS WALL

c. TWO-WAY

Fig. 5.3

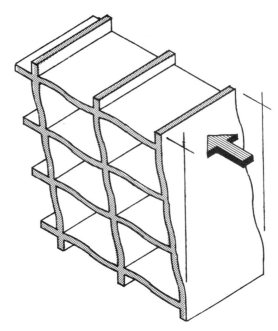

Fig. 5.4

7.2). However if the wall pattern is such that the resultant wind pressure does not act through the centroid of the resisting walls, torsion is generated, increasing the shear in certain walls (Problem 4.1).

The response of a shear wall to lateral loading depends greatly on its shape in plan, that is, the inertia it provides against bending. Some common linear shear wall forms are presented in Fig. 5.5.

Shear walls are rarely solid walls, since they are mostly penetrated, thus weakened by some openings. The number, size, and arrangement of these openings may severely affect the wall's behavior. Some tyical shear walls with openings are illustrated in Fig. 5.6.

If the wall has small window openings only (Fig. 5.6*a*), it behaves like a solid wall under lateral loading. The high gravity loads induce so much compression in the wall that the rotation (i.e., flexure) caused by wind is never able to overcome it on the windward side.

A similar result is obtained through the staggered arrangement of door openings in an interior shear wall (Fig. 5.6*b*), in which the wall rotates as a unit. However in the other extreme in which a slot of openings divides the wall into two separate units (Fig. 5.6*e*), each one behaves as an individual wall carry-ing one-half the load. In this case, because of the relatively

Fig. 5.5. Typical shear wall forms.

  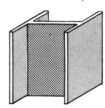 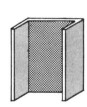

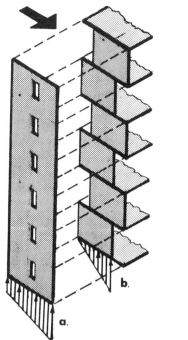
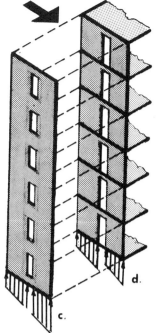
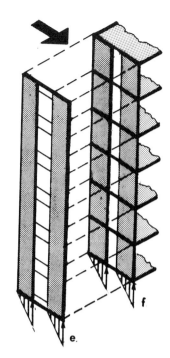

Fig. 5.6

small gravity loads, the wind may very well induce tension in the wall. Also, for the interior shear wall (Fig. 5.6f), where continuity across the corridor is provided only by the slab system, individual wall action may be safely assumed. Owing to the larger dead weight, however, no tension may be generated by the wind.

It is rather difficult to determine the response of a wall system somewhere between the extreme cases just discussed. The behavior of the wall system depends on the amount of rigidity offered by the spandrels against vertical shear wracking. One may visualize the wall as being made up of two distinct segments interacting to some extent in resisting the lateral loads. This is indicated by the continuous stress diagram at the base of Figs. 5.6c and d.

This discussion has assumed that bearing walls are solid flat, and in vertical planes. However they may consist of a lacework of diagonal or closely spaced linear column members (Fig. 5.20). They also may be curved or warped, and positioned in inclined planes.

For further discussion of bearing wall behavior, refer to Problems 7.1 and 7.2, which deal with the approximate analysis and design of two brick buildings.

THE SHEAR CORE STRUCTURE

The linear bearing wall system works quite well for apartment buildings in which functions and utilitarian needs are fixed. Commercial buildings, however, require maximum flexibility in layout, calling for large open spaces that can be subdivided by movable partitions. A common solution is to gather vertical transportation and energy distribution systems (e.g., elevators, stairs, toilets, mechanical shafts) to form a core or cores, depending on size and function of the building. These cores are utilized as shear wall systems to provide the necessary lateral stability for the building.

Several examples of shear core buildings are given in Fig. 5.7. There seems to be no restriction with respect to shape and location of the core within the building form. Characteristics of core systems are as follows; letters in parentheses refer to individual diagrams of Fig. 5.7.

* Shape of core (Chapter 4).

  ** Open core (n) versus closed core (b).
  ** Single core versus core in combination with linear walls (a).

* Number of cores: single versus multiple.

* Location of cores: internal (c) versus perimeter (j) versus external (m).

* Arrangement of cores: symmetrical (f) versus asymmetrical (j).

* Geometry of building as generator of core form: direct (k) versus indirect generators (p).

The building types in Fig. 5.7 do not include systems using cores in combination with other structural systems; they are discussed later in this chapter.

Cores can be made of steel, concrete, or a combination of both. The steel framed core may utilize the principle of a Vierendeel truss to achieve its lateral stability. The Vierendeel frame system is rather flexible, thus is only used for relatively low-rise applications. Diagonal bracing of the Vierendeel frame (i.e., vertical trussing) is used to achieve the necessary core stiffness for taller buildings (Fig. 4.9). The advantage of steel framed cores lies in the relatively rapid assemblage of the prefabricated members.

The concrete core, on the other hand, encloses space in addition to carrying loads, and no extra considerations need to be given to fireproofing. The lack of ductility inherent in concrete as a material is a disadvantage with respect to earthquake loading.

Shear cores may be visualized as resisting lateral loads like huge beams cantilevering out of the ground. Thus the bending and shear stresses generated in a core are similar to those of a box section beam, assuming the section does not warp (Problems 4.2 and 4.3). Since the core also carries gravity loads, it has the advantage of being prestressed by the induced compres-

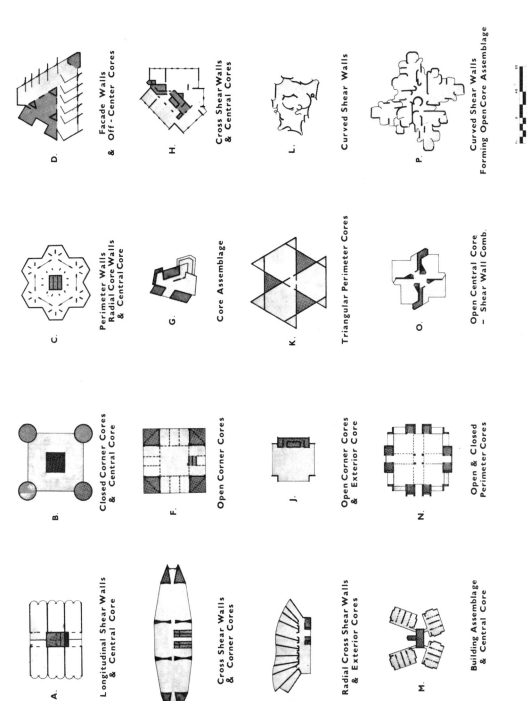

A. Longitudinal Shear Walls & Central Core

B. Closed Corner Cores & Central Core

C. Perimeter Walls Radial Core Walls & Central Core

D. Facade Walls & Off - Center Cores

E. Cross Shear Walls & Corner Cores

F. Open Corner Cores

G. Core Assemblage

H. Cross Shear Walls & Central Cores

I. Radial Cross Shear Walls & Exterior Cores

J.

K. Triangular Perimeter Cores

L. Curved Shear Walls

M. Building Assemblage & Central Core

N. Open & Closed Perimeter Cores

O. Open Central Core – Shear Wall Comb.

P. Curved Shear Walls Forming Open Core Assemblage

Fig. 5.7. Wall-core building systems.

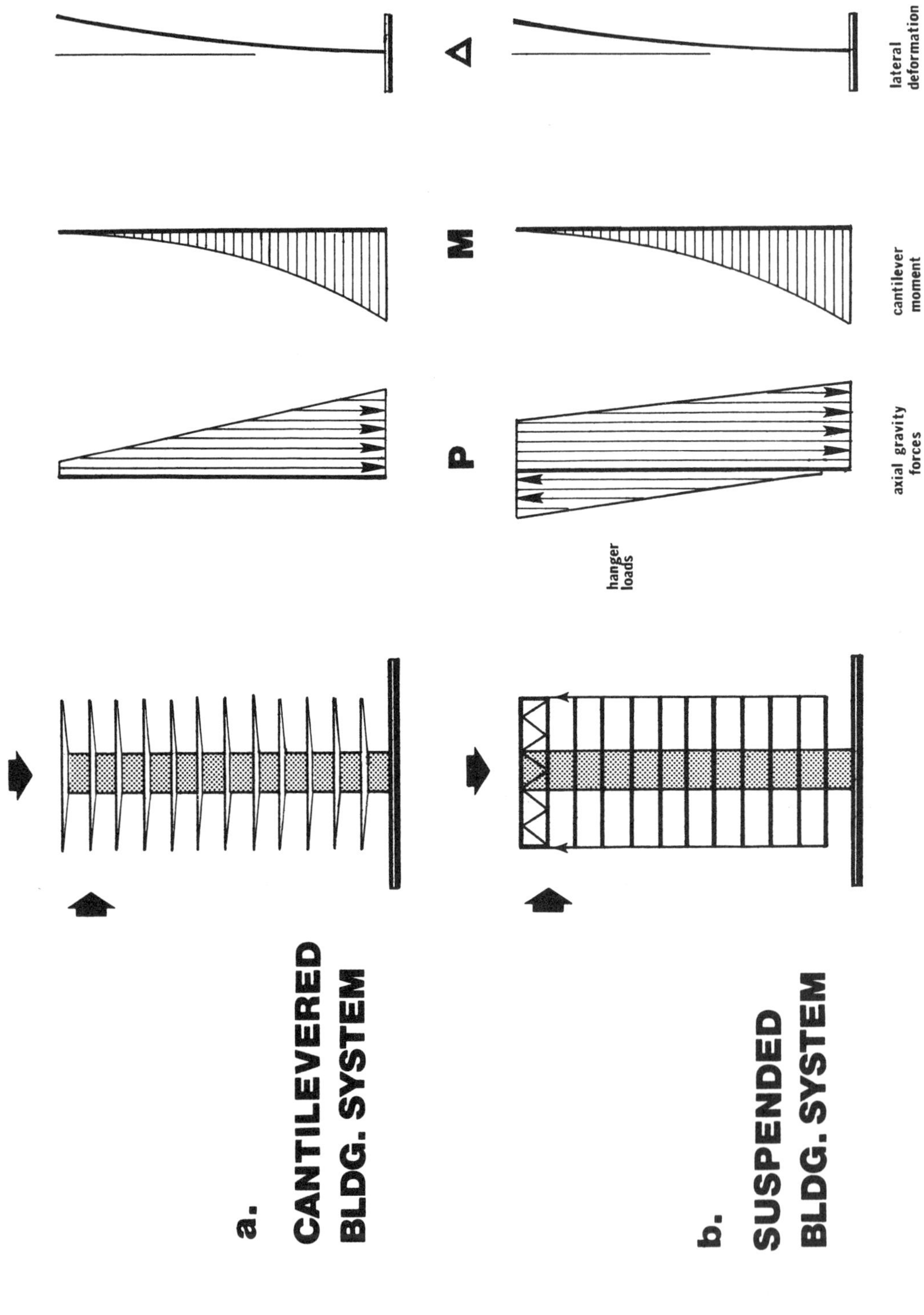

a. CANTILEVERED BLDG. SYSTEM

b. SUSPENDED BLDG. SYSTEM

P — axial gravity forces

hanger loads

M — cantilever moment

Δ — lateral deformation

Fig. 5.8

sive forces, thus may not have to be designed for tensile stresses due to the bending caused by lateral loads; this is especially true for heavy concrete cores. In addition, the capacity of the core material to resist shear stresses is increased.

The cantilevered system (Fig. 5.8a) is not a common building type because of the flexibility of the cantilevered floor structure and the relatively high amount of reinforcing steel needed to resist the negative slab moments. If the floor structure is supported at the perimeter by hangers suspended from story-high truss systems (Fig. 5.86b), the overall stiffness of the building is improved; the architectural expression of the building remains open and light. Obviously the attraction of all the loads within the building to a relatively small core area requires exceptional soil conditions with high bearing capacity.

Figure 5.8 illustrates how both central core systems respond to gravity and wind loads. The gravity loads in the cantilevered system increase progressively from zero at the top to maximum at the base, while the hanger loads in the suspended system first must be brought to the top of the core, thus inducing much more prestress force in the upper region of the core. Both systems respond similarly to lateral loads in bending, neglecting the difference of the induced compression due to gravity. The moment pattern is that of a uniformly loaded cantilever beam with maximum moment at the fixed end.

The response of a core to lateral loading is dependent on its shape, the degree of homogeneity and rigidity, and the direction of the load. At every floor level there are openings in the core, and the amount of continuity provided by the spandrels determines the behavior of the core. It may act like an open section and distort (i.e., warp) in its upper portion with no restraint, especially under asymmetrical loading causing twisting (Fig. 5.9). Thus additional torsional shearing stresses are generated at the top of the core along with additional lateral bending and shear in the flanges at the base. The effect of asymmetrical arrangement of cores within the building is also discussed in Chapter 4.

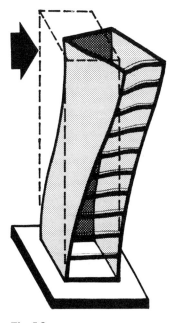

Fig. 5.9

RIGID FRAME SYSTEMS

Rigid frame skeletons generally consist of a rectangular grid of horizontal beams and vertical columns connected together in the same plane by means of rigid joints. The frame may be in plane with an interior wall of the building, or in plane with the facade. The rigid frame principle seems to be economical up to approximately 30 stories for steel framing and up to 20 stories for concrete framing.

Some typical rigid frame buildings appear in Fig. 5.10. Since this comparative study emphasizes the organization of typical column layouts as related to building form, laterally stiffened

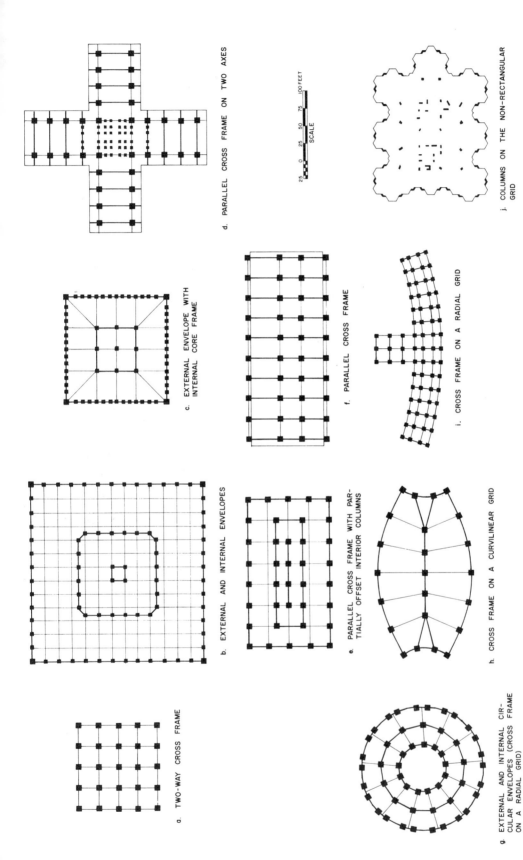

a. TWO-WAY CROSS FRAME

b. EXTERNAL AND INTERNAL ENVELOPES

c. EXTERNAL ENVELOPE WITH INTERNAL CORE FRAME

d. PARALLEL CROSS FRAME ON TWO AXES

e. PARALLEL CROSS FRAME WITH PAR- TIALLY OFFSET INTERIOR COLUMNS

f. PARALLEL CROSS FRAME

g. EXTERNAL AND INTERNAL CIR- CULAR ENVELOPES (CROSS FRAME ON A RADIAL GRID)

h. CROSS FRAME ON A CURVILINEAR GRID

i. CROSS FRAME ON A RADIAL GRID

j. COLUMNS ON THE NON-RECTANGULAR GRID

SCALE

Fig. 5.10.   Frame structure systems.

rigid frame buildings are also shown (e.g., Fig. 5.10f). This study reveals several major frame categories:

- Parallel cross frames (Figs. 5.10d–i).

- Envelope frames (Figs. 5.10b, c, g).

- Two-way cross frames (Fig. 5.10a).

- Frames on polygonal grids (Fig. 5.10j).

The plan figures show the application of these structural systems to various building plan forms organized by various types of grid patterns, including the following.

- Parallel cross frames.
  - •• On typical rectangular grid (Fig. 5.10f).
  - •• On rectangular grid with offset interior grid (Fig. 5.10e).
  - •• On radial grid (Fig. 5.10g, i).
  - •• On curvilinear grid (Fig. 5.10h).
  - •• On two axes (Fig. 5.10d).

- Envelope frames.
  - •• External envelopes with core cross frames (Fig. 5.10c).
  - •• External and internal envelopes on a square grid (Fig. 5.10b).
  - •• External and internal envelopes on a circular grid (Fig. 5.10g).

- Two-way frames: square grid (Fig. 5.10a).

- Frames on polygonal grids: complex form, almost organic in nature (Fig. 5.10j).

The few examples indicate the potential of subdividing a building form with frame systems.

Because of its continuity, the rigid frame responds to lateral loads primarily through flexure of the beams and columns (Fig. 5.11). This continuous character of the rigid frame is dependent on the rotational resistance of the member connections not to permit any slippage.

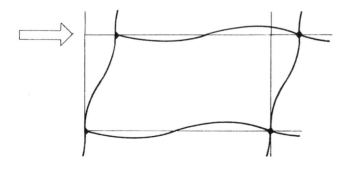

Fig. 5.11

The load capacity of the frame relies very much on the strength of the individual beams and columns; its capacity decreases as story height and column spacing become larger.

The lateral deflection of rigid frames is caused by two factors.

• DEFLECTION DUE TO CANTILEVER BENDING (FIG. 5.12a). This phenomenon is known as chord drift. In resisting the overturning moment, the frame acts as a vertical cantilever beam that bends through axial deformation of its fibers. In this case lengthening and shortening of the columns produce the lateral sway. This mode of deflection accounts for about 20% of the total drift of the structure.

• DEFLECTION DUE TO BENDING OF BEAMS AND COLUMS (FIG. 5.12b). This phenomenon is known as shear lag, or frame wracking. Horizontal and vertical shear forces acting on columns and beams, respectively, cause bending moments to be introduced into these members. As they bend, the entire frame distorts. This mode of deformation accounts for about 80% of the total sway of the structure, that is, 65% due to beam flexure and 15% due to column flexure. The curvature of the deflection corresponds to the external shear diagram: the slope of the deformation is maximum at the base of the structure, where the largest shear occurs.

• ACTUAL, TOTAL DEFORMATION OF THE STRUCTURE. Superposition of deflection curves of Figs. 5.12a and b yields the final deformation of the structure.

For further discussion of rigid frame behavior refer to Problems 7.3 to 7.6.

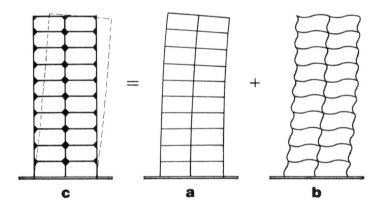

Fig. 5.12   c   a   b

THE WALL–BEAM STRUCTURE: INTERSPATIAL AND STAGGERED TRUSS SYSTEMS

The potential usage of wall-beam systems is discussed in more detail in Chapter 10. Here we are primarily concerned with story-high beams spanning across the short direction of a building. Supported on rows of columns along the exterior walls (Fig. 5.13), the beams may be trusses made of steel or concrete, or they may be solid concrete walls.

The most common wall beam structures are the interspatial and staggered truss systems. A typical interspatial building is illustrated in Fig. 5.13a. Trusses are used at every other floor. They support the floor slabs on both their top and bottom chords. The free space that is generated at alternate floors is advantageous for certain building types that require flexibility in planning.

The staggered truss building (Fig. 5.13b) is much stiffer than the interspatial system. Here trusses are used at every floor, arranged in a staggered pattern. By staggering the story-high wall beams at alternate floors, relatively large clear spaces are generated, while the floor slabs are made to span only half the truss spacing. These floor slabs rest on the top chord of one

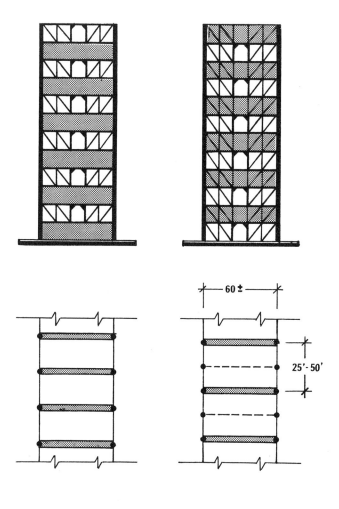

a. interspatial   b. staggered truss   Fig. 5.13

truss and hang from the bottom chord of the next, on the floor above. The elevation of the truss pattern looks rather similar to a running bond of brickwork (Fig. 4.2i).

The principle of staggering trusses is very efficient when applied to the resisting of horizontal and vertical loads. It uses about 40% less steel than a conventional braced frame in high-rise applications and calls for considerably fewer field connections. The system has already been applied to buildings in the 30-story range.

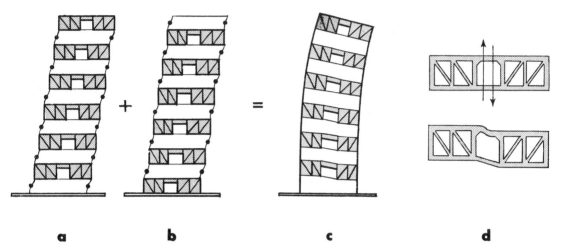

Fig. 5.14

The behavior of interspatial wall beam structures (Fig. 5.14a) reveals trussed levels that are extremely stiff, like rigid slices, and hardly deform. The open stories, however, can utilize only the columns in resisting the lateral load. These columns wrack in the mode of deformation similar to columns in a conventional rigid frame (Problem 7.10).

In staggered truss structures the floor slabs are assumed to act as infinitely stiff horizontal diaphragms, thus all points on any one floor will have equal horizontal displacement. Hence adjacent trussed frames (Figs. 5.14a, b) are forced to act together as a unit. That is, superposition of their separate modes of behavior yields approximately the deformed state of the entire system (Fig. 5.14c). The deflection of the building is that of a rigid cantilever beam. The deformation curve indicates that the columns need not be designed for bending moments across the short direction of the building. Therefore the floor slabs, acting as rigid diaphragms, transmit the entire wind shear to the trusses, which in turn translate the load to the columns, to be resisted axially. Since the trusses must resist vertical shear, any opening in the wall beams causes wracking (Fig. 5.14d), thus will lessen the rigidity of the beams.

The exterior columns may be turned with their webs perpendicular to the trusses, thereby utilizing their strong axes to resist wind in the longitudinal direction. The lateral stiffness in that direction may be increased, for instance, by adding spandrel panels to generate frame action.

FRAME–SHEAR WALL BUILDING SYSTEMS

Pure rigid frame systems are not practical in buildings higher than 30 stories; systems have been used that employ a shear wall of some type within the frame to resist lateral loads. The shear walls are either of concrete or trussed steel bracing. They may be closed interior cores, as around elevator shafts or stairwells, or parallel walls within the building, or they may be vertical facade trusses.

Some typical high-rise buildings using cores and frames appear in plan in Fig. 5.15. The discussion is based on purely geometrical considerations. From a behavioral point of view, these plan forms can very well apply to flat slab systems or frame–shear wall systems with belt trusses.

The different plan forms suggest a variety of possible layout solutions. The core systems as related to building form are organized from the following points of view; letters in parentheses refer to individual diagrams in Fig. 5.15.

- Location of cores.

  •• Exterior facade cores (*i*).
  •• Interior cores: facade cores (*j*), cores within the building (*a–c*, *f–h*, etc.).
  •• Eccentric cores (*d*, *i*).

- Number of cores.

  •• Single cores (*a, b, d, e,* etc.).
  •• Split cores (*h, s, t*).
  •• Multiple cores (*c, j, l*).

- Shapes of cores.

  •• Closed forms: square, rectangular, circular, triangular.
  •• Open forms: X-shaped, I-shaped, and [-shaped.
  •• Core shape as related to building form (*j, o, t*).

The frame–shear wall systems are classified with respect to their response to lateral loading, which may be one of the following three types.

Hinged Frame–Shear Wall Systems (Fig. 5.19a)

Since the frame girders are hinged, the frame can carry only gravity loads. The shear wall resists all lateral loads.

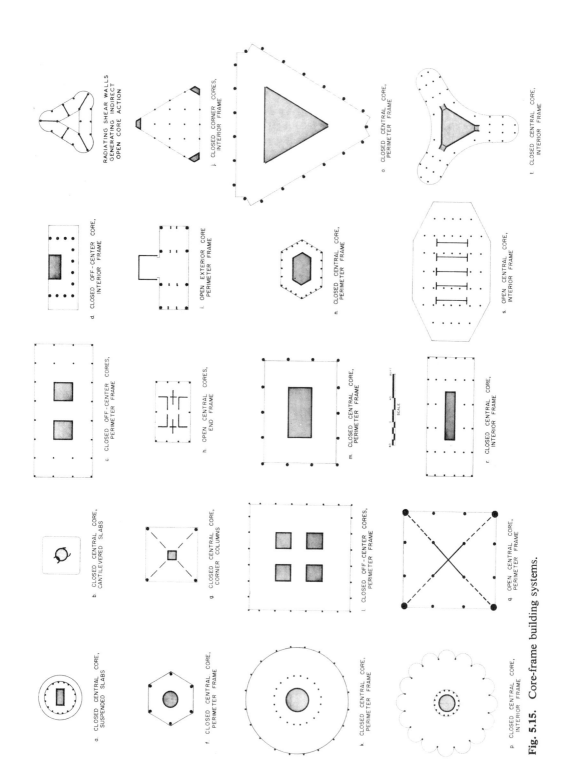

Fig. 5.15. Core-frame building systems.

RADIATING SHEAR WALLS GENERATING INDIRECT OPEN CORE ACTION

j. CLOSED CORNER CORES, INTERIOR FRAME

o. CLOSED CENTRAL CORE, PERIMETER FRAME

t. CLOSED CENTRAL CORE, INTERIOR FRAME

d. CLOSED OFF-CENTER CORE, INTERIOR FRAME

i. OPEN EXTERIOR CORE, PERIMETER FRAME

n. CLOSED CENTRAL CORE, PERIMETER FRAME

s. OPEN CENTRAL CORE, INTERIOR FRAME

c. CLOSED OFF-CENTER CORES, PERIMETER FRAME

h. OPEN CENTRAL CORES, END FRAME

m. CLOSED CENTRAL CORE, PERIMETER FRAME

r. CLOSED CENTRAL CORE, INTERIOR FRAME

SCALE

b. CLOSED CENTRAL CORE, CANTILEVERED SLABS

g. CLOSED CENTRAL CORE, CORNER COLUMNS

l. CLOSED OFF-CENTER CORES, PERIMETER FRAME

q. OPEN CENTRAL CORE, PERIMETER FRAME

a. CLOSED CENTRAL CORE, SUSPENDED SLABS

f. CLOSED CENTRAL CORE, PERIMETER FRAME

k. CLOSED CENTRAL CORE, PERIMETER FRAME

p. CLOSED CENTRAL CORE, INTERIOR FRAME

Hinged Frame–Vierendeel–Shear Wall Interaction Systems

The lateral forces are resisted by a shear wall and rigid frame (i.e., Vierendeel) system. In the example of Fig. 5.16 the two facade walls across the short direction of the building carry one-half of the total wind, and the core carries the other half. The interior and longitudinal facade frames carry only gravity loads.

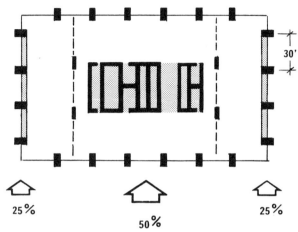

30'

25%   50%   25%

Fig. 5.16

Rigid Frame–Shear Wall Interaction

Using only shear walls to respond to lateral loads is impractical above about 500 ft. To be sufficiently strong, cores have to become too large and do not correspond to their functions for vertical transportation and energy distribution. Furthermore, deflection may be large enough to cause cracking of partitions and windows or even to evoke unpleasant psychological reactions among the building's occupants. The lateral rigidity is greatly improved by using not only the shear wall system but also the rigid frame to resist lateral forces. The total deflection of the interacting shear wall and rigid frame systems is obtained by superimposing the individual modes of deformation (Fig. 5.17).

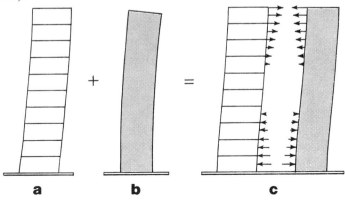

a   +   b   =   c

Fig. 5.17

- RIGID FRAME SHEAR MODE DEFORMATION. This deflection is indicated schematically only in Fig. 5.17a. Note that the slope of the deformation is greatest at the base of the structure where the maximum shear is acting.

- SHEAR WALL BENDING MODE DEFORMATION. The shear wall in Fig. 5.17b may be a solid concrete wall or a vertical steel truss; it may be an interior core, parallel internal walls, or a facade wall. The system acts as a vertical cantilever beam, bending as such. Note that the slope of the deflection is greatest at the top of the building, indicating that in this region, the shear wall system contributes the least stiffness.

- INTERACTION OF FRAME AND SHEAR CORE. The interaction of frame and shear wall (Fig. 5.17c) is obtained by superimposing the separate deflection modes resulting in a flat-S-curve. Because of the different deflection characteristics of shear wall and frame, the shear wall is pulled back by the frame in the upper portion of the building, and pushed forward in the lower. Hence wind shear is carried mostly by the frame in the upper portion of the building and by the shear wall in the lower portion. The interaction of the two structural systems is investigated mathematically in Problem 7.7.

FLAT SLAB BUILDING STRUCTURES

Flat slab systems consist of solid or waffle-type concrete slabs supported directly on columns, thus eliminating the need for floor framing. This results in minimum story height, an obvious economic advantage. Drop panels and/or column capitals are frequently used because of high shear concentrations around the colunms. Slabs without drop panels are commonly called flat plates. The system is adaptable to an irregular support layout.

Some of the disadvantages of flat slab systems are as follows:

- Large dead load is undesirable when difficult foundation conditions are encountered.

- Small depth-to-span ratios can cause the appearance of excessive deflection of slabs.

- The relatively short span capability (15–25 ft, or up to 35 ft if posttensioned) limits applicability to building types with frequent partition layout, such as apartment buildings.

Depending on the height-to-width ratio of the building, flat slab structures may have only colunms as bearing elements, or they may use shear walls in addition to the columns to increase lateral stiffness.

The monolithic character of the concrete structure forces the entire building to react to lateral loads as a unit. It is not realistic to assume that lateral loads are resisted entirely by the more rigid core or shear wall and that the slabs and columns contribute no strength at all.

The flat slab itself, though relatively flexible, provides strength to the system because of its continuity with the shear walls and columns. One can visualize that a portion of the slab will act as a shallow beam continuous with the columns, thus behaving as a rigid frame.

Hence the behavior of the total system is similar to that of a core-frame system; Fig. 5.17 also serves to show the behavior of flat slab buildings. The lateral forces are primarily resisted by frame action in the upper portion of the structure and by the shear wall or core system in the lower portion.

SHEAR WALL–FRAME INTERACTION SYSTEM WITH RIGID BELT TRUSSES

The braced frame (i.e., frame–shear wall building) becomes inefficient above about 40 stories, since large amounts of material are needed to make the bracing sufficiently stiff and strong. The efficiency of the building structure may be improved by about 30% by using horizontal belt trusses to tie the frame to the core. The trusses are fixed rigidly to the core and are simply connected to the exterior colunms. When the shear core tries to bend, the belt trusses act as lever arms that put direct axial stresses into the perimeter columns. These colunms, in turn, act as struts to resist the deflection of the core. That is the core fully develops the horizontal shears, and the belt trusses transfer the vertical shear from the core to the facade frame. Thus the building is made to act as a unit, very similar to the cantilever tube.

The building can have one or several belt trusses; the more trusses used, the better the integration of core and facade columns. They can be placed at locations within the building where the diagonal bracing will not interfere with the building's function (e.g., at mechanical levels). The structural principle of employing belt trusses at the top and center of a building seems to be economical in applications up to approximately 60 stories.

The stress diagram in Fig. 5.18 illustrates the relative efficiency of hinging the belt trusses to the perimeter columns rather than fixing them rigidly. If the trusses were to be continuously connected to these columns, the entire system would act as a unit, thus utilizing only a small percentage of the moment-resisting capacity of the core, whose walls are relatively close to the neutral axis of the building. This is indicated by the continuous distribution of stresses shown for the rigid system (Fig. 5.18a).

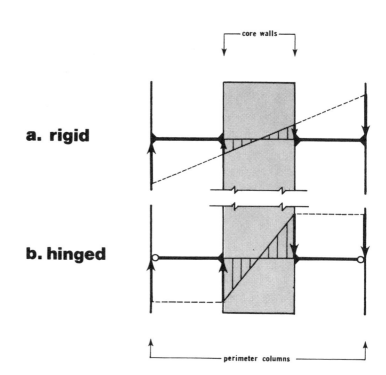

a. rigid

b. hinged

— core walls —

perimeter columns

Fig. 5.18

On the other hand, elastic arms, cantilevered from the core and hinged to the perimeter columns, better develop the moment resisting capacity of the core, and engage the exterior columns like the rigid system (Fig. 5.18b). Yet since the hinged shear connections induce no bending moments into the columns, the axial capacity of the columns is increased.

The response of a core frame building with belt trusses to lateral loading is given in Fig. 5.19. When the frame is hinged to the core of a structure (Fig. 5.19a), the core behaves like a cantilever and its top is free to rotate. The frame hardly resists any rotation. If the frame is tied to the core by a belt truss (Fig. 5.19b), however, any rotation at the top of the system is

Fig. 5.19

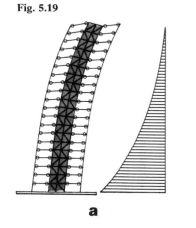
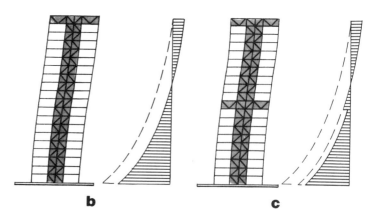

a   b   c

restricted, since the perimeter columns tie the belt truss down; there is no bending moment in the columns. The partial fixity provided at the top of the system is reflected in the moment diagram. The system no longer acts as a pure cantilever because it is restrained at the top as well as at the bottom. The resulting deflection is a flat S-curve, with a zero moment at the point of inflection. The bending moment at the base of the building is less than is the case for Fig. 5.19a.

The strength and stiffness of the system is further increased by adding additional belt trusses at intermediate levels within the building (Fig. 5.20c). At each trussed level the system is restrained from rotating. The fixity provided at these levels pulls the moment diagram back. The bending moment at the base of the building is further reduced due to the greater translation of lateral forces to axial forces; the building sway is further decreased.

TUBULAR SYSTEMS

A recent development in structural design is the concept of tubular behavior introduced by Fazlur Khan of S.O.M. At present, four of the world's five tallest buildings are tubular systems. They are the Hancock Building, the Sears Building, and the Standard Oil Building in Chicago, and the World Trade Center in New York (Figs. 5.20e, h, f, and g, respectively). Tubular systems are so efficient that in most cases the amount of structural material used per square foot of floor space is comparable to that used in conventionally framed buildings half the size.

Tubular design assumes that the facade structure responds to lateral loads as a closed hollow box beam cantilevering out of the ground. Since the exterior walls resist all or most of the wind load, costly interior diagonal bracing or shear walls are eliminated.

The tube's walls consist of closely spaced colunms around the perimeter of the building tied together by deep spandrel beams. This facade structure looks like a perforated wall. The stiffness of the facade wall may be further increased by adding diagonal braces, causing trusslike action. The rigidity of the tube is so high that it repsonds to lateral loading similar to a cantilever beam.

As we see later, the exterior tube alone can resist all lateral loads entirely, or it can be further stiffened by adding interior bracing of some kind. The following discussion deals with different applications of tubular design that have been used to date, and the section is subdivided into the following topics:

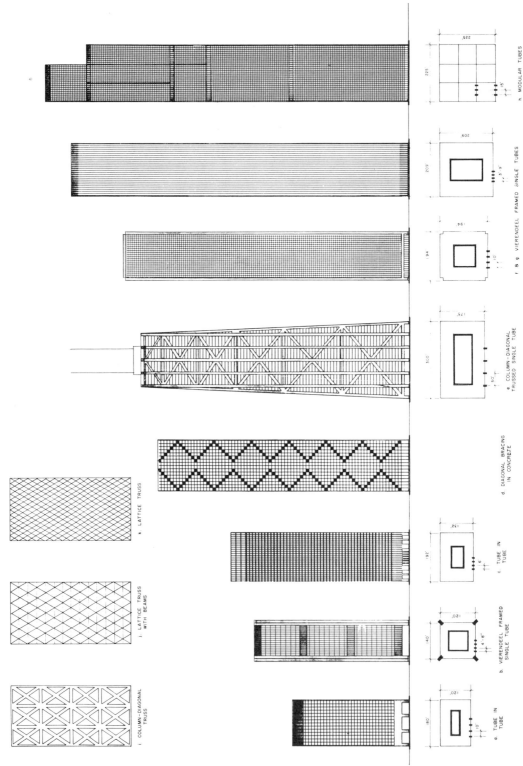

Fig. 5.20. Tubular building structures.

- Hollow tube
    - Framed tube
    - Trussed tube:
        - Column–diagonal trussed tube
        - Lattice trussed tube
- Interior braced tube
    - Tube with parallel shear walls
    - Tube in tube
    - Modified tube
        - Framed tube with rigid frames
        - Tube in semitube
    - Modular tubes

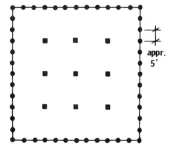

Fig. 5.21. Framed hollow tube.

Hollow Tube

Framed Tube

The framed tube, the earliest application of the tubular concept, was first used in the 43-story Dewitt Chestnut Apartment Building in Chicago (S.O.M., 1961). In this Vierendeel tube system the exterior walls of the building, consisting of a closely spaced rectangular grid of beams and columns rigidly connected together, resist lateral loads through cantilever tube action without using interior bracing. The interior columns are assumed to carry gravity loads only and do not contribute to the exterior tube's stiffness (Fig. 5.21). The stiff floors act as diaphragms with respect to distributing the lateral forces to the perimeter walls.

Other examples of hollow framed tube buildings are the 83-story Standard Oil Building in Chicago and the 110-story World Trade Center in New York (Figs. 5.20*f, g*). Although these buildings have interior cores, they act as hollow tubes because the cores are not designed to resist lateral loads.

The Vierendeel tube evolves logically from the conventional rigid frame structure. The system possesses lateral stiffness and torsional qualities while retaining flexible interior possibilities. The facade grid is so closely spaced that it can serve as mullions for the glazing (Fig. 5.21).

It would be ideal in the design of framed tube systems if the exterior walls were to act as a unit, responding to lateral loads in pure cantilever bending. If this were the case, all columns that make up the tube, analogous to the fibers of a beam, would be either in direct axial tension or in compression. The linear stress distribution that would result is indicated by broken lines in Fig. 5.22.

However the true behavior of the tube lies somewhere between that of a pure cantilever and a pure frame. The sides of the tube parallel to the wind tend to act as independent multibay rigid frames, given the flexibility of the spandrel beams. This flexibility results in wracking of the frame due to shear, called

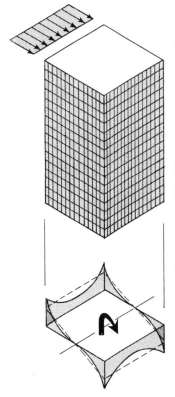

Fig. 5.22

shear lag. Hence bending takes place in columns and beams. This type of behavior, characteristic of rigid frames, has been discussed previously (Fig. 5.12*b*).

The effect of shear lag on the tube action results in nonlinear pressure distribution along the column envelope; the columns at the corners of the building are forced to take a higher share of the load than the columns in between (Fig. 5.22). Furthermore, the total deflection of the building no longer resembles a cantilever beam, as shear mode deformation becomes more significant.

The shear problem severely affects the efficiency of tubular systems, and all later developments of tubular design attempt to overcome it. The framed tube principle seems to be economical for steel buildings up to 80 stories and for concrete buildings up to 60 stories. The approximate behavior of a single tube is analytically investigated in Problem 7.11.

Trussed Tube

The inherent weakness of the framed tube lies in the flexibility of its spandrel beams. Its rigidity is greatly improved by adding diagonal members. The shear is now primarily absorbed by the diagonals, not by the spandrels. The diagonals carry the lateral forces directly in predominantly axial action. This reduction of shear lag provides for nearly pure cantilever behavior (Fig. 5.23).

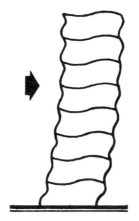 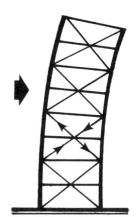

Fig. 5.23

Column–Diagonal Trussed Tube

This system uses diagonals within the rectangular grid of beams and columns (Figs. 5.20*e, i*). The diagonals together with the spandrel beams create a wall-like rigidity against lateral loads. Not only do the diagonals carry the major portion of wind loads, they act as inclined columns supporting gravity loads, as well.

Normally the compression induced by gravity loads is not overcome by the tension caused by lateral loads. This dual function of the diagonal members makes this system rather efficient for very tall buildings (up to about 100 stories in steel). It allows much larger spacing of columns than the framed tube.

An essential characteristic of the system is its capability to distribute a concentrated load evenly through the entire structure, as indicated in Fig. 5.24 for the first 56 stories of the John Hancock Building in Chicago. The spandrels carry gravity loads between the colunms and act as ties preventing the floors from stretching. In this way they improve the effectiveness of the diagonals in acting as a primary load distribution system.

An interesting approach to achieving diagonals in an exterior concrete wall has been proposed in a student project at I.I.T. (Fig. 5.20d) in which diagonals are created by filling window openings in a diagonal pattern.

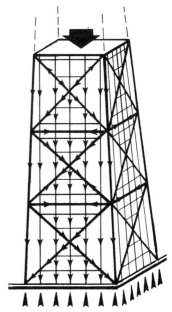

Fig. 5.24

Lattice Trussed Tube

In this system the tube is made up of closely spaced diagonals with no vertical columns (Figs. 5.20j, k). The diagonals act as inclined columns, carry all gravity loads, and stiffen the structure against wind. The diagonals may be tied together by horizontal beams.

The diagonals are extremely efficient in responding to lateral loads, but they are less efficient than vertical columns in transmitting gravity loads to the ground. Furthermore, the large number of joints required between diagonals and the problems related to window details make the lattice truss system generally impractical.

Interior Braced Tube

The framed exterior tube may be stiffened in plane by adding diagonals, or it may be stiffened from within the building by adding shear walls or interior cores. Several approaches to interior bracing are discussed in the following sections.

Tube with Parallel Shear Walls

The exterior tubular wall can be stiffened by incorporating interior shear walls into the plan. One can visualize the exterior tube walls as the flanges of a huge built-up beam system in which the shear walls represent the webs. The stresses in the exterior tube walls are primarily axial, since shear lag is minimized.

The examples in Figs. 5.25a and b, respectively, illustrate two approaches: wide spacing of facade columns, requiring a shear wall for every column, and close spacing of facade colunms, requiring only two shear walls.

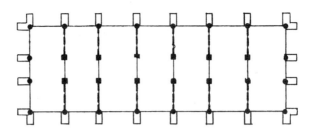

a

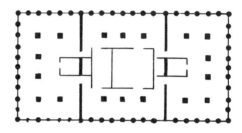

Fig. 5.25   **b**

Tube in Tube

The stiffness of a hollow tube system is very much improved by using the core not only for gravity loads but to resist lateral loads, as well. The floor structure ties the exterior and interior tubes together, and they respond as a unit to lateral forces.

The reaction of a tube in tube system to wind is similar to that of a frame and shear wall structure. However the framed exterior tube is much stiffer than a rigid frame.

Figure 5.26 indicates that the exterior tube resists most of the wind in the upper portion of the building, whereas the core carries most of the loads in the lower portion.

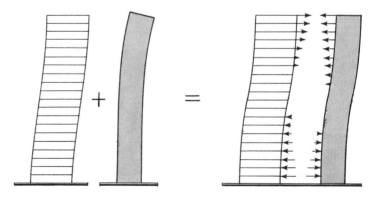

Fig. 5.26

The tube in tube approach has been used in the 38-story Brunswick Building in Chicago, and the 52-story One Shell Plaza Building in Houston (Fig. 5.20c).

Taking the tube-in-tube concept one step further, the designers of a 60-story office building in Tokyo (Fig. 5.27) used a triple tube. In this system the exterior tube alone resists wind loads, but all three tubes, connected by the floor systems (i.e., diaphragms) interact in resisting earthquake loads, a significant design factor in Japan.

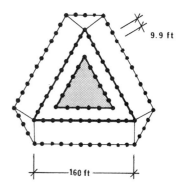

Fig. 5.27

Modified Tube

Tubular action is most efficient in round and nearly square buildings. Buildings deviating from these forms present special structural considerations when tubular action is desired. The following two examples describe such conditions.

Framed Tube with Rigid Frames

The hexagonal shape of a 40-story office building in Charlotte, N.C. (Fig. 5.28), forced the designers to modify the tubular principle. The pointed ends of this hexagonal building exhibited excessive shear lag, making it impossible to get effective tubular response. Adding rigid frames in the transverse direction served to tie the exterior walls together. Thus the end walls in triangular arrangement were reinforced by the rigid frames. By tying together the perimeter walls, effective tubular action was achieved.

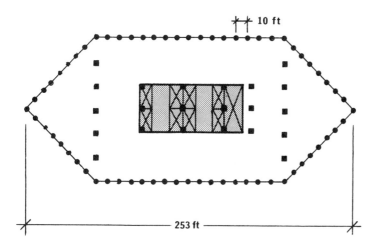

Fig. 5.28

Tube in Semitube

The irregular plan of the 32-story Western Pennsylvania National Bank in Pittsburgh (Fig. 5.29) gave rise to still another special solution of tubular design. In most tubular buildings, the tubular effect is generated by the exterior walls. In this building, however, the two intersecting octagons form a structural tube in the central part of the building.

The two end portions of the building are stiffened by channel-like wall frame systems. The wind is resisted by the combination of interior tube and the huge exterior end-wall channels.

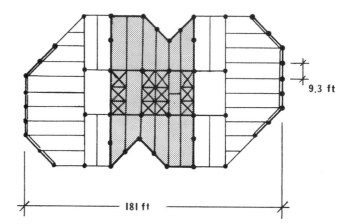

Fig. 5.29

9.3 ft

181 ft

Modular Tubes

The latest development in tubular design is the modular or bundled tube principle. This system has been used for the Sears Building in Chicago (Fig. 5.20*h*), currently the tallest building in the world.

The exterior framed tube is stiffened by interior cross diaphragms in both directions (Fig. 5.30); an assemblage of cell tubes is formed. These individual tubes are independently strong, therefore may be bundled in any configuration and discontinued at any level. A further advantage of this bundled tube system lies in the extremely large floor areas that may be enclosed.

The interior diaphragms act as webs of a huge cantilever beam in resisting shear forces, thus minimizing shear lag. In addition, they contribute strength against bending.

The behavior of this system is shown in the stress distribution diagram in Fig. 5.30. The diaphragms parallel to the wind (i.e., webs) absorb shear, thereby generating points of peak stress at points of intersection with perpendicular walls (i.e., flanges). indicating the individual action of each tube. Note the difference in axial stress distribution if there are no internal stiffeners—that is, a single tube (Fig. 5.22). The vertical diaphragms tend to distribute the axial stresses equally, although shear lag still occurs to some extent. However the deviation from ideal tubular behavior, indicated by broken lines, does not seem to be very significant.

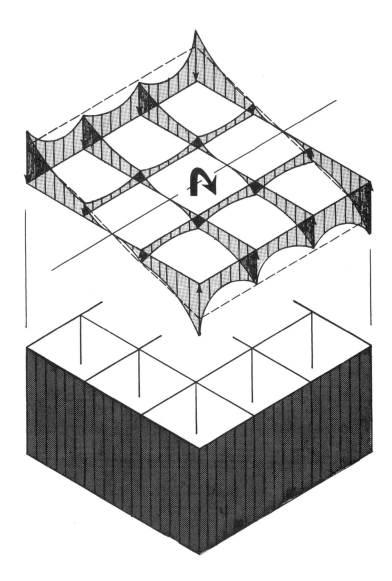

Fig. 5.30

COMPOSITE BUILDINGS

In the hybrid structure, a recent development aimed at increasing the lateral stiffness of framed skyscrapers, concrete and steel act together as a structural unit. This concept has been applied for several years to individual structural members such as floors (Chapter 8) and columns. However designing the entire building by composite construction is a completely new approach. Following are two distinctive solutions involving the application of applying this concept.

Tubular Composite Buildings

In a system developed by Skidmore, Owings, and Merrill, the exterior steel frame is stiffened against lateral deformation by a cast-in-place concrete, perforated perimeter wall. The resulting

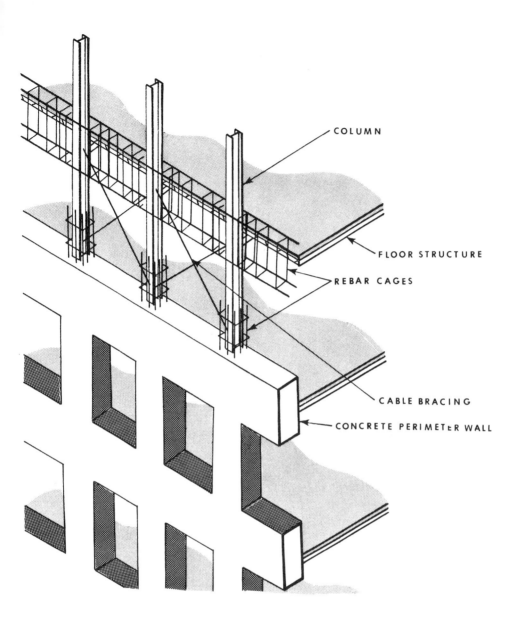

COLUMN

FLOOR STRUCTURE

REBAR CAGES

CABLE BRACING

CONCRETE PERIMETER WALL

SCHEMATIC SKETCH OF
A TUBULAR COMPOSITE BUILDING

Fig. 5.31

sway of the building resembles that of a rigid tube cantilevering out of the ground. This approach combines the fast erection and high strength (thus the interior space flexibility) of steel construction, with the fireproofing, insulating, lateral rigidity, and moldability of the concrete curtain wall. It has been used for the 36-story Gateway III in Chicago, the 50-story One Shell Square Tower in New Orleans, and the 24-story CDC Building in Houston, where precast concrete panels became the formwork for the cast-in-place concrete.

The construction process consists of first erecting the steel frame for 8 to 10 stories. Since the exterior columns only carry construction loads, they are lighter than the interior ones. The outer frame is temporarily cable braced for lateral stability. Next cellular steel decking is laid and the concrete floor is poured, to stabilize the skeleton and to allow interior work to begin. After reinforcing cages and formwork are placed around the columns and for the spandrels, concrete is cast to form a continuous perforated wall. This process is repeated in increments of 8 to 10 stories (Fig. 5.31).

However the difference in movement between the exterior steel-concrete columns and the interior steel columns causes a problem. An adjustment in the placement of girders must be made to overcome the unequal shortening of the columns due to elastic behavior, shrinkage, and creep (Fig. 5.32).

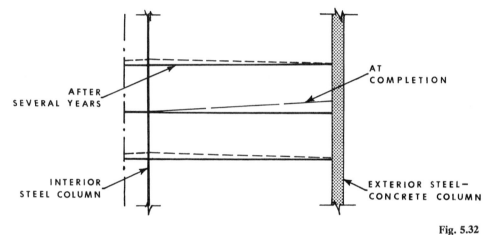

AT COMPLETION

AFTER SEVERAL YEARS

INTERIOR STEEL COLUMN

EXTERIOR STEEL– CONCRETE COLUMN

Fig. 5.32

Since in this system the tubular skin resists all lateral forces, the columns and girders framing the utility core can be lighter because they carry gravitational loads only. Also, the net usable floor area in the upper stories is increased where the core area is reduced.

Reid and Tarics Associates of San Francisco developed another tubular composite building system. As facade structure they use steel spandrel girders and tubular steel columns filled with concrete (Fig. 5.33). Again the envelope provides enough stiffness to carry all lateral loading. The prefabricated tree consists of a one tubular column two stories high and two cantilevering steel girders. The trees are bolted to each other at midspan of the beams and midheight of the columns; these connection points are the least stressed with respect to lateral loading. The natural continuity of the girders is not interrupted at the columns where stresses are highest; they pierce the columns with only the web connected to the tube. Thus the

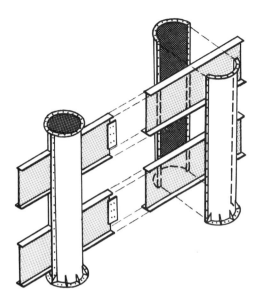

Fig. 5.33

number of highly stressed building connections is greatly reduced.

Plate Wall Cladding

Curtain walls of panels are usually attached to steel framed
structures. They are nonstructural and serve solely as environmental control devices. Mies van der Rohe was one of the first
architects to introduce steel cladding as a facade treatment to

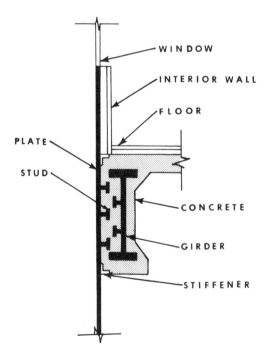

Fig. 5.34

high-rise buildings. In his 860 Lake Shore Drive apartment buildings he used 5/16 in. painted steel plates to cover the concrete that fireproofed the steel frame. When the cladding is bonded with studs to the reinforced concrete, it provides not only weather proofing, window framing, and the desired architectural expression, but also structural stiffness (Fig. 5.34). Primary resistance to lateral drift is provided by the girders in most rigid frame buildings. However the composite action of the steel skin and concrete-steel frame improves the lateral resistance so much that the interior girders need less stiffness. Moreover, the sway of the building is reduced by 20 to 50% without increasing the weight of the structure. Since the steel cladding is not fireproofed, codes do not allow its use for supporting gravity loads.

The approach of using the curtain wall efficiently to carry lateral loads and combining the best qualities of concrete and steel in construction and structure is just beginning to be explored. With the interest in more economical systems, this area will continue to develop.

COMPARISON OF HIGH–RISE STRUCTURAL SYSTEMS

This chapter discusses different types of high-rise framing concepts, and each structural system is shown to be suitable for certain building heights, or rather, for certain building height-to-width ratios. Figure 5.35, according to Fazlur Khan, compares most of these structural concepts. Steel and concrete systems are presented separately. The structural systems given for certain heights should not be considered an absolute rule. In fact, the 102-story Empire State Building is characterized by a rigid frame–shear wall interaction system, indicated as applying to buildings less than 40 stories high. The chart is organized according to structural efficiency (i.e., optimization) as measured by the weight per square foot; that is, the weight of the total building structure divided by the total square footage of gross floor area.

Low- to medium-rise buildings are normally designed for gravity loads, then checked for their ability to resist lateral loads. However high-rise buildings are much more susceptible to lateral force action. Figure 5.36 reveals the drastic increase in the amount of material needed for resistance of lateral forces for a five-bay rigid steel frame building. With respect to gravity loads, the weight of the structure increases almost linearly with the number of stories. However the amount of material needed

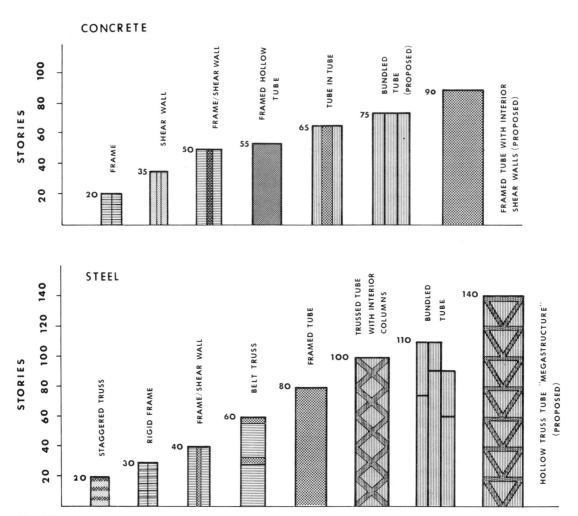

Fig. 5.35

for resistance of lateral forces increases at a drastically accelerating rate. The example shows the infeasibility of using the rigid frame principle with about 55 psf for a 90-story building, instead of the tubular system with only 34 psf (e.g., Standard Oil Building, Chicago). The most efficient structure is one in which the wind stresses superimposed on the gravity amount to an increase of less than 33% over the gravity stresses; the codes sanction an increase of 33% in allowable stresses if gravity and wind or earthquake act together. The selection of a particular structural system for a certain building height approaches that condition, as indicated by the broken line in Fig. 5.36.

Weight-to-area ratios for some typical high-rise buildings are given in Table 5.1 The frame–shear wall system of the Empire State Building is far from an optimum solution, as indicated by the 42.2 psf in contrast to the 29.7 psf of the tubular John

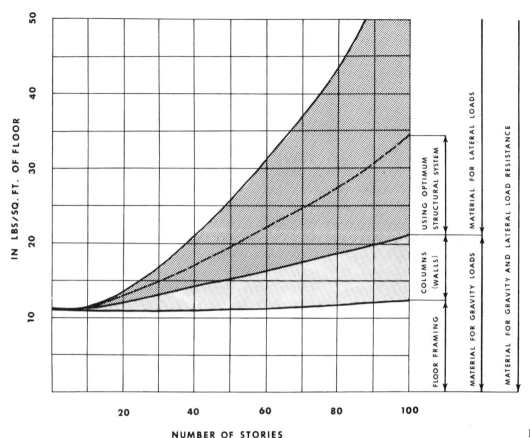

IN LBS/SQ. FT. OF FLOOR

NUMBER OF STORIES

FLOOR FRAMING

COLUMNS (WALLS)

USING OPTIMUM STRUCTURAL SYSTEM

MATERIAL FOR GRAVITY LOADS

MATERIAL FOR LATERAL LOADS

MATERIAL FOR GRAVITY AND LATERAL LOAD RESISTANCE

Fig. 5.36

Hancock Center. An even larger contrast is the 60-story Chase Manhattan Building with 55 psf and the slightly lower 54-story IDS Building with only 17.9 psf. The Chase Manhattan Building is a long-span rigid frame that needs huge girders to resist wind forces. The IDS Building owes its efficiency to the belt truss system. Disproportionate amounts of steel do not necessarily indicate that the structural design of the building is poor. For instance, the Civic Center in Chicago uses about twice as much steel as other buildings in its height range. However it has to satisfy the functional requirements of size and location of courtrooms. Thus the girder spans are 87 ft and the floor heights are much larger than usual (i.e., 30 stories for 640 ft). Buildings that solely house office space have high loads and high story heights (12–14 ft); those containing some apartment units have lower loads and their story heights are less (9–11 ft.).

An optimum solution seems to be available for any building type, considering the wide variety of structural systems discussed in this chapter.

Table 5.1

Year	Stories	Height/Width	psf	Building
1930	102	9.3	42.2	Empire State Building, New York
1968	100	7.9	29.7	John Hancock Center, Chicago
1972	110	6.9	37.0	World Trade Center, New York
1974	109	6.4	33.0	Sears & Roebuck, Chicago
1963	60	7.3	55.2	Chase Manhattan, New York
1969	60	5.7	38.0	First National Bank, Chicago
1971	64	6.3	30.0	U.S. Steel Building, Pittsburgh
1971	57	6.1	17.9	I.D.S. Center, Minneapolis
1957	42	5.1	28.0	Seagram Building, New York
1970	41	4.1	21.0	Boston Co. Building, Boston
1965	30	5.7	38.0	Civic Center, Chicago
1969	26	4.0	26.0	Alcoa Building, San Francisco
1971	10	5.1	6.3	Low Income Housing, Brockton, Mass.

CHAPTER SIX

Other Design Approaches Controlling Building Drift

In recent years wind and earthquake loading have become determining factors in high-rise building design. Chapter 2 indicated that the introduction of high strength structural materials resulted in reduction of member sizes or building weight, which in turn caused buildings to be more flexible and more susceptible to aerodynamic action. The skyscrapers of today sway and oscillate, in contrast to the heavyweight high rise of the past. For instance, the Empire State Building (1931) deflects only 6.5 in., then vibrates 7.2 in., resulting in a maximum deflection of 10.1 in. at an 80 mph wind.

The control of the dynamic response of a high-rise building can be achieved in the following ways:

- By increasing stiffness through the use of an efficient structural system (Chapter 5).

- By increasing the weight of the structure (not feasible).

- By increasing building density through the addition of more structural and fill-in materials (not feasible).

- By selecting an efficient building shape.

- By generating additional forces in the building to counteract the external lateral action.

The last two approaches are briefly discussed in the following sections.

EFFICIENT BUILDING FORMS

Generally, architects are limiting high-rise building forms to rectangular prisms, which from a geometrical point of view are rather susceptible to lateral drift. Other building shapes are not as responsive to lateral force action. Having inherent strength in their geometrical form, they provide higher structural efficiency or allow greater building height at a lower cost. Some of these building forms are discussed in the following sections.

The rigidity of a building can be greatly increased by sloping the exterior columns, resulting in a truncated pyramid, a rather stiff, closed form (John Hancock Center in Chicago, Fig. 5.20e). The reductions in lateral drift range from 10 to 50%, with the greatest influence in the taller and narrower building structures. A computer study showed that a slope of only 8% in the exterior columns produced 50% reduction in the lateral displacement of a 40-story building. (Reference 6.2)

A variation of the John Hancock Building's truncated pyramid is the full pyramid of the 50-story Transamerica Building in San Francisco (Fig. 6.1e). This 853 ft high building consists of a moment-resisting facade frame having only the four corner columns joined at the spire, achieving A-frame action. The vertical interior columns do not intersect with the sloping exterior columns; they are discontinued 15 ft before intersection and support only the floors.

Reduction of lateral building displacement can also be achieved by tapering the exterior frame, as in the 60-story First National Bank of Chicago (Fig. 6.d). The structural benefits are greatest when the taper extends the full height of the building. In the First National Bank the taper of the exterior steel columns starts at one-third the way down from the top of the building.

A cyclindrical building form provides true tubular geometry and true- three-dimensional response to lateral loading. The Marina City Towers (Figs. 6.1f and 5.15p) in Chicago are prime examples of that type of form. A typical tower consists of a ring of columns at the perimeter and around the corridor adjacent to the central concrete core. These columns reduce the required size of the radial beams and distribute the loads to the caisson footings. Approximately 70% of the lateral loads will be carried by the core. To preserve the lateral stiffness of the core, the openings in the core were staggered from floor to floor.

In addition to the structural advantage of three-dimensional action, the cylindrical building offers less surface area perpendicular to the wind direction, thus the magnitude of the wind pressure is greatly reduced, compared to what a prismatic building experiences. Building codes permit a reduction of the wind pressure design loads for circular buildings by 20 to 40% of the usual values for comparably sized rectangular buildings.

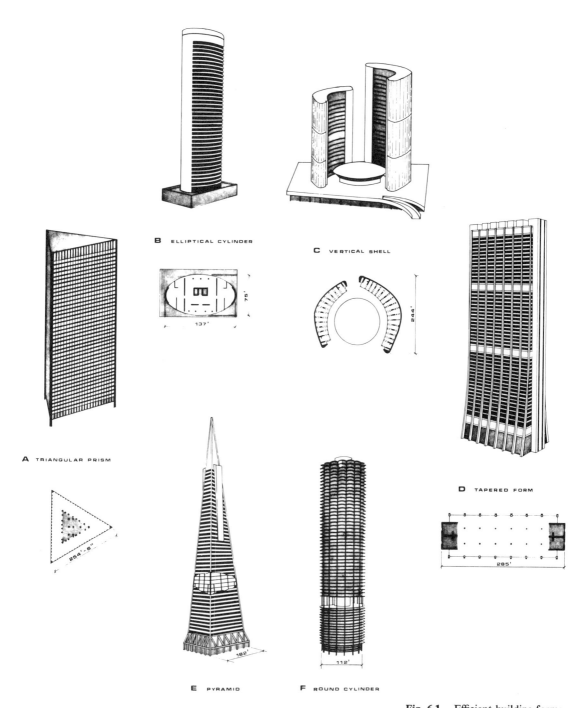

B ELLIPTICAL CYLINDER

75'

137'

C VERTICAL SHELL

244'

A TRIANGULAR PRISM

254'-6"

E PYRAMID

182'

F ROUND CYLINDER

112'

D TAPERED FORM

285'

Fig. 6.1. Efficient building forms.

The elliptical building offers advantages similar to the circular one. The architect of the Le France Building in Paris (Fig. 6.1*b*) claims a 27% reduction of wind loading attributable to the elliptical shape. The building's lateral loads are resisted by a central core and interior and exterior shear walls. Only shallow foundations were required, since the shear wall system distributes lateral forces across a wide area. Again building codes offer a reduction of the wind load requirements by 20 to 40% of the values required for a rectangular building.

The triangular prism is another structurally efficient building form. The U.S. Steel Building in Pittsburgh (Fig. 8.3*l*) uses an equilateral prism with notched corners to aid in reducing the building's lateral response to wind.

The American Broadcasting Company Building in Los Angeles (Fig. 6.1*a*) also has a triangular, prismatic shape. The tower rises 576 ft, and the exterior walls act as Vierendeel trusses. The trussed facade girders transmit gravity loads to the corner columns, and lateral loads are transferred by the floor diaphragm to the central core.

A building can be a crescent or serpintine shape to increase its stiffness with respect to lateral forces. Its action is analogous to corrugated steel flooring and folded or undulating roof shells efficiently resisting gravity loading.

The Toronto City Hall (Fig. 6.1*c*), consisting of two crescent-shaped towers rising 20 stories (261 ft) and 27 stories (327 ft) above a two-story podium, uses this approach. The structure of a typical tower consists of an exterior, windowless vertical shell wall from which radial beams extend to a central row of columns and beyond to cantilever $6\frac{1}{2}$ ft to the curtain wall. The floor slab spans between the radiating beams. The gravity loads are carried by the column-shell-frame. Lateral loads are resisted by the vertical shell, which is stiffened by the ribbing action of the floor structure.

The crescent shell form is efficient in resisting lateral forces acting symmetrically on it. However it is rather inefficient when considering asymmetrical loading. This produces torsional stresses, which in the Toronto City Hall were counteracted by thick, vertical edge beams at the ends of the towers. The curved shape of the shell combined with the close proximity of the towers, greatly amplifies the wind pressure. Wind tunnel tests showed suction pressures at the sides of the building nearly four times higher than specified by codes.

THE COUNTERACTING FORCE OR DYNAMIC RESPONSE

There have been several examples of controlling building sway and oscillation in nonconventional ways. Each of these allows the building to respond dynamically rather than statically in withstanding external lateral action.

Eugene Freyssinet of France and Lev Zetlin of the United States proposed to control lateral deflection of a building by introducing stressed tendons within the structure to generate an opposing deformation (Fig. 6.2). This eliminates the need to achieve the lateral stiffness of a building by additional material,

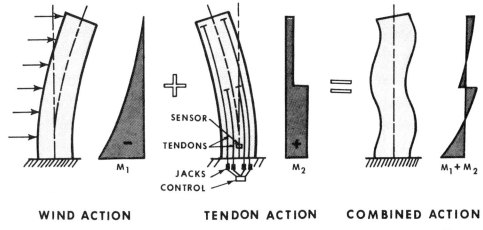

WIND ACTION   TENDON ACTION   COMBINED ACTION

Fig. 6.2

most of which may be used only once in 100 years to absorb maximum wind velocities.

Cables near the exterior facade are attached to jacks at their base. A sensor unit measures the wind velocity and direction. This information is transmitted to a control unit at the base, which causes the jacks to tension the cables. This off-center tensioning induces a bending moment opposing the wind moment. Thus the moments are neutralized and the lateral deformation is greatly reduced. The amounts of tension in the cables and in the building side being stressed vary according to the magnitude and direction of the wind pressure. The concept is analogous to the tension felt in the muscles of an outstretched arm when the hand accepts a heavy object and the arm attempts to maintain its position.

Damping is another approach toward the reduction of the gusty wind effects on a high-rise structure. Like the dampers used for slowing down the closing of doors, nonstructural energy absorbers can be employed to decrease the swaying and oscillating motions of a building.

In New York's World Trade Center viscoelastic dampers were attached to the bottom chord ends of the open web steel joists and to the adjacent columns (Fig. 6.3). As the name suggests, viscoelastic material is both elastic (returns to its original position like a rubber band) and viscous (tends to flow under pressure like a liquid). Viscoelastic material resists forces in shear; it does not store energy like a spring, however, but converts it into heat that is diffused to the surrounding environment. Hence after the forces are released, the material does not snap back and forth like a spring but slowly returns to its unstressed position. The building does not oscillate with damping; instead, gust winds emit heat inside the building because of the response of the dampers (Reference 6.3).

The principle can also be applied to a building whose primary structure supports a secondary structural frame, as in the U.S.

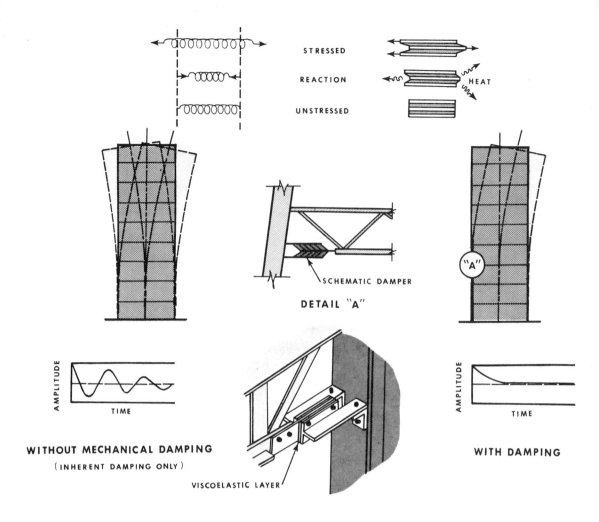

STRESSED

REACTION

UNSTRESSED

HEAT

SCHEMATIC DAMPER

DETAIL "A"

"A"

AMPLITUDE

TIME

WITHOUT MECHANICAL DAMPING

(INHERENT DAMPING ONLY)

VISCOELASTIC LAYER

AMPLITUDE

TIME

WITH DAMPING

VISCOELASTIC DAMPING

Fig. 6.3

Steel Building in Pittsburgh. The secondary floor structure system, which is rather susceptible to lateral sway, can be attached to the columns through viscoelastic dampers, thus making it possible for the dampers to convert energy of oscillation into heat energy as the building laterally sways (Fig. 6.4). In another proposal expansion joints with viscoelastic dampers would be inserted between floor structure and building core. Again, the relative movement of floor structure and rigid core causes energy of oscillation to be dissipated in the dampers (Reference 6.3).

Fazlur Khan of Skidmore, Owings, and Merrill and Mark Fintel of the Portland Cement Association developed a concept that permits the control of damage caused by earthquake. In their "Shock Absorbing Soft Story Concept," the first story is allowed to deform with the earthquake while the upper portion of the building remains almost unaffected, thus in the elastic

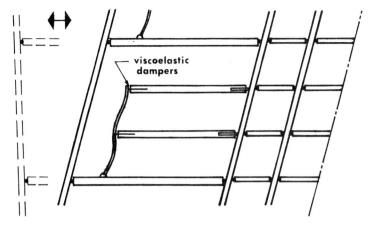

viscoelastic dampers

Fig. 6.4

range. The bottom story consists of a series of stability walls (Fig. 6.5) that are predesigned for forces greater than earthquake action, thus controlling excessive displacement of the upper stories (Reference 6.2).

Other ideas have been considered, but neither technology nor the precise understanding of the phenomenon has been developed to apply them as solutions. For instance, since the positive pressure on the windward building face generates suction on the leeward side, the pressure difference could be overcome through discharge of air on the leeward side. Thus not only is the magnitude of the lateral action reduced, there is also a diminution of the oscillations that form after a change in wind velocity allows air to rush into the negative pressure region and push the building in the opposite direction.

It has also been proposed to use the wind pressure as a source of energy for building maintenance by allowing the wind to enter the building at certain locations.

The principle of resisting wind pressure in any manner other than static is still in its infancy. The future will bring many new developments in this area.

Fig. 6.5

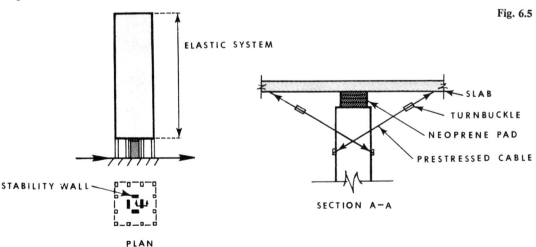

ELASTIC SYSTEM

SLAB

TURNBUCKLE

NEOPRENE PAD

PRESTRESSED CABLE

SECTION A—A

STABILITY WALL

PLAN

CHAPTER SEVEN

Approximate Structural Analysis and Design of Buildings

This chapter investigates analytically high-rise buildings using typical support structures, dealing with the following structural systems:

• The bearing wall.

• The rigid frame.

• The rigid frame–shear wall.

• The interspatial building using Vierendeel trusses.

• The tube.

APPROXIMATE ANALYSIS OF BEARING WALL BUILDINGS

Problems 7.1 and 7.2 deal with bearing wall buildings using the typical wall arrangement of the cross wall–long wall principle (Fig. 5.3).

PROBLEM 7.1. THE CROSS WALL STRUCTURE

Design a typical interior cross wall for a 10-story brick building. The walls are spaced 15 ft apart (Fig. 7.1), and the story height is 10 ft. The cross walls will act as bearing walls for gravity loads as well as shear walls for wind loads acting parallel to them.

The lateral forces acting against the short side of the building (i.e., perpendicular to cross walls) will be resisted by a system of longitudinal shear walls along the corridor (broken lines in Fig. 7.1).

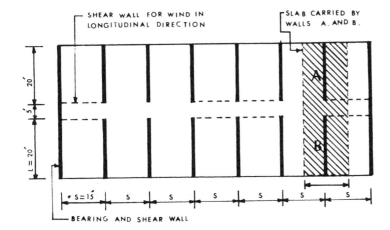

SHEAR WALL FOR WIND IN LONGITUDINAL DIRECTION

SLAB CARRIED BY WALLS A. AND B.

BEARING AND SHEAR WALL

Fig. 7.1

For building dimensions refer to Figs. 7.1 and 7.2 The allowable compressive stress of brick is $f_m = 300$ psi based on 8000 psi compressive strength and type N mortar (without inspection). The allowable shear stress is $v = 18$ psi. Assume a constant wall thickness of $t = 12$ in. The masonry weighs 120 lb/ft³ (Reference 7.13). Assume the following loads:

DEAD LOAD OF THE SLAB

5 in. hollow core =	40 psf
2 in. topping =	20 psf
	60 psf

LIVE LOAD

Corridor =	100 psf
Floor =	40 psf

Assume in this approximate approach that each wall has the same stiffness, hence carries the same amount of wind pressure. Thus design only one typical cross wall.

A. Loading

Wind Loads Acting Parallel to Cross Walls. The wind loads are based on New York State Construction Code (Chapter 2). The distribution of the wind pressure for a typical cross wall is shown in Fig. 7.2.

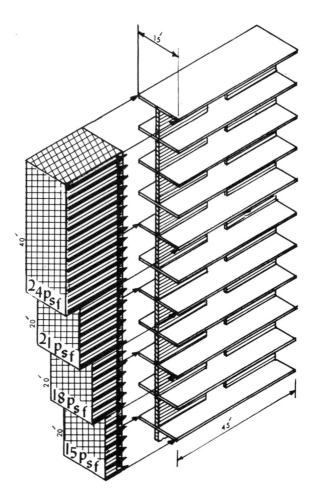

Fig. 7.2

The resultants of the wind pressure are

$$W_1 = 15(2 \times 10)15 = \quad 4,500 \text{ lb}$$
$$W_2 = 18(2 \times 10)15 = \quad 5,400 \text{ lb}$$
$$W_3 = 21(2 \times 10)15 = \quad 6,300 \text{ lb}$$
$$W_4 = 24(4 \times 10)15 = 14,400 \text{ lb}$$
$$\overline{\qquad\qquad\qquad W_{tot} = 30,600 \text{ lb} = 30.6 \text{ k}}$$

The magnitude and location of wind forces are given in Fig. 7.3.

Gravity Loads Carried by Cross Walls (Fig. 7.3)

DEAD LOADS. The dead loads each cross wall must carry consist of slab weight and its own weight.

$$P_{DL_1} = 60(20)15 + 120(1)(10)20$$

$$= 18,000 + 24,000 = 42,000 \text{ lb} = 42 \text{ k/floor}$$

$$P_{DL_2} = 60(5)15 = 4500 \text{ lb} = 4.5 \text{ k/floor}$$

Summing up the weight of all floors yields

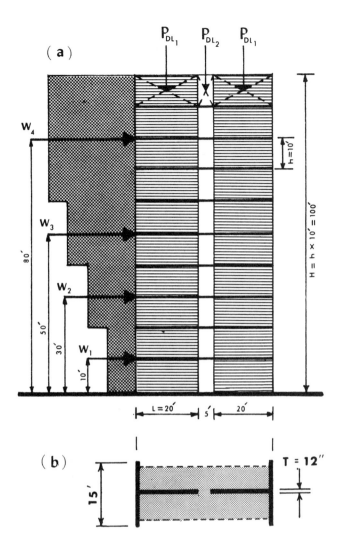

(a)

(b)

T = 12"

Fig. 7.3

$$\sum P_{DL_1} = 42(10) = 420 \text{ k}$$
$$\sum P_{DL_2} = 4.5(10) = 45 \text{ k}$$

The total dead load the wall has to carry is

$$P_{totDL} = 45 + 2(420) = 885 \text{ k}$$

LIVE LOADS. Live loads are loads other than dead loads acting vertically.

$$P_{LL_1} = 40(20)15 = 12,000 \text{ lb} = 12 \text{ k}$$
$$P_{LL_2} = 100(5)15 = 7500 \text{ lb} = 7.5 \text{ k}$$

Summing up the live loads of all floors and neglecting load reduction yields

$$\sum P_{LL_1} = 12(10) = 120 \text{ k}$$
$$\sum P_{LL_2} = 7.5(10) = 75 \text{ k}$$

The total live load the wall has to carry is

$$P_{totLL} = 75 + 2(120) = 315 \text{ k}$$

The total loads the wall has to carry are

$$\text{TOTAL LOADS} = P_{totDL} + P_{totLL} = 885 + 315 = 1200 \text{ k}$$

B. Analysis and Design Check

Overturning (Figs. 7.4 and 7.5). The code requires the moment of stability of the structure above the horizontal plane under consideration to be not less than 1.5 times the overturning moment due to wind.

Stability of the cross wall will be checked at the base of the building only.

Figure 7.4 indicates that overturning may appear at different floor levels, especially where the dead load is reduced (e.g., less wall thickness).

It will be a conservative assumption to neglect the interaction of the cross walls across the corridor (Fig. 7.5).

The overturning moment generated by wind is

$$M_{act} = W_1 h_1 + W_2 h_2 + W_3 h_3 + W_4 h_4$$

$$= 4.5(10) + 5.4(30) + 6.3(50) + 14.4(80) = 1674 \text{ ft-k}$$

It is assumed that each wall A and B carries one-half the overturning moment.

The resisting moment due to dead load considering only one wall is

$$M_{react} = P_{DL}\left(\frac{L}{2}\right) = \frac{885}{2}\left(\frac{20}{2}\right) = 4425 \text{ ft-k}$$

Check stability: $\dfrac{M_{react}}{M_{act}} = \dfrac{4425}{837} = 5.31 > 1.5$ OK

Sliding and Shear Stresses. Codes require the sliding force due to lateral forces to be resisted by the structure above the horizontal plane under consideration or by anchors or soil friction, providing a total resisting force not less than 1.5 times the sliding force.

The total lateral force due to wind is

$$W_{tot} = 30.6 \text{ k}$$

The critical shear stress generated by the wind at the base of the building (Fig. 7.6) is

$$v_{act} = \frac{W_{tot}}{A_{wall}} = \frac{30,600}{2(20 \times 12)12} = 5.32 \text{ psi} < 18(1.33)$$

The actual shear stress is much less than the allowable one.

Note: The beneficial aspect of dead weight increasing the

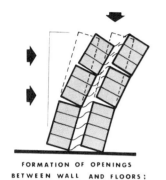

FORMATION OF OPENINGS
BETWEEN WALL AND FLOORS:
INSTABILITY DUE TO OVERTURNING

Fig. 7.4

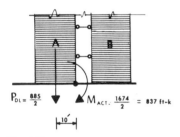

$P_{DL} = \dfrac{885}{2}$ $M_{ACT.} \dfrac{1674}{2} = 837 \text{ ft-k}$

Fig. 7.5

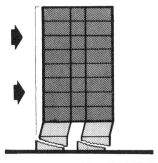

HORIZONTAL SHEAR WRACKING
(i.e. DIAGONAL TENSION ACTION)

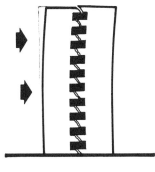

VERTICAL SHEAR WRACKING

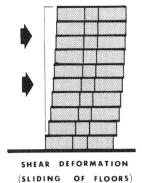

SHEAR DEFORMATION
(SLIDING OF FLOORS)

Fig. 7.6

shear capacity through increase of frictional resistance was neglected.

The resisting shear capacity is

$$V_{wall} = 18(2 \times 20 \times 12)12 = 103,680 \text{ lb}$$

The acting lateral force is

$$W_{tot} = 30,600 \text{ lb}$$

$$\frac{V_{wall}}{W_{tot}} = \frac{103,680}{30,600} = 3.39 > 1.5 \qquad \text{OK}$$

Compressive Stresses. The critical compressive stresses are generated by dead and live loads and wind rotation (Fig. 7.7). The maximum compressive stress as generated by axial and bending stresses is

$$f = P/A + M/S$$

It is assumed that the allowable stresses for axial and bending action are the same, and reduction of allowable stresses due to buckling is not critical (see discussion, Problem 7.2).
The wall area is

$$A = 2(20 \times 12)12 = 5760 \text{ in.}^2$$

The section modulus for one wall is

$$S = \frac{tL^2}{6} = \frac{12(20 \times 12)^2}{6} = 115,200 \text{ in.}^3$$

The total live and dead loads are

$$P_{tot} = 1200 \text{ k}$$

Rotation due to wind on both walls is

$$M_{act} = 1674 \text{ ft-k}$$

Hence the maximum compressive stress is

$$f = \frac{P}{A} + \frac{M}{S}$$

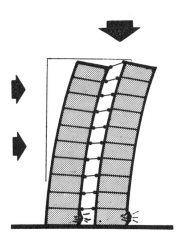

FAILURE DUE TO EXCESSIVE COMPRESSION AT THE BASE

Fig. 7.7

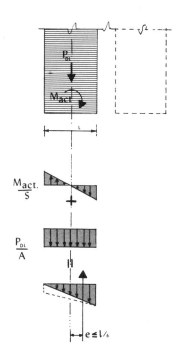

Fig. 7.8

$$= \frac{1200}{5760} + \frac{(1674)12}{(115,200)2}$$

$$= 0.208 + 0.087 = 0.295 \text{ ksi} < 1.33(0.3) \qquad \text{OK}$$

The bearing without wind action is

$$f = 0.208 < 0.3 \qquad \text{OK}$$

Notice that compression is the controlling design factor, since the actual stress comes close to the allowable one.

Tensile Stresses. Tensile stresses should be avoided (Fig. 7.8). This is achieved by keeping the resultant force in the middle third of the wall.

The critical tensile stress is generated by bending due to wind and counteracting axial forces due to dead load. Assuming no tensile stresses, we have

$$f = \frac{M_{\text{act}}}{S} - \frac{P_{DL}}{A} \leq 0$$

Replacing the moment by an eccentric axial force yields

$$M_{\text{act}} = P_{DL}(e)$$

$$\frac{P_{DL}(e)}{S} - \frac{P_{DL}}{A} \leq 0$$

The maximum allowable eccentricity not yielding any tension is

$$e \leq \frac{S}{A} = \frac{tL^2}{6(tL)} = \frac{L}{6} \qquad \text{or} \qquad e_{\text{max}} = \frac{L}{6} \qquad (7.1)$$

The actual eccentricity of the dead load is

$$e_{\text{act}} = \frac{M_{\text{act}}}{P_{DL}} = \frac{1674/2}{885/2} = 1.89$$

$$e_{\text{max}} = \frac{L}{6} = \frac{20}{6} = 3.33 > 1.89$$

There will be no tensile stresses at first floor level. A similar approach should be used for checking possible tensile stresses at other floor levels, especially where the wall thickness is reduced.

PROBLEM 7.2. THE LONG WALL STRUCTURE

Design a typical exterior long wall for a 10-story brick building. The long walls are $7\frac{1}{2}$ in. thick and are supporting a steel joist floor system (Fig. 7.9). The perforated exterior long walls are assumed to behave under loading as a series of individual 5 ft wide vertical walls (e.g., wall MN in Fig. 7.9). Thus only 50% of the facade wall will be available as bearing area.

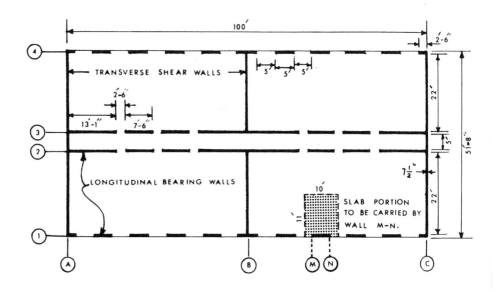

PLAN VIEW

Fig. 7.9

In this problem the wind against the short side of the building is not considered; walls 1-(A–C), 2-(A–C), 3-(A–C), and 4-(A–C) behave as a cross wall system (see Problem 7.1), resisting the wind according to their relative stiffness, assuming a rigid diaphragm action of the floors. Because of the high inertia in the long wall direction of the building and the increase of allowable stresses by 33%, the combined stresses generated by the wind and gravity will probably not control the wall design.

The building dimensions are given in Figs. 7.9 and 7.10. The allowable compressive stress of brick is $f_m = 400$ psi based on 8000 psi compressive strength with type N mortar (with inspection). The allowable shear stress is $v = 22$ psi. The actual wall thickness is $t = 7\frac{1}{2}$ in.. The masonry weighs $120 \, \text{lb/ft}^3$ (Reference 7.13).

Assume the following loads:

DEAD LOAD

    roof = 45 psf
    floor = 55 psf

LIVE LOAD

    roof = 30 psf
    floor = 40 psf

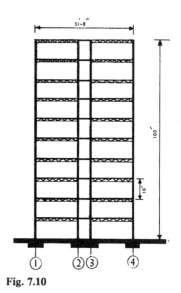

Fig. 7.10

The wind acting perpendicular to the long side of the building will be carried first in bending by the longitudinal walls to the floor diaphragms, which in turn distribute the wind to the six transverse walls (Fig. 7.11). The transverse shear walls will resist the wind according to their relative stiffness. Since the shear

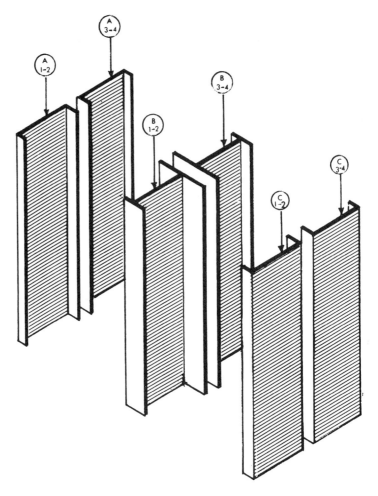

Fig. 7.11   TRANSVERSE   SHEAR   WALLS

walls are tied to the longitudinal bearing walls, a portion of the bearing wall will act as the flange of the shear wall in resisting overturning due to lateral forces.

The transverse shear walls are not checked in this example, since their behavior is rather similar to the typical interior cross wall of Problem 7.1. However we do investigate the distribution of the wind according to the relative stiffness of the transverse shear walls, assuming rigid diaphragm action of the slab.

A.   Relative Stiffness of Transverse Shear Walls

Wall A-(1–2).   Wall A-(1–2) is assumed to have the same stiffness as walls A-(3–4), C-(1–2), and C-(3–4). The wall, whose dimensions appear in Fig. 7.12, is to be investigated at first floor level.

According to the building code requirements for engineered brick masonry, the effective width of flanges for L-shaped or

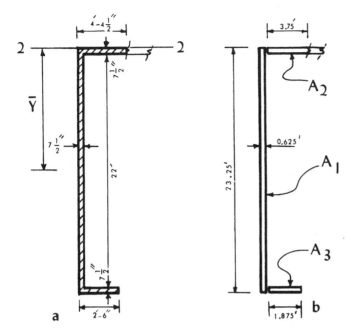

a

b

Fig. 7.12

[-shaped walls shall be taken as: $6t \geq b_e \leq h/16$ for [-shaped walls and $h/6$ for I-shaped walls, where

h = total wall height above the level to be analyzed = 100 ft
t = wall thickness at level to be checked = 7.5 in.

Thus

$$b_e = \frac{100}{16}(12) = 75 \text{ in.}$$

$$b_e = 6(7.5) = 45 \text{ in.} < 75 \text{ in.}$$

The effective flange width at the corridor is

$$b_e = 45 + 7\tfrac{1}{2} = 52\tfrac{1}{2} \text{ in.} = 4 \text{ ft } 4\tfrac{1}{2} \text{ in.}$$

The actual flange width at the exterior of the building is

$$b = 2 \text{ ft } 6 \text{ in.}$$

The wall system is subdivided into three walls, as in Fig. 7.12b. The wall areas are

$A_1 = 23.25(0.625) = 14.53 \text{ ft}^2$
$A_2 = 3.75(0.625) = 2.34 \text{ ft}^2$
$A_3 = 1.86(0.625) = 1.17 \text{ ft}^2$
$A_{tot} = 18.04 \text{ ft}^2$

The centroidal axis of the wall system is found by taking moments with the individual wall areas about axis 2-2. Those moments must be equal to the moments generated by the total wall area about the same axis:

$$\overline{Y}(A_{tot}) = \sum A_n Y_n = A_1 Y_1 + A_2 Y_2 + A_3 Y_3$$

$$\bar{Y} = \frac{A_1 Y_1 + A_2 Y_2 + A_3 Y_3}{A_{tot}}$$

$$= \frac{14.53(11.62)}{18.04} + \frac{2.34(0.31)}{18.04} + \frac{1.17(22.94)}{18.04}$$

$$= \frac{168.84 + 0.73 + 26.83}{18.04} = \frac{196.40}{18.04} = 10.88 \text{ ft}$$

The moment of inertia of the wall system about its centroidal axis as based on the parallel axis theorem is

$$I_x = \sum I_g + \sum A_n Y_n^2 \qquad \text{or} \qquad I_g = \sum I_x - A_{tot}\bar{Y}^2$$

Figuring first the moments of inertia of the individual areas ($\sum I_x$) about axis 2-2 yields

wall A_1: $\quad I_{x_1} = tL^3/3 = A_1 L^2/3 = 14.53(23.25)^2/3 = 2616.79 \text{ ft}^4$
wall A_2: $\quad I_{x_2} = tL^3/3 = A_2 L^2/3 = 2.34(0.625)^2/3 \approx \quad 0$
wall A_3: $\quad I_{x_3} \approx A_3 Y_3^2 \qquad\qquad = 1.17(22.94)^2 \quad = \quad 615.70 \text{ ft}^4$

$$\sum I_{xn} = 3232.49 \text{ ft}^4$$

Hence the moment of inertia of the wall system about the centroidal axis is

$$I_{c_1} = \sum I_x - A_{tot}\bar{Y}^2$$

$$= 3232.49 - 18.04(10.88)^2$$

$$= 3232.49 - 2135.47 = 1097.02 \text{ ft}^4$$

Wall B-(1–2). Since wall B-(1–2) is assumed to have the same stiffness as wall B-(3–4), only wall B-(1–2) is investigated at first floor level. For dimensions refer to Fig. 7.13. The approach is similar to that used for wall 1–2.

$$b_e = \frac{h}{6} = \left(\frac{100}{6}\right) 12 = 200 \text{ in.}$$

$$b_e = 6t \text{ to be added on each side} = 6(7.5) = 45 \text{ in.}$$

The effective flange width at the corridor is

$$b_e = 2(45) + 7.5 = 97.5 < 200 \text{ in.}$$

The actual flange width at the exterior of the building is

$$b = 5 \text{ ft}$$

The wall system is subdivided as shown in Fig. 7.13b. The wall areas are

$A_1 = (0.625)23.25 = 14.53 \text{ ft}^2$
$A_2 = (0.625)7.5 \quad = \quad 4.70 \text{ ft}^2$
$A_3 = (0.625)4.37 \quad = \quad 2.73 \text{ ft}^2$

$$A_{tot} = 21.96 \text{ ft}^2$$

The location of the centroidal axis of the wall system is

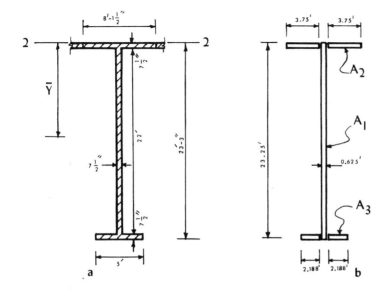

Fig. 7.13

$$\bar{Y} = \frac{A_1 Y_1 + A_2 Y_2 + A_3 Y_3}{A_{tot}}$$

$$= \frac{14.53(11.62) + 4.70(0.31) + 2.73(22.94)}{21.96} = 10.61 \text{ ft}$$

Figuring the moment of inertias of the individual areas $\sum I_x$ about axis 2-2 yields

wall A_1: $I_{x_1} = tL^3/3 = A_1 L^2/3 = 14.53(23.25)^2/3 = 2615.51 \text{ ft}^4$
wall A_2: $I_{x_2} = tL^3/3 = A_2 L^2/3 = 4.70(0.625)^2/3 \approx 0$
wall A_3: $I_{x_3} \approx A_3 Y_3^2 \qquad\quad = 2.73(22.94)^2 = 1436.65 \text{ ft}^4$

$$\sum I_{xn} = 4052.16 \text{ ft}^4$$

Hence the moment of inertia of the wall system is

$$I_{c_1} = \sum I_x - A_{tot}\bar{Y}^2$$
$$= 4052.16 - 21.96(10.61)^2$$
$$= 4052.16 - 2472.08 = 1580.08 \text{ ft}^4$$

Lateral Load Distribution. The relative stiffness of each transverse wall is dependent on its own inertia as related to the inertia of the total cross wall system: $I_i/\sum I_n$.

The results in Table 7.1 indicate that based on rigid diaphragm action (Fig. 7.14a), each end wall carries 14.53% of the total lateral load and each central transverse wall carries 20.88%.

Based on facade geometry, that is, assuming semirigid (flexible) diaphragm action of the floors (Fig. 7.14b), the outside walls resist 12.5% and inside walls 25% each. Notice that this fast approximation, however, assigns less forces to the outside walls (12.5% vs. 14.53%) and more forces to the inside walls (25% vs. 20.88%).

Table 7.1

Wall	I (ft⁴)	$I/\sum I$	Wind Distribution $I/\sum I(100)$ (%)	Length of Building L (ft)	Portion of Load Carried as Based on: Relative Stiffness $L(I/\sum I)$ (ft)	Tributory Area (ft)
A(1–2)	1097.02	0.1453	14.53	100	14.53	12.50
A(3–4)	1097.02	0.1453	14.53	100	14.53	12.50
C(1–2)	1097.02	0.1453	14.53	100	14.53	12.50
C(3–4)	1097.02	0.1453	14.53	100	14.53	12.50
B(1–2)	1580.08	0.2088	20.88	100	20.88	25.00
B(3–4)	1580.08	0.2088	20.88	100	20.88	25.00
$\sum I =$	7548.24	0.9988	99.88	100	99.88	100.00

WIND PRESSURE
WALL DEFLECTION
R1
R2
R1
a. RIGID DIAPHRAGM ACTION OF SLAB
DIAPHRAGM DEFLECTION
R1
R2
R1
b. SEMI - RIGID DIAPHRAGM ACTION OF SLAB

Fig. 7.14

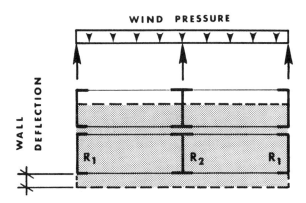

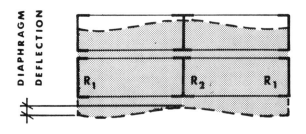

If, for approximation purposes, the same stiffness (i.e., $R_1 = R_2 = R$) is assumed for each wall together with rigid diaphragm action, then each wall resists an equal proportion of the total load. In other words, the 100 ft of facade width will be laterally supported by the six walls, or one wall will carry one-sixth of the width, or 16.67% of the total load.

B. Loads Acting on Wall M-N

The floor area supported by wall M-N is

$$A = 10(11) = 110 \text{ ft}^2$$

The dead load per floor carried by the wall (Fig. 7.15) is

roof: $P_{DL_1} = 0.045(110) = 4.95 \text{ k}$
floor: $P_{DL_2} = 0.055(110) = 6.05 \text{ k}$
wall: $P_W = 0.08 (5 \times 10 + 4 \times 2.5 \times 2.5) = 6.00 \text{ k}$

The total dead load acting on first floor level is

$$\sum P_{DL} = 4.95(1) + (6.05 + 6.0)9 = 113.4 \text{ k}$$

The live load per floor carried by the wall is

roof: $P_{LL_1} = 0.03(110) = 3.3 \text{ k}$
floor: $P_{LL_2} = 0.04(110) = 4.4 \text{ k}$

The total live load acting on first floor level is

$$\sum P_{LL} = 3.3(1) + 9(4.4) = 42.9 \text{ k}$$

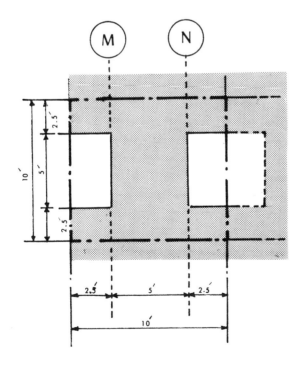

TYPICAL WALL PANEL

Fig. 7.15

Problem 7.2. The Long Wall Structure   137

The reduced total live load acting on first floor level as based on Chapter 2 is

$$\sum P_{RLL} = 3.3(0.8) + 4.4(0.8)2 + 4.4(0.75) + 4.4(0.7)$$
$$+ 4.4(0.65) + 4.4(0.6) + 4.4(0.55) + 4.4(0.5)2$$

$$= 3.3(0.8) + 4.4[0.82(2) + 0.75 + 0.7 + 0.65$$
$$+ 0.6 + 0.55 + 0.5(2)] = 28.38 \text{ k}$$

This value is equivalent to a reduction of the total live load by 34%. The total load acting on first floor level is

$$P_{RTL} = P_{DL} + P_{RLL} = 113.4 + 28.38 = 141.78 \text{ k}$$
$$P_{TL} = P_{DL} + P_{LL} = 113.4 + 42.9 = 156.30 \text{ k}$$

The wind pressure at first floor level is 15 psf.

C. Gravity Action on the Wall: Case $DL + RLL$ at First Floor Level

Bending will be induced into the bearing wall at the floor-wall connection due to eccentric transition of gravity loads. The wall may be assumed to behave as a continuous vertical member restrained by the floor diaphragms from moving laterally (Fig. 7.16).

It is further assumed that the floor loads bend the walls only locally and redistribute as they travel downward, ensuring that the load action will coincide with the centroidal axis of the wall.

The wall is checked at first floor level for critical compressive stresses. Tensile stresses may develop at the top story. However at the other floor levels no tension will develop in the wall, since it is prestressed by the gravity loads.

The true action of the slab on the wall is indeterminate: a triangular pressure distribution may be assumed as based on the bearing length b of the slab or joist (Fig. 7.17).

The eccentricity of the slab reaction with respect to the

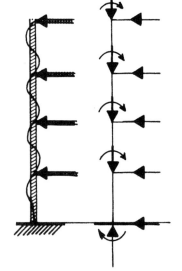

Fig. 7.16

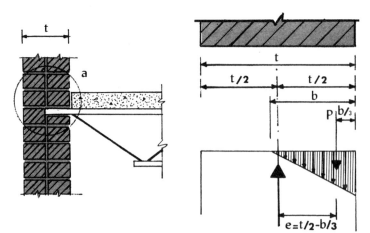

Fig. 7.17

DETAIL AT a

principal wall axis normal to the wall length for $b = 4$ in. is

$$e = \frac{t}{2} - \frac{b}{3} = \frac{7.5}{2} - \frac{4}{3} = 2.42 \text{ in.}$$

Thus the acting moment at second floor level is

$$M_{2act} = e(P_{DL_2} + P_{LL_2})$$
$$= 2.42\, P_{tot} = 2.42(6.05 + 4.4) = 25.30 \text{ in.-k}$$

The rotational capacity of the wall (Fig. 7.18b) is

$$M_{cap} = P_{tot} \left(\frac{2}{3}\right) t = P_{tot} \left(\frac{2}{3}\right) 7.5 = 5 P_{tot}$$

Thus

$$M_{cap} \approx 2 M_{act}$$

Hence one may assume that half the moment is carried up the wall and half the moment is carried down the wall. That is not true at roof level for a wall having no parapet.

The moment acting on top of the wall at first floor level is

$$M_2 = \frac{25.30}{2} = 12.65 \text{ in.-k}$$

The total axial load acting at second floor level is

$$P_2 = \sum P_{DL} + \sum P_{RLL} = 141.78 \text{ k}$$

The weight of the wall is

$$P_W = 6.0 \text{ k}$$

Figure 7.19 shows the free body of the wall at first floor level

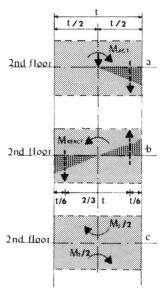

Fig. 7.18

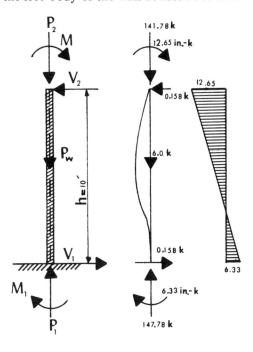

Fig. 7.19

as based on the assumed behavior of the building wall in Fig. 7.16.

Vertical equilibrium of forces yields

$$\sum V = 0 = P_2 + P_W - P_1$$

$$P_1 = P_2 + P_W = 141.78 + 6.0 = 147.78 \text{ k}$$

The horizontal shears acting at first and second floor levels are equal, as based on horizontal equilibrium.

$$V_1 = V_2 = V$$

The following relationship can be obtained from beam tables: Half the moment applied at the simple support of a beam will be carried to the restrained support of that beam:

$$M_1 = \frac{M_2}{2} = \frac{12.65}{2} = 6.33 \text{ in.-k}$$

Taking rotational equilibrium about P_1 gives

$$\sum M_1 = 0 = V_2(h) - M_2 - M_1$$

$$V_2 = \frac{M_2 + M_1}{h} = \frac{3M_2}{2h} = \frac{3(12.65)}{2(10)12} = 0.158 \text{ k}$$

The compressive stresses generated in the wall are checked only approximately. The decrease of allowable compressive stress due to the slenderness of the wall and bending action is neglected. The decrease of stresses is in the range of 15%.

Note that the effect of bending is rather small and the double curvature of the deformed wall beneficial (i.e., stiffness factor $k < 1.0$).

The compressive stresses at first floor level are

$$f = \frac{P}{A} + \frac{M}{S} = \frac{147.78}{5(12)7.5} + \frac{6.33}{5(12)7.5^2/6}$$

$$f = 0.327 + 0.011 = 0.338 \text{ ksi} < 0.40 \text{ ksi} \qquad \text{OK}$$

Even if the actual stress is increased by 20%, it still is below the allowable stress. Hence the wall can be assumed satisfactory with respect to compressive stresses. The shear stresses are

$$v = \frac{V}{A} = \frac{158}{5(12)7.5} = 0.35 \text{ psi} < 22 \text{ psi}$$

Shear is no problem.

D. Wind Action on the Wall: Case $DL + LL + $ Wind

The external longitudinal wall must transmit lateral forces in bending to the slab diaphragms, which in turn transmit the forces to the shear walls. The longitudinal wall may be considered as a continuous vertical member behaving under lateral loads as indicated in Fig. 7.20.

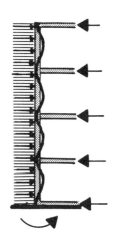

Fig. 7.20

The critical compressive stresses in the wall will be checked at first floor level. Note that because there are no counteracting gravity loads, tensile stresses may appear in the wall at top floor level.

From the deformed configuration of the wall (Fig. 7.20) one may assume that the wall behaves under wind (i.e., assuming the loads to be equally distributed across the height of the building) as a continuous beam restrained at the different floor levels from rotating. Figure 7.21 shows the assumed wall condition for lateral loads.

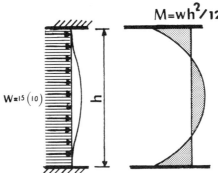

Fig. 7.21

The wind moments at floor levels are

lower two stories: $M_2 = \dfrac{wh^2}{12}$

$$= \frac{[15(10)10^2/12]12}{1000} = 15 \text{ in.-k}$$

upper four stories: $M_1 = \dfrac{[24(10)10^2/12]12}{1000} = 24 \text{ in.-k}$

The moment acting on the wall at second floor level due to eccentric action of joists is

$M_2 = 12.65$ in.-k (see discussion under $DL + RLL$)

The total moment due to wind and gravity at second floor level (Fig. 7.22a) is

$$M_{2\,tot} = 12.65 + 15.0 = 27.65 \text{ in.-k}$$

The total axial load acting at second floor level is

$$P_2 = \sum P_{DL} + \sum P_{LL} = 156.3 \text{ k}$$

Figure 7.22 shows the free body of the wall at first floor level and the forces acting on it as a result of superimposing the wind case on the gravity case (Figs. 7.22b and c, respectively).

The compressive stresses will only be checked approximately. Note that the deformations of the wall due to wind and gravity counteract each other, thus causing an increase of wall stiffness. Neglecting the influence of slenderness and bending on reduction of allowable stresses is less severe for this case than for case $DL + RLL$.

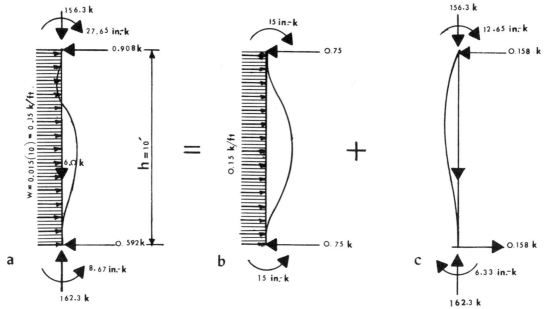

Fig. 7.22

The compressive stress at first floor level is

$$f = \frac{P}{A} + \frac{M}{S}$$

$$= \frac{156.6}{5(12)7.5} + \frac{27.65}{5(12)7.5^2/6} = 0.348 + 0.049$$

$$= 0.397 \text{ ksi} < 0.4(1.33)$$

The actual stress is below the allowable one.

The shear stress is

$$v = \frac{V}{A} = \frac{908}{5(12)7.5} = 2.02 \text{ psi} < 22(1.33) \text{ psi}$$

Shear is no problem.

THE RIGID FRAME STRUCTURE

The rigid frame structure is made up of columns and girders rigidly connected to one another. The rigidity of the building due to the continuity of its members is necessary for the resistance to lateral forces and asymmetrical vertical force action.

Under equally distributed vertical loads, the rigid frame will deform as shown in Fig. 7.23a. The frame is highly indeterminate. To find the degree of indeterminacy, visualize a statically determinate building (e.g., Fig. 7.24b). The columns together with the cantilevering girder stubs form a statically determinate tree system supporting simple beams. Comparison of this system with the continuous frame (Fig. 7.24a) reveals that it has been generated by cutting the continuous beams and removing at the roller support rotational and translational resistance and at the pin support rotational resistance.

One may conclude that to transform a rigid frame into a determinate one, three unknown conditions have to be removed for every girder. The summation of all unknown conditions is equal to the degree of indeterminancy of the building structure. For instance, the frame in Fig. 7.23a has 35 girders. Each girder is three times indeterminate. Hence the building is 35(3) = 105 times indeterminate.

Because of the high degree of indeterminacy of rigid frame buildings, it will be advantageous to develop approximate methods of analysis that are very helpful for a first approximation of member sizes in the early stage of design. Separate approximations will be developed for vertical and horizontal load action, since the rigid frame responds quite differently to each of these loads.

Approximate Analysis for Vertical Loading

A rigid frame deforms under vertical loads as indicated in Fig. 7.23a. The deflected shape of a typical girder shows two points of contraflecture (Fig. 7.23b) where moments are zero. If the location of these points is known, the structure is determinate.

An approximate analysis is dependent on the selection of the inflection points. To gain some understanding about the location of these points, boundary restraints and various loading conditions have to be considered.

Boundary Restraints

Full restraint (Fig. 7.23c) yields inflection points at $0.21L$ from the support. The same deformation curvature is obtained for a continuous beam supporting an equally distributed load.

No restraint (Fig. 7.23d) moves the inflection points to the ends of the beam, thus yielding a simply supported beam.

Partial restraint, the investigated case (Fig. 7.23b), yields inflection points somewhere between $0.21L$ and $0.00L$.

Loading Conditions

An envelope of various moment diagrams is presented in Fig. 7.23e, based on ACI Code 318-63. The maximum positive mo-

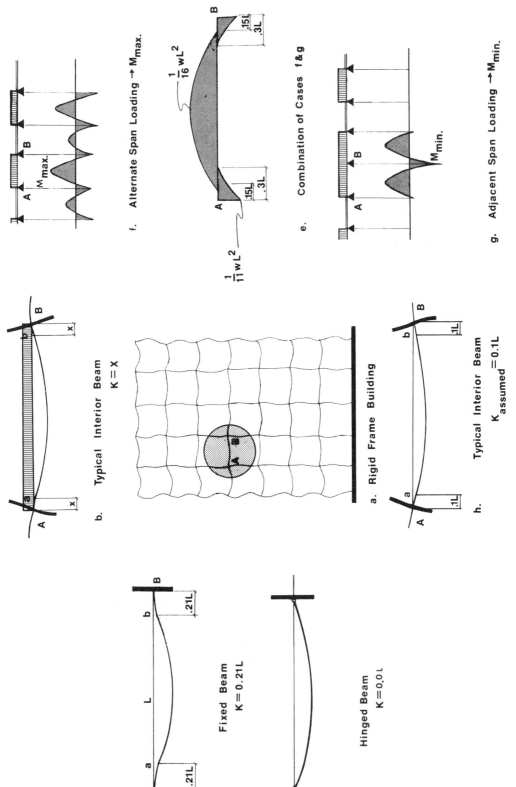

f. Alternate Span Loading → M_{max}.

$\frac{1}{16} wL^2$

.15L
.3L

.15L
.3L

e. Combination of Cases f & g

g. Adjacent Span Loading → M_{min}.

M_{min}.

$\frac{1}{11} wL^2$

b. Typical Interior Beam
K = X

x

x

a. Rigid Frame Building

h. Typical Interior Beam
$K_{assumed}$ = 0.1L

.1L

.1L

c. Fixed Beam
K = 0.21L

.21L

.21L

L

d. Hinged Beam
K = 0,0 L

Fig. 7.23

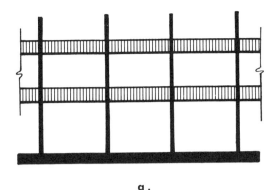

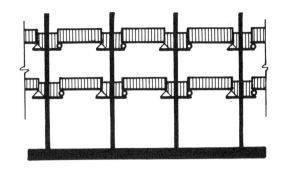

a.

b.

Fig. 7.24

ment is obtained by loading alternate spans of the continuous girder (Fig. 7.23*f*). The maximum negative moments are obtained by loading adjacent spans (Fig. 7.23*g*). Only typical interior spans are considered; end span conditions are neglected. The inflection points for the two cases are located at 0.3*L* and 0.15*L*.

The unpredictability of live loads may make it impossible to foresee true hinge location. However it is reasonable to assume that the hinges of the partially restrained girder are at 0.1*L* from the support. This approximation is conservative with respect to the absolute maximum moment in the beam.

In other words, the selected beam size as based on the maximum field moment is conservative; the magnitude of the support moment is in reality larger, however, and should not be used for the design of the negative support reinforcing in concrete beams. The assumed hinge locations make the building frame determinate for vertical loads. One may visualize the rigid frame replaced by column trees supporting simple beams (Fig. 7.24*b*).

Design Assumptions for Vertical Loading Conditions

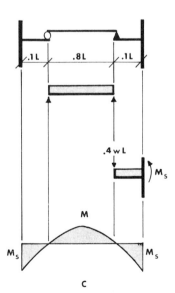

- Girders

  -- The axial force is considered zero because of its relative small magnitude.
  -- Inflection points are assumed at one-tenth of the span measured from each support.

The maximum moment for the beam supported by the column stubs in a typical building girder (Fig. 7.25) is

$$M = \frac{w(0.8L)^2}{8} = 0.08wL^2 \qquad (7.2)$$

The reaction R of the beam is

$$R = \frac{0.8L(w)}{2} = 0.4wL$$

Fig. 7.25

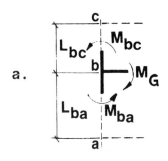

a.

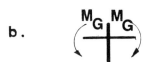

b.

Fig. 7.26

The minimum support moment is

$$M_s = -\left(0.4wL(0.1L) + \frac{w(0.1L)^2}{2}\right) = -0.045wL^2 \quad (7.3)$$

• Columns

•• Maximum loads for interior columns are obtained by loading the bays on both sides of the column. In general, moments in interior columns may be neglected, since the end moments of the girders tend to cancel each other as shown in Fig. 7.26b.

•• The end column has to carry the girder moment, which is divided between the columns in proportion to their stiffness (Fig. 7.26a).

The moment equations for columns of variable heights and inertias are

$$M_{bc} = M_G \frac{I_{bc}/L_{bc}}{I_{bc}/L_{bc} + I_{ba}/L_{ba}}$$

$$M_{ba} = M_G \frac{I_{ba}/L_{ba}}{I_{bc}/L_{bc} + I_{ba}/L_{ba}} \quad (7.4)$$

Rotational equilibrium about joint b yields

$$M_{ba} + M_{bc} = M_G$$

PROBLEM 7.3

Find moments and axial forces for the two-story rigid frame building shown in Fig. 7.27. Assume the column inertias at ground level to be 50% higher than those of the columns on the second floor.

A. Axial Column Forces

It is assumed that the columns carry one-half the respective girder loads.

at column line Ⓐ

$N_2 = 1.5(12.5) = 18.75$ k
$N_1 = 18.75 + 2.5(12.5) = 50.00$ k

at column line Ⓑ

$N_2 = 18.75 + 1.5(7.5) = 30.00$ k
$N_1 = 30.0 + 2.5(12.5 + 7.5) = 80.00$ k

at column line Ⓒ

$N_2 = 1.5(7.5) = 11.25$ k
$N_1 = 2.5(7.5) + 11.25 = 30.00$ k

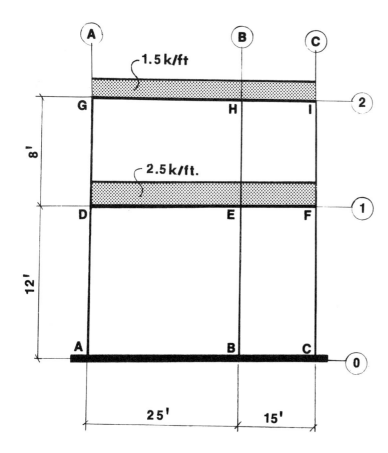

Fig. 7.27

B. Beam Moments

Field moments (bottom fibers in tension):

$$M = 0.08wL^2 \tag{7.2}$$

$M_{GH} = 0.08(1.5)(25)^2 = 75.00 \text{ ft-k}$
$M_{HI} = 0.08(1.5)(15)^2 = 27.00 \text{ ft-k}$
$M_{DE} = 0.08(2.5)(25)^2 = 125.00 \text{ ft-k}$
$M_{EF} = 0.08(2.5)(15)^2 = 45.00 \text{ ft-k}$

Support moments (top fibers in tension):

$$M = 0.045wL^2 \tag{7.3}$$

$M_{GH} = M_{HG} = 0.045(1.5)(25)^2 = 42.2 \text{ ft-k}$
$M_{HI} = M_{IH} = 0.045(1.5)(15)^2 = 15.2 \text{ ft-k}$
$M_{DE} = M_{ED} = 0.045(2.5)(25)^2 = 70.4 \text{ ft-k}$
$M_{EF} = M_{FE} = 0.045(2.5)(15)^2 = 25.3 \text{ ft-k}$

C. Column Moments (FIG. 7.28)

The exterior columns must carry the rotation caused by the end restraint of the girders.

$$M_{DA} = M_{DE} \frac{I_{DA}/L_{DA}}{I_{DA}/L_{DA} + I_{DG}/L_{DG}} \tag{7.4}$$

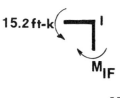

$$M_{DA} = 70.4 \frac{1.5I_{DG}/12}{1.5I_{DG}/12 + I_{DG}/8} = 70.4(0.5) = 35.2 \text{ ft-k}$$

$$M_{DG} = M_{DE} \frac{I_{DG}/L_{DG}}{I_{DA}/L_{DA} + I_{DG}/L_{DG}}$$

$$M_{DG} = 70.4 \frac{I_{DG}/8}{1.5I_{DG}/12 + I_{DG}/8} = 70.4(0.5) = 35.2 \text{ ft-k}$$

Check: $\sum M_D = 0 = M_{DG} + M_{DA} - M_{DE}$
$$= 35.2 + 35.2 - 70.4 \qquad \text{OK}$$

The moments have to balance about joints G and I.

$$\sum M_G = 0 = 42.2 - M_{GD} \qquad M_{GD} = 42.2 \text{ ft-k}$$

$$\sum M_I = 0 = 15.2 - M_{IF} \qquad M_{IF} = 15.2 \text{ ft-k}$$

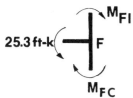

The approach used to find the column moments at joint F is similar to that employed for joint D.

$$M_{FC} = M_{FI} = 0.5(25.3) = 12.65 \text{ ft-k}$$

In general, the end girder moments at an interior column tend to cancel. In this specific case, however, unequal bay sizes and constant loading cause an unbalanced moment of $70.4 - 25.3 = 45.1$ ft-k to be generated at joint E (Fig. 7.29). This moment must be carried by the columns EH and EB. Using the same stiffness relationships found for the exterior columns yields

$$M_{EB} = M_{EH} = 0.5(45.1) = 22.55 \text{ ft-k}$$

$$M_{HE} = 42.2 - 15.2 = 27.0 \text{ ft-k}$$

The resulting force flow through the building frame is shown in Fig. 7.30.

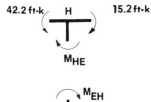

Fig. 7.28

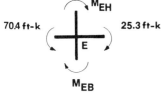

Fig. 7.29

Approximate Analysis for Lateral Loading

As buildings become taller the importance of lateral forces (wind and earthquake) increases. A rigid frame responds quite differently to lateral loading and to vertical loading (Figs. 7.31 and 7.23a, respectively). Hence the assumptions made for the analysis of frame elements reacting to vertical loads are not applicable to horizontal load action. A rigid frame deformed by lateral loads (Fig. 7.31) reveals that inflection points form near the midspans of beams and columns. The "portal method" of analysis for lateral loads utilizes this aspect of behavior. It is the simplest method for determining approximate stresses in frame members due to lateral loads. The portal method is considered to be applicable to building bents of regular geometry up to 25 stories high with a height-to-width ratio of less than 5. Variations in beam spans and column heights should be small. Also, the building should be of uniform strength (i.e., one end

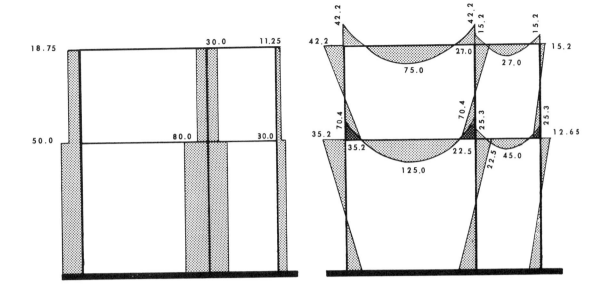

a. Axial Forces (k)   b. Bending Moments (ft-k)

Fig. 7.30. Force diagrams.

should not be stiffer than the other), for when the center of pressure does not coincide with the center of resistance, torsion will occur. Although the optimum building height for the application of the portal method seems to be about 25 stories, it has been used for much taller buildings, such as the 700 ft high Lincoln Center Building in New York City, built in the late 1920s.

The portal method makes the following assumptions:

- Lateral forces are resisted entirely by the building frame. Any stiffening due to floors, walls, or other fill in materials is neglected.

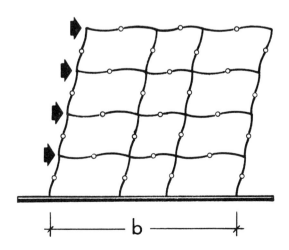

b

Fig. 7.31

- The frame deforms such that inflection points form exactly at midheight of columns and midspan of beams.

- A bent of a frame acts as a series of independent portals. A typical story of the frame in Fig. 7.31 is presented in Fig. 7.32a.

The three-bay, one-story frame is considered as a series of three individual portals (Fig. 7.32b), where each has one or two columns common to an adjacent portal. Each separate portal is three times indeterminate. Because of the assumed inflection points in columns and beams (i.e., three additional conditions), however, the portal is statically determinate.

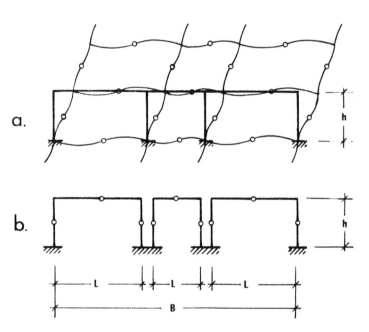

Fig. 7.32

The free bodies of the three individual portals taken at midheight of columns (i.e., assumed location of inflection points) appear in Fig. 7.33.

The portal method arbitrarily assumes that each portal carries a load proportional to its span, or

$$\frac{W_1}{L_1} = \frac{W_2}{L_2} = \frac{W_3}{L_3} = \cdots = \frac{W}{B}$$

or

$$W_1 = \frac{WL_1}{B} \qquad W_2 = \frac{WL_2}{B} \qquad W_3 = \frac{WL_3}{B} \qquad \text{(a)}$$

Taking moments about the hinge of the right column of the portal in Fig. 7.33a and replacing the portal loads by equation (a) yields

$$W_1\left(\frac{h}{2}\right) = N_1(L_1) \qquad N_1 = \frac{W_1 h}{2L_1} = \frac{Wh}{2B} \qquad \text{(b)}$$

The equation for the other axial force is similar.

$$N_2 = \frac{W_2 h}{2L_2} = \frac{Wh}{2B}$$

Interior columns as a rule do not carry any axial forces due to wind. This can easily be seen by summing up N_1 and N_2 to obtain the resultant axial load for the interior column (Fig. 7.33a).

Hence in general the wind moment is resisted by a couple composed of the axial forces of the exterior columns.

To find the column shears, the moment is taken about the midspan of the girder in Fig. 7.33b.

$$N_1\left(\frac{L_1}{2}\right) = V_1\left(\frac{h}{2}\right) \cdots V_1 = \frac{N_1 L_1}{h} \qquad \text{(c)}$$

Substituting equation (b) in (c) yields

$$V_1 = \frac{W_1 h}{2L_1}\frac{L_1}{h} = \frac{W_1}{2} = \frac{W}{2}\frac{L_1}{B}$$

Similarly:

$$V_2' = \frac{W_2}{2} = \frac{W}{2}\frac{L_2}{B}$$

$$V_3' = \frac{W_3}{2} = \frac{W}{2}\frac{L_3}{B}$$

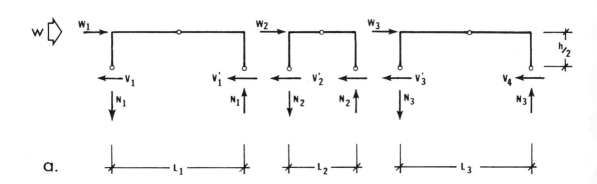

a.

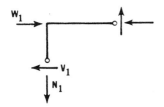

b.

Fig. 7.33

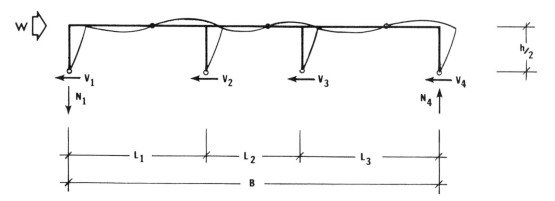

Fig. 7.34

Hence the column shears at mid story height (Fig. 7.34) are

$$V_1 = \frac{WL_1}{2B} \qquad (7.5)$$

$$V_2 = V_1' + V_2' = \frac{W(L_1 + L_2)}{2B}$$

$$V_3 = V_2' + V_3' = \frac{W(L_2 + L_3)}{2B}$$

$$V_4 = \frac{WL_3}{2B}$$

In other words, *the total wind shear is distributed to the columns in direct proportion to the width (i.e., floor area) that each column is supporting.* Note that for equal bay spacing the shear in the exterior columns is half the shear in interior columns, all of which have the same value. Hence for $L_1 = L_2 = L_3 = L$:

$$V_1 = V_4 = \frac{WL}{2B} \qquad (7.6)$$

$$V_2 = V_3 = \frac{WL}{B}$$

It has been assumed that column sizes are approximately equal at any one floor level. If column sizes were to vary considerably, however, the shear would have to be distributed in proportion to their inertias.

One should be aware of the potential inaccuracies inherent to the portal method. The assumed location of inflection points at midheight of columns and midspan of beams is quite reasonable for the middle portion of a rigid frame building, where the stiffness of the columns ($\sum I_c/L_c$) is approximately equal to the stiffness of the beams ($\sum I_g/L_g$). However in the upper two stories or so the stiffness of the columns is relatively small in comparison to the beams. Here the inflection points of the columns move downward and are often assumed to be at about $0.4h$. In the lower three stories the opposite is true, since column

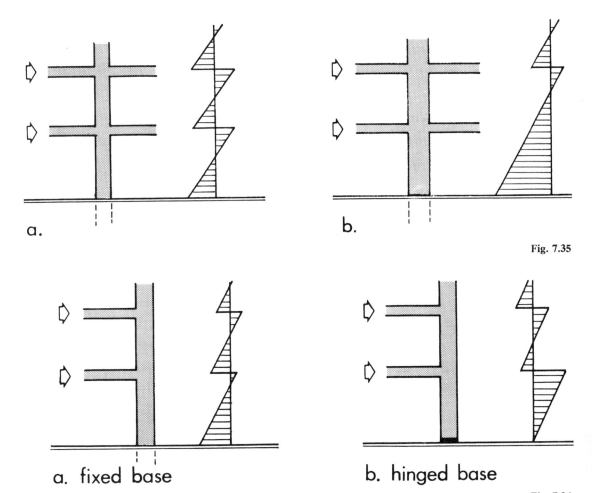

a.

b.

Fig. 7.35

a. fixed base　　　　　　b. hinged base

Fig. 7.36

stiffness is much larger than beam stiffness. Hence the points of contraflexure move upward. For a typical frame building, they are at about $0.6h$ (Fig. 7.35a). In extreme cases, where the column stiffness is greatly increased, the inflection point may very well move up into the next story (Fig. 7.35b).

The foregoing discussion assumes that the ground floor height is equal to the typical story height. An increase in the first floor height also causes the inflection point to move upward.

Another factor to be considered is the amount of restraint provided by the foundations. This too can affect the location of the hinge. With release of restraint at the base of the first floor column, the inflection point moves downward until it forms a hinged base (Fig. 7.36b).

The portal method also neglects the possibility that joints may not provide true continuity between members. Joint slippage may occur and reduce the amount of fixity. Furthermore, secondary stresses generated by the deformation of frame members are neglected. For instance, the difference in axial deformations between interior and exterior columns will cause additional bending stresses in the girders connected to them. However these factors may be neglected for buildings not higher than 25 stories and with slenderness ratios not greater than 5. Somehow these assumptions empirically recognize that the true three-dimensional action of the finished building is neglected.

PROBLEM 7.4

Determine the stress distribution due to wind for the six-story rigid frame building shown in Fig. 7.37. The frame bents are spaced 20 ft apart. Use lateral wind pressures according to the New York State Construction Code (Fig. 2.6).

A. Loading

The distribution of wind pressure according to the New York State Construction Code is given in Fig. 7.37b. Replacing the wind pressure by resultant forces acting at the joints yields

$$
\begin{aligned}
W_6 &= 20(0.024 \times 5) & &= 2.4 \text{ k} \\
W_5 &= 20[(0.024 \times 5) + (0.021 \times 5)] &&= 4.5 \text{ k} \\
W_4 &= 20(0.021 \times 10) & &= 4.2 \text{ k} \\
W_3 &= 20[(0.021 \times 5) + (0.018 \times 5)] &&= 3.9 \text{ k} \\
W_2 &= 20[(0.018 \times 5) + (0.015 \times 5)] &&= 3.3 \text{ k} \\
W_1 &= 20[0.015 \times (5 + 7)] & &= 3.6 \text{ k}
\end{aligned}
$$

B. Analysis of Frame Stresses

Given the symmetrical frame geometry, only half the frame is considered.

Fig. 7.37

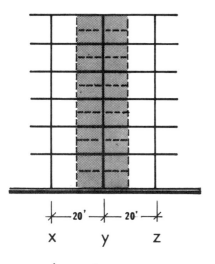

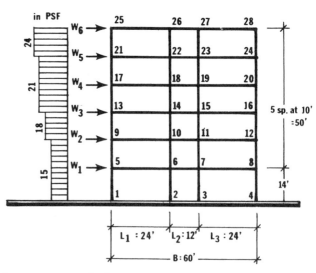

a. elevation   b. typical frame bent "y"

Column Shear Forces. According to equation 7.5, the total shear is distributed to the columns in direct proportion to the floor area each column is supporting. The shears acting at the column inflection points for the top floor (Fig. 7.38) are

$$V_{25-21} = \frac{2.4 \times 24}{2 \times 60} = 0.48 \text{ k}$$

$$V_{26-22} = \frac{2.4 \times (24 + 12)}{2 \times 60} = 0.72 \text{ k}$$

Similarly, the column shears for the fifth floor (Fig. 7.38b) are

$$V_{21-17} = 0.48 + \frac{4.5 \times 24}{2 \times 60} = 0.48 + 0.90 = 1.38 \text{ k}$$

$$V_{22-18} = 0.72 + \frac{4.5 \times (24 + 12)}{2 \times 60} = 0.72 + 1.35 = 2.07 \text{ k}$$

The same procedure is used in finding the column shears for the other stories.

$$V_{17-13} = 1.38 + \frac{4.2 \times 24}{2 \times 60} = 1.38 + 0.84 = 2.22 \text{ k}$$

$$V_{18-14} = 2.07 + \frac{4.2 \times (24 + 12)}{2 \times 60} = 2.07 + 1.26 = 3.33 \text{ k}$$

$$V_{13-9} = 2.22 + \frac{3.9 \times 24}{2 \times 60} = 2.22 + 0.78 = 3.00 \text{ k}$$

$$V_{14-10} = 3.33 + \frac{3.9 \times (24 + 12)}{2 \times 60} = 3.33 + 1.17 = 4.50 \text{ k}$$

$$V_{9-5} = 3.00 + \frac{3.3 \times 24}{2 \times 60} = 3.00 + 0.66 = 3.66 \text{ k}$$

$$V_{10-6} = 4.50 + \frac{3.3 \times (24 + 12)}{2 \times 60} = 4.50 + 0.99 = 5.49 \text{ k}$$

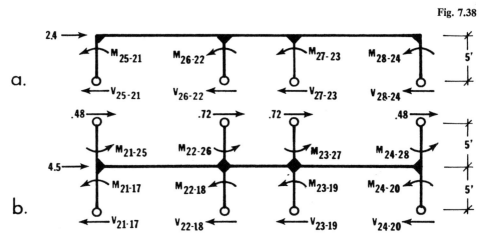

Fig. 7.38

$$V_{5-1} = 3.66 + \frac{3.6 \times 24}{2 \times 60} = 3.66 + 0.72 = 4.38 \text{ k}$$

$$V_{6-2} = 5.49 + \frac{3.6 \times (24 + 12)}{2 \times 60} = 5.49 + 1.08 = 6.57 \text{ k}$$

The column shears can also be found by using the free bodies represented in Fig. 7.40.

Column Moments at Joints. Based on rotational equilibrium of the column free body, a typical column moment is easily found by multiplying the column shear by one-half the column height (Fig. 7.39). Some of the column moments are identified in Fig. 7.38.

$$\begin{aligned}
M_{25-21} &= -M_{21-25} = 0.48 \times 5 = 2.40 \text{ ft-k} \\
M_{26-22} &= -M_{22-26} = 0.72 \times 5 = 3.60 \text{ ft-k} \\
M_{21-17} &= -M_{17-21} = 1.38 \times 5 = 6.90 \text{ ft-k} \\
M_{22-18} &= -M_{18-22} = 2.07 \times 5 = 10.35 \text{ ft-k} \\
M_{17-13} &= -M_{13-17} = 2.22 \times 5 = 11.10 \text{ ft-k} \\
M_{18-14} &= -M_{14-18} = 3.33 \times 5 = 16.65 \text{ ft-k} \\
M_{13-9} &= -M_{9-13} = 3.00 \times 5 = 15.00 \text{ ft-k} \\
M_{14-10} &= -M_{10-14} = 4.50 \times 5 = 22.50 \text{ ft-k} \\
M_{9-5} &= -M_{5-9} = 3.66 \times 5 = 18.30 \text{ ft-k} \\
M_{10-6} &= -M_{6-10} = 5.49 \times 5 = 27.45 \text{ ft-k} \\
M_{5-1} &= -M_{1-5} = 4.38 \times 7 = 30.66 \text{ ft-k} \\
M_{6-2} &= -M_{2-6} = 6.57 \times 7 = 45.99 \text{ ft-k}
\end{aligned}$$

Axial Column Forces. The wind moment is resisted by a couple composed of the axial forces of the exterior columns. The interior columns do not carry any axial forces. The axial column force N_{25-21} at the top floor level is found by taking moments about the column inflection point in the other exterior column (Fig. 7.40*a*).

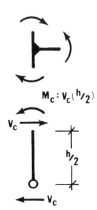

$$M_c = V_c\left(\frac{h}{2}\right)$$

Fig. 7.39

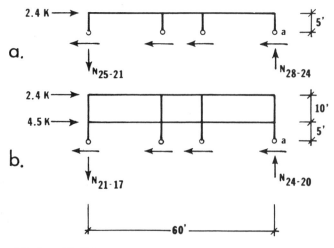

Fig. 7.40

$$\sum M_a = 0 = 2.4(5) - N_{25-21}(60) \qquad N_{25-21} = 0.2 \text{ k (T)}$$

Vertical equilibrium yields

$$\sum V = 0 = 0.2 - N_{28-24} \qquad N_{28-24} = 0.2 \text{ k (C)}$$

The same approach is used for finding the column axial forces at the fifth floor level (Fig. 7.40b).

$$\sum M_a = 0 = 2.4(15) + 4.5(5) - (60)N_{21-17}$$
$$N_{21-17} = 0.98 \text{ k (T)}$$
$$N_{24-20} = 0.98 \text{ k (C)}$$

Similarly, for the axial column forces at the other floor levels:

$$N_{17-13} = -N_{20-16} = \frac{2.4(25) + 4.5(15) + 4.2(5)}{60} = 2.48 \text{ k}$$

$$N_{13-9} = -N_{16-12} = \frac{[2.4(35) + 4.5(25) + 4.2(15) + 3.9(5)]}{60} = 4.64 \text{ k}$$

$$N_{9-5} = -N_{12-8} = \frac{[2.4(45) + 4.5(35) + 4.2(25) + 3.9(15) + 3.3(5)]}{60} = 7.42 \text{ k}$$

$$N_{5-1} = -N_{8-4} = \frac{[2.4(57) + 4.5(47) + 4.2(37) + 3.9(27) + 3.3(17) + 3.6(7)]}{60} = 11.51 \text{ k}$$

Beam Shear Forces. The shear forces in the beams are found simply by summing up the vertical forces in the free bodies in Fig. 7.41.

from Fig. 7.41a: $\sum V = 0 = 0.2 - V_{25-26}$ $\qquad V_{25-26} = 0.2 \text{ k}$
from Fig. 7.41b: $\sum V = 0 = 0.2 - V_{26-27}$ $\qquad V_{26-27} = 0.2 \text{ k}$
from Fig. 7.41c: $\sum V = 0 = 0.98 - 0.2 - V_{21-22}$ $\qquad V_{21-22} = 0.78 \text{ k}$
from Fig. 7.41d: $\sum V = 0 = 0.78 - V_{22-23}$ $\qquad V_{22-23} = 0.78 \text{ k}$

Similarly, for the other beams:

$$V_{17-18} = V_{18-19} = V_{19-20} = 2.48 - 0.98 = 1.50 \text{ k}$$
$$V_{13-14} = V_{14-15} = V_{15-16} = 4.64 - 2.48 = 2.16 \text{ k}$$
$$V_{9-10} = V_{10-11} = V_{11-12} = 7.42 - 4.64 = 2.78 \text{ k}$$
$$V_{5-6} = V_{6-7} = V_{7-8} = 11.51 - 7.42 = 4.09 \text{ k}$$

Note: Since there are no axial forces in interior columns, beam shears at a specific floor level remain constant across the entire width of the frame.

Beam Moments at Joints. The beam end moments are now found by multiplying the beam shear by half the beam span. Some of the beam moments are identified in Fig. 7.41. Notice the similarity to the column moment approach.

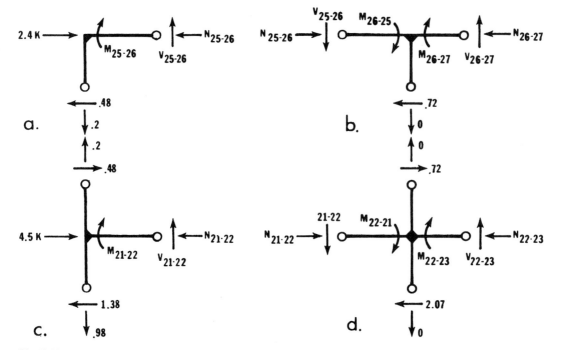

a.

b.

c.

d.

Fig. 7.41

$$
\begin{aligned}
M_{25-26} &= -M_{26-25} = 0.20 \times 12 = & 2.4 \text{ ft-k} \\
M_{26-27} &= -M_{27-26} = 0.20 \times 6 = & 1.2 \text{ ft-k} \\
M_{21-22} &= -M_{22-21} = 0.78 \times 12 = & 9.36 \text{ ft-k} \\
M_{22-23} &= -M_{23-22} = 0.78 \times 6 = & 4.68 \text{ ft-k} \\
M_{17-18} &= -M_{18-17} = 1.50 \times 12 = & 18.00 \text{ ft-k} \\
M_{18-19} &= -M_{19-18} = 1.50 \times 6 = & 9.00 \text{ ft-k} \\
M_{13-14} &= -M'_{14-13} = 2.16 \times 12 = & 25.92 \text{ ft-k} \\
M_{14-15} &= -M_{15-14} = 2.16 \times 6 = & 12.96 \text{ ft-k} \\
M_{9-10} &= -M_{10-9} = 2.78 \times 12 = & 33.36 \text{ ft-k} \\
M_{10-11} &= -M_{11-10} = 2.78 \times 6 = & 16.68 \text{ ft-k} \\
M_{5-6} &= -M_{6-5} = 4.09 \times 12 = & 49.08 \text{ ft-k} \\
M_{6-7} &= -M_{7-6} = 4.09 \times 6 = & 24.54 \text{ ft-k}
\end{aligned}
$$

Moments obtained for columns and beams are checked by using the principle of rotational equilibrium around a joint. For instance, the rotational equilibrium for joint 22 (Fig. 7.42) yields

$$\sum M_{22} = 0 = 9.36 - 10.35 + 4.68 - 3.6 = 0.09 \approx 0 \quad \text{OK}$$

A similar approach may be used for checking other joints.

Beam Axial Forces. The axial forces in the beams are found by summing up the horizontal forces in the free bodies shown in Fig. 7.41.

$$
\begin{aligned}
N_{25-26} &= 2.40 - 0.48 = 1.92 \text{ k} \\
N_{26-27} &= 1.92 - 0.72 = 1.20 \text{ k}
\end{aligned}
$$

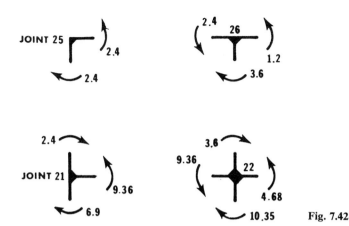

Fig. 7.42

$N_{27-28} = 1.20 - 0.72 = 0.48$ k

$N_{21-22} = (4.50 + 0.48) - 1.38 = 3.60$ k

$N_{22-23} = (3.60 + 0.72) - 2.07 = 2.25$ k

$N_{23-24} = (2.25 + 0.72) - 2.07 = 0.90$ k

$N_{17-18} = (4.20 + 1.38) - 2.22 = 3.36$ k

$N_{18-19} = (3.36 + 2.07) - 3.33 = 2.10$ k

$N_{19-20} = (2.10 + 2.07) - 3.33 = 0.84$ k

$N_{13-14} = (3.90 + 2.22) - 3.00 = 3.12$ k

$N_{14-15} = (3.12 + 3.33) - 4.50 = 1.95$ k

$N_{15-16} = (1.95 + 3.33) - 4.50 = 0.78$ k

$N_{9-10} = (3.30 + 3.00) - 3.66 = 2.64$ k

$N_{10-11} = (2.64 + 4.50) - 5.49 = 1.65$ k

$N_{11-12} = (1.65 + 4.50) - 5.49 = 0.66$ k

$N_{5-6} = (3.60 + 3.66) - 4.38 = 2.88$ k

$N_{6-7} = (2.88 + 5.49) - 6.57 = 1.80$ k

$N_{7-8} = (1.80 + 5.49) - 6.57 = 0.72$ k

The force flow through every member of the rigid frame as initiated by the lateral wind pressure is given in Fig. 7.43.

Approximate Design of Rigid Frame Buildings

For the sizing of frame members, two loading cases will be considered:

- Only gravity loads are acting.

- Gravity loads are acting together with wind or earthquake forces, for this case codes allow a 33% increase of allowable stresses.

Typical frame members must resist compression and bending. The method of design is determined by the relative magnitudes of these axial and rotational forces.

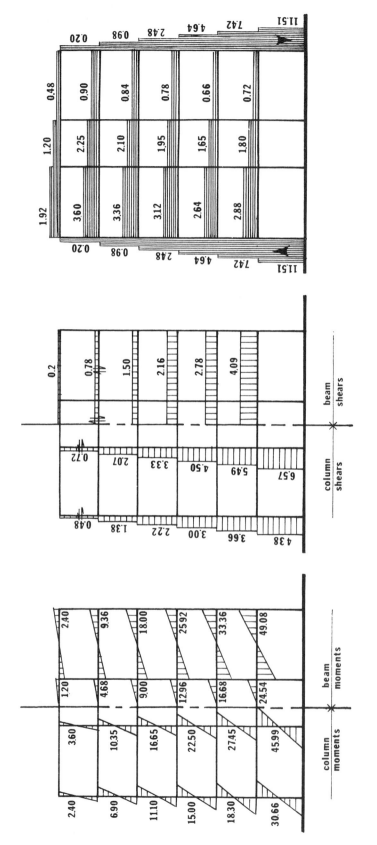

a. bending moments (ft-k)

b. shear forces (k)

c. axial forces (k)

Fig. 7.43. Force diagrams.

Beams

Since the axial forces in frame girders are relatively small, their design is based primarily on bending.

The section modulus for a symmetrical, rolled steel beam section is determined by the following formula:

$$S_{req} = \frac{M}{F_b} \qquad (7.7)$$

where S_{req} = required section modulus (in.³)

M = maximum acting moment (in.-k)

F_b = allowable bending stress (ksi) for a laterally supported section (e.g., F_b = 24 ksi for A36 steel)

In using equation 7.7 it is assumed that bending is indeed the critical factor and that no other criteria (e.g., shear, deflection, crippling, or instability due to lack of lateral support or compactness) will control.

Size of concrete beams is dependent on the amount of reinforcement used in the section. The depth of the concrete beam may be reasonably approximated as based on shear and deflection criteria (ACI 318-71). For a typical concrete with a strength of f'_c = 4000 psi the minimum beam height is

$$\frac{L}{18.5} \leq h \geq \frac{V_u}{323b} + 2.5 \qquad (7.8)$$

where V_u = ultimate shear force at distance d from the face of the support (lb)

b = beam width (in.)

L = span length of beam from center to center support (in.)

h = beam height (in.)

The amount of steel reinforcement may be approximated from

$$A_s = \frac{M_u}{\phi f_y z} = \frac{M_u}{0.9 f_y (0.9d)} = \frac{M_u}{0.81(d) f_y} \qquad (7.9)$$

where A_s = area of tensile reinforcement required (in.²)

M_u = ultimate moment (in.-k)

d = distance from extreme compression fiber to centroid of tension reinforcement (in.); for a single layer of tension reinforcement d may be approximated by $d = h - 2.5$ in. (see equation 7.8)

f_y = yield strength of steel reinforcement (ksi)

Columns

Most rigid frame columns are rather slender. They carry high axial forces and high primary rotational forces. Secondary moments are caused by lateral displacement of the column. As the column deflects laterally, additional moments are developed by the axial forces. The discussion in this section is restricted to the approximate design of steel columns.

The failure of typical beam columns is due to inelastic buckling. The formula used for the design of these beam columns, assuming bending about one principal axis only, according to AISC Specifications (1969, 1.6-1a), is

$$\frac{f_a}{F_a} + \frac{C_m}{1 - (f_a/F'_e)} \frac{f_b}{F_b} \leq 1 \tag{a}$$

For a first approximation of the column size, the amplification of the moments due to lateral deformation and the effects of boundary conditions are neglected. That is:

$$\frac{C_m}{1 - (f_a/F'_e)} = 1$$

Thus the interaction equation (a) is of a simple percentage type:

$$\frac{f_a}{F_a} + \frac{f_b}{F_b} \leq 1 \tag{b}$$

Note: The AISC Specifications allow the use of this formula for members with little axial forces ($f_a/F_a \leq 0.15$).

Multiplying equation (b) by F_a yields

$$f_a + f_b \frac{F_a}{F_b} \leq F_a \tag{c}$$

Substituting $f_a = P/A$, $f_b = M/S$, $F_a = P_{all}/A$, we write

$$\frac{P}{A} + \frac{M}{S} \frac{F_a}{F_b} \leq \frac{P_{all}}{A} \tag{d}$$

Multiplying equation (d) by A yields

$$P + \frac{A}{S} M \frac{F_a}{F_b} \leq P_{all}$$

The *AISC Manual of Steel Construction* lists in its column tables values for the ratio A/S, known as the bending factor B.

$$P + BM \frac{F_a}{F_b} \leq P_{all} \tag{e}$$

For an initial estimate of section size, the ratio of allowable axial and bending stresses is conservatively assumed to be 1. Thus

$$P_{all} \geq P + BM$$

The product of BM is considered as a fictitious axial column load P'. Thus the column tables of the *AISC Manual* can be used to select a section

$$P + P' = P + BM = P_{all} \qquad (7.10)$$

where P = the acting axial force (k)
$\quad\quad B$ = bending factor (in.$^{-1}$)
$\quad\quad M$ = maximum acting moment (in.-k)
$\quad\quad P_{all}$ = required tabular column load

Equation 7.10 is based on an equivalent axial load and always overestimates the size of the section. Therefore it is common procedure to select not the section required but the next smaller one.

Another approximate design approach sometimes used is based on the same design assumptions developed earlier. Equation (d) with $F_a/F_b = 1$ yields

$$F_a \geq \frac{P}{A} + \frac{M}{S} \qquad (a)$$

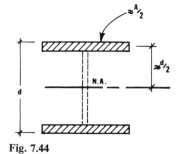

Fig. 7.44

Since bending stresses are resisted primarily by the flanges of a W-section, it is assumed that the total area of the section is concentrated in the two flanges. Thus the web is considered to be nonexistent (Fig. 7.44).

The moment of inertia of such a hypothetical section consisting of flanges only may be expressed as

$$I = \left[\frac{A}{2} \left(\frac{d}{2} \right)^2 \right] 2 = \frac{Ad^2}{4}$$

or in terms of the section modulus

$$S = \frac{I}{d/2} = \frac{Ad}{2}$$

Substituting the section modulus into equation (a) yields

$$F_a \geq \frac{P}{A} + \frac{M}{Ad/2}$$

Thus the minimum required area for the wide-flange section is

$$A_{min} = \frac{1}{F_a} (P + 2M/d) \qquad (7.11)$$

To design a typical column in a rigid frame building, we must know the allowable compression stress F_a (i.e., the capacity of the column). The capacity is directly related to the slenderness of the column (KL/r), which takes into account column size and geometry (radius of gyration r), column span L, and end restraint K. The problem lies in the evaluation of the end restraint as provided by the floor girders attached to the column at the upper and lower ends. The effective column length (i.e., the shape of the laterally displaced column) depends on that end restraint (i.e., the amount of rotational fixity provided at

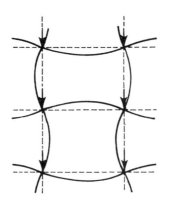
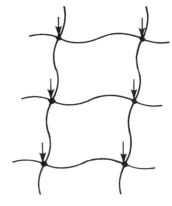

Fig. 7.45

a. no sidesway   b. sidesway

the column boundaries). The amount of restraint is measured by the stiffness factor K as based on an equivalent pinned-end laterally braced column ($K = 1$).

To be able to approximate the stiffness factor K, it is necessary to distinguish between the two types of rigid frame buildings discussed below.

• A rigid frame building that is laterally stabilized by shear walls (e.g., concrete cores) or trussed bents deforms under vertical loads as shown in Fig. 7.45a. It is assumed that all columns at any one story will buckle simultaneously. Depending on the rotational rigidity of the girders, the stiffness factor K for the columns is in the range of 0.5 to 1.0. For purposes of approximation, the effective column length KL may be safely assumed equal to the unbraced length of the column ($K = 1$). This assumption is correct for frames with hinged connections between beams and columns but is rather conservative for rigid frame action. For instance, the stiffness factor K for the bottom story of a high-rise rigid frame is in the range of 0.8.

• Rigid frame buildings with only light curtain wall systems and no lateral bracing are laterally unstable. That is, they displace laterally under vertical loading. For such conditions, known as sidesway, column stiffness factors are always larger than 1 (Fig. 7.45b).

For the ideal case in which infinite restraint is provided by floor girders, the stiffness factor is $K = 1$ (Fig. 7.46a).

As the restraint against end rotation is reduced, the effective length of the columns will increase and always will be larger than the actual length. The amount of end restraint is also dependent on the type of girder-to-column connection (hinged vs. semirigid vs. rigid connection).

In rigid frame structures, the effective length or the stiffness factor K increases as the stiffness of the girders decreases, assuming no change in column stiffness. For example, for a bending stiffness of the girders ($\sum I_g / \sum L_g$) equal to that of

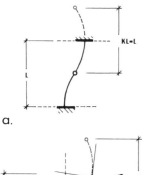

a.

b.

Fig. 7.46

the columns $(\sum I_c / \sum L_c)$ the stiffness factor $K = 1.3$ (Fig. 7.46b). The typical stiffness factor for the lower stories of a high-rise rigid frame building is in the range of 1.60, increasing slightly toward the upper stories. In general, it is conservative to use $K = 2$ as a rough, first approximation.

In a frame building where the girders are hinged to the columns, however, K is generally larger than 2. Using $K = 2.50$ as a first approximation is not necessarily conservative!

The previous discussion applies to the effective column length about either axis (i.e., K_x, K_y). Both axes have to be checked. If the column is free to sway about its x-axis but is restrained from displacing laterally about its y-axis, it may be assumed as a first approximation that the weak axis controls; that is, $K_x L / r_x = L / r_y$.

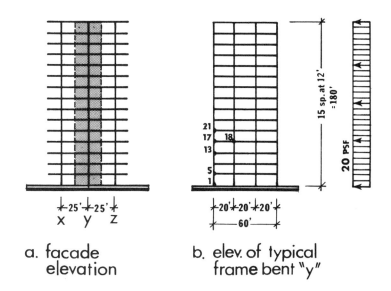

a. facade elevation

b. elev. of typical frame bent "y"

Fig. 7.47

PROBLEM 7.5

The steel frame shown in Fig. 7.47b is a typical interior bent of a 15-story building. The frame bents are spaced 25 ft apart. The wind pressure is approximated as 20 psf (see Fig. 2.6 for accurate values). Floor live and dead loads are 80 psf each. The weight of the columns is assumed to be equivalent to 14 psf. For the design of the columns, use a reduction of 20% for the floor live loads (see Chapter 2 for accurate live load reduction). The roof load is assumed to be two-thirds of the typical floor load. Neglect reduction of live loads for girder design.

Design columns 1–5 and 13–17 and beam 17–18, using A36 steel.

A. Analysis

Wind Loads. To find the required column axial and shear forces, free bodies of the building frame are taken at midheight (assumed hinge location) of the first, fourth, and fifth floors as in Fig. 7.48.

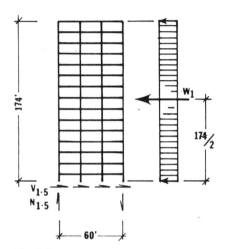

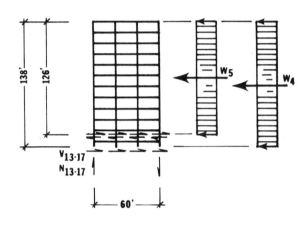

Fig. 7.48

The total wind pressure for each of the free bodies is

$$W_1 = (0.02 \times 25)174 = 87 \text{ k}$$
$$W_4 = (0.02 \times 25)138 = 69 \text{ k}$$
$$W_5 = (0.02 \times 25)126 = 63 \text{ k}$$

The axial forces are found by taking moments about the exterior columns on the windward side.

$$N_{1-5}(60) = 87\left(\frac{174}{2}\right) \qquad N_{1-5} = 126.15 \text{ k}$$

$$N_{13-17}(60) = 69\left(\frac{138}{2}\right) \qquad N_{13-17} = 79.35 \text{ k}$$

$$N_{17-21}(60) = 63\left(\frac{126}{2}\right) \qquad N_{17-21} = 66.15 \text{ k}$$

The column shears at the respective floor levels are found according to equation 7.5.

The shear for a typical exterior column is

$$V_{1-5} = \frac{W_1 L_1}{2B} = \frac{87 \times 20}{2 \times 60} = 14.50 \text{ k}$$

$$V_{13-17} = \frac{69 \times 20}{2 \times 60} = 11.50 \text{ k}$$

$$V_{17-21} = \frac{63 \times 20}{2 \times 60} = 10.50 \text{ k}$$

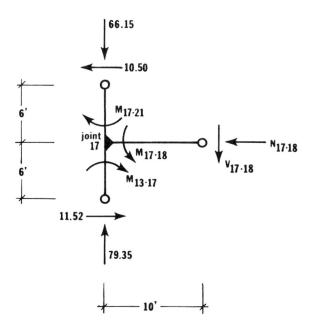

66.15

10.50

6'

joint 17

$M_{17\text{-}21}$

$M_{17\text{-}18}$

$N_{17\text{-}18}$

$V_{17\text{-}18}$

6'

$M_{13\text{-}17}$

11.52

79.35

10'

Fig. 7.49

Figure 7.49 gives the known column shear and axial forces. From this free body, taken at joint 17, all other required beam and column forces are found.

Vertical equilibrium of the free body yields the beam shear:

$$\sum V = 0 = 79.35 - 66.15 - V_{17-18} \qquad V_{17-18} = 13.2 \text{ k}$$

Horizontal equilibrium yields the axial force in the beam:

$$\sum H = 0 = 11.52 - 10.50 - N_{17-18} \qquad N_{17-18} = 1.02 \text{ k}$$

The moments in the members at joint 17 are found by multiplying the member shears acting at the assumed hinge location by their respective distances to the joint.

$$M_{13-17} = 11.52(6) \quad = \quad 69.12 \text{ ft-k}$$

$$M_{17-21} = 10.50(6) \quad = \quad 63.00 \text{ ft-k}$$

$$M_{17-18} = 13.20(10) = 132.00 \text{ ft-k}$$

$$M_{1-5} = 14.50(6) \quad = \quad 87.00 \text{ ft-k}$$

Check if joint 17 is in rotational equilibrium

$$\sum M = 0 = 69.12 + 63.00 - 132.00 = 0.12 \approx 0 \quad \text{OK}$$

Gravity Loads. The total gravity load carried by beam 17–18 is

$$w = 25(0.08 + 0.08) = 4.00 \text{ k/ft}$$

According to equation 7.2, the maximum field moment is

$$M = 0.08wL^2 = 0.08(4)20^2 = 128 \text{ ft-k}$$

According to equation 7.3, the maximum support moment is

$$-M = 0.045wL^2 = 0.045(4)20^2 = 72 \text{ ft-k}$$

According to equation 7.4, the column moment, as caused by the beam support moment, assuming same column stiffness, is

$$M_{17-21} = M_{13-17} = \frac{72}{2} = 36 \text{ ft-k} \qquad (\text{see Fig. 7.50})$$

$$M_{1-5} = 36 \text{ ft-k}$$

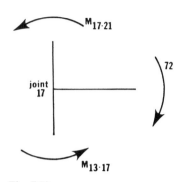

Fig. 7.50

A typical exterior column must support the following floor area at every story:

$$A = 25(10) = 250 \text{ ft}^2$$

A typical floor load with reduced live load acting on this area is

$$w = 80 + 0.8(80) + 14 = 158 \text{ psf}$$

A typical floor load with full live load acting on this area is

$$w' = 80 + 80 + 14 = 174 \text{ psf}$$

The exterior column 1–5 at the first floor level has to carry the following load:

$$N_{1-5} = 250[0.158(14) + (0.66)(0.158)(1)] = 578.00$$
$$(\text{with reduced live load})$$

$$N'_{1-5} = 250[0.174(14) + 0.66(0.174)(1)] = 637.75 \text{ k}$$
$$(\text{with full live load})$$

Similarly, the exterior column 13–17 at the fourth floor has to carry

$$N_{13-17} = 250[0.158(11) + (0.66)(0.158)(1)] = 461.00 \text{ k}$$
$$N'_{13-17} = 250[0.174(11) + 0.66(0.174)(1)] = 507.25 \text{ k}$$

B. Design

Beam 17–18

Wind loads:	$-M =$	132.00 ft-k
	$N =$	1.02 k (is neglected)
Gravity loads:	$M =$	128.00 ft-k
	$-M =$	72.00 ft-k
Wind + gravity loads:	$-M = 132.00 + 72.00 =$	204.00 ft-k

For the case of wind acting together with gravity loads, codes allow an increase in allowable stresses of 33%, which is equivalent to a load reduction of 25%.

$$-M = 204.00(0.75) = 153 \text{ ft-k}$$

Since the moment for the combined loading case is larger than that for gravity only, it controls the design of the beam. The required section modulus is

$$S_{\text{req}} = \frac{M}{F_b} = \frac{153.00(12)}{24} = 76.50 \text{ in.}^3$$

Select as a trial section

$$W\ 21 \times 44 \qquad A = 13.00 \text{ in.}^2, \qquad I_x = 843 \text{ in.}^4$$

Column 13–17

| Wind loads: | $N = 79.35$ k |
| | $M = 69.12$ ft-k |

Gravity loads: $N = 461.00$ k $N' = 507.25$ k
                                    $M = 36.00$ ft-k

Wind + gravity loads: $N = 79.35 + 507.25 = 586.60$ k
                                $M = 69.12 + 36.00 = 105.12$ ft-k

DESIGN FOR THE COMBINED LOADING CASE. The column tables in the *AISC Manual* are used for design. The stiffness factor is assumed as $K = 2$ assuming an unbraced frame. A bending factor of $B_x = 0.185$ is selected.

Note: There is hardly any change in the magnitude of the bending factor; as a comparison of the values on the bottom of pages 3–15, 3–16 in the *AISC Manual* indicates.

The equivalent axial force is

$$P + P' = P + B_x M_x = [586.60 + 0.185(105.12)12]0.75 \quad (7.10)$$

$$= 614.98 \text{ k}$$

For an effective column length of $KL = 2(12) = 24$; try

$$W\ 14 \times 127 \qquad P_{\text{all}} = 587.00\ k, \qquad B_x = 0.185$$

CHECK FOR GRAVITY LOADS

$$P + B_x M_x = 461 + 0.185(36)12 = 540.92 \text{ k} < 587.00 \text{ k}$$

Hence the combined loading case controls.

Select as trial section

$$W\ 14 \times 127 \qquad I_x = 1480 \text{ in.}^4, \qquad A = 37.30 \text{ in.}^2$$

Column 1–5

Wind loads: $N = 126.15$ k
                                 $M = 87.00$ ft-k

Gravity loads: $N = 578.00$ k $N' = 637.75$ k
                                  $M = 36.00$ ft-k

Wind + gravity loads: $N = 126.15 + 637.75 = 763.90$ k
                                $M = 87.00 + 36.00 = 123.00$ ft-k

DESIGN FOR COMBINED LOADING CASE. See AISC Manual, page 3–15:

$$KL = 2(12) = 24 \text{ ft}$$

$$P + B_x M_x = [763.90 + 0.184(123.00)12]0.75 = 776.61 \text{ k}$$

Try a

$$W \; 14 \times 158 \qquad P_{\text{all}} = 754.00 \; k, \qquad B_x = 0.184$$

CHECK FOR GRAVITY LOADS

$$P + B_x M_x = 578.00 + 0.184(36.00)12 = 657.49 \text{ k} < 754.00 \text{ k}$$

Hence the combined loading case controls. Select as a trial section

$$W \; 14 \times 158 \qquad I_x = 1900 \text{ in.}^4, \qquad A = 46.5 \text{ in.}^2$$

Lateral Deformation of Rigid Frame Buildings

The total drift of a building must be limited to ensure the comfort of the occupants and the protection of mechanical and architectural systems. The commonly accepted range for drift is from 0.0016 to 0.0035 times the height of the building, depending on the building height and the magnitude of the wind pressure. The Committee on Wind Bracing of the American Society of Civil Engineers has recommended that the maximum sway be less than 0.002 times the height of the building for normal wind pressure.

As shown in Fig. 5.12, the lateral drift of rigid frame buildings is caused by shear wracking resulting in bending of columns and girders and by cantilever behavior of the frame causing axial deformations of the columns. The highest stresses are carried by the exterior columns and girders because they are the furthest from the neutral axis of the building.

In the derivation of the formula for approximate lateral building sway, the stiffness provided by adjacent frames and filler materials is neglected. Also, the reduction of rigidity due to joint slippage and deformation is not considered.

Lateral Deformation of Rigid Frame Due to Bending of Beams and Columns

The assumptions of the portal method can be used to obtain an approximate solution of lateral drift of the frame due to shear wracking. Figure 7.51 shows the deformed state of a typical bent bay with the assumed hinge location at midspan of girders and midheight of columns,

where ϕ = angle of rotation due to the bending of girders
θ = angle of rotation due to the bending of columns
Δ_c = deflection due to the bending of columns
Δ_g = deflection due to the bending of girders

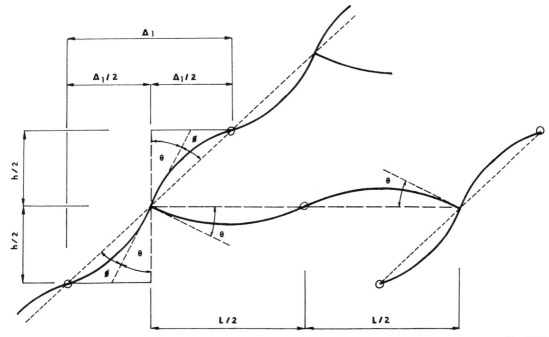

Fig. 7.51

The relationship between girder rotation and deformation (Fig. 7.52b) is

$$\frac{\Delta_g/2}{L/2} = \tan \theta \approx \theta \qquad \text{or} \qquad \theta = \frac{\Delta_g}{L} \qquad \text{(a)}$$

The relationship between column rotation and deformation (Fig. 7.52a) is

$$\frac{\Delta_c/2}{h/2} = \tan \phi \approx \phi \qquad \text{or} \qquad \phi = \frac{\Delta_c}{h} \qquad \text{(b)}$$

The total deformation of a typical bent is

$$\frac{\Delta_1}{h} = \tan (\theta + \phi) \approx \theta + \phi \qquad \text{(c)}$$

Substituting equations (a) and (b) in (c) yields

$$\frac{\Delta_1}{h} = \frac{\Delta_g}{L} + \frac{\Delta_c}{h} \qquad \text{(d)}$$

Deflection Due to Bending of Columns

The lateral sway of the columns is represented in Fig. 7.52a. The girders are assumed to be infinitely rigid. The lateral deformation caused by the column shear acting at the assumed hinge, as based on a simple cantilever, is

$$\Delta_c = 2 \frac{V_c (h/2)^3}{3EI_c} = \frac{V_c h^3}{12EI_c} \qquad (7.12)$$

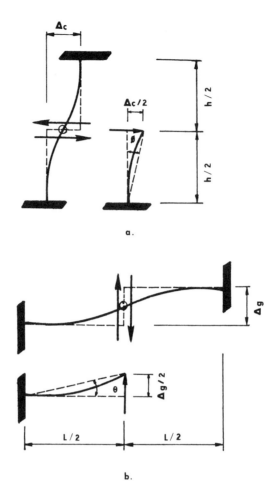

Fig. 7.52

b.

Deflection Due to Bending of Girders (Fig. 7.52b)

Assuming that columns are infinitely rigid, the deflection of a simple cantilever caused by the girder shear at midspan of the bay yields

$$\Delta_g = 2\,\frac{V_g(L/2)^3}{3EI_g} = \frac{V_g L^3}{12EI_g} \qquad (7.13)$$

Substituting equations 7.12 and 7.13 in equation (d) gives

$$\frac{\Delta_1}{h} = \frac{V_g L^3}{12EI_g L} + \frac{V_c h^3}{12EI_c h}$$

It is assumed that the ratio of Δ_1/h of each building floor will be constant. This, however, is not true in the transition zone from the fixed building base to the assumed constant slope of the deflected bent. Neglecting conservatively the effects of the base zone as based on the foregoing assumptions, the ratio of story drift to story height is equal to the ratio of building sway $\Delta_{1\,\max}$ to the building height H. Because I_g and I_c of the base floors are greater than those of the floors beyond the third or

172   Approximate Structural Analysis and Design of Buildings

fourth level, the ratios of V_c/I_c and V_g/I_g are taken from the upper stories and used in equation 7.14.

$$\frac{\Delta_1}{h} = \frac{\Delta_{1\,max}}{H} = \frac{V_g L^2}{12EI_g} + \frac{V_c h^2}{12EI_c}$$

$$\Delta_{1\,max} = \frac{V_g L^2 H}{12EI_g} + \frac{V_c h^2 H}{12EI_c} \qquad (7.14)$$

Rigid Frame Deformation Due to Axial Deformation of Columns

Since gravity forces increase in a linear manner toward the base of the building, column areas may be considered to increase proportionally in the same way. In other words, the wind stresses in the columns may be assumed to increase linearly from zero at the top of the structure to maximum at the base. Hence the resultant wind pressure, assuming that equally distributed wind pressure acts at the top of the building, thus causing a linear increase of axial column stress.

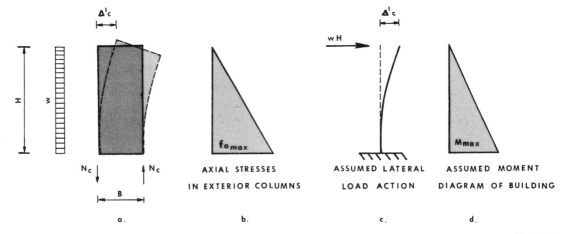

a. b. c. d.

AXIAL STRESSES IN EXTERIOR COLUMNS

ASSUMED LATERAL LOAD ACTION

ASSUMED MOMENT DIAGRAM OF BUILDING

Fig. 7.53

The maximum deformation of a cantilever due to a single load (Fig. 7.53c) is

$$\Delta_c' = \frac{(wH)H^3}{3EI_B} = \frac{wH^4}{3EI_B} = \frac{M_{max}H^2}{3EI_B} \qquad (a)$$

where the maximum moment at the base of the building is

$$M_{max} = wH(H) = wH^2$$

The maximum wind stresses in the exterior columns for a symmetrical frame are

$$f_{max} = \frac{M_{max}(B/2)}{I_B} \quad \text{or} \quad M_{max} = \frac{2f_{max}I_B}{B} \qquad (b)$$

Substituting equation (b) in (a) yields

$$\Delta'_c = \frac{2f_{max}H^2}{3EB} \qquad (7.15)$$

The maximum axial column stress at the building base as caused by the wind is

$$f_{max} = \frac{N_c}{A_c}$$

Hence the lateral deformation caused by axial force action is

$$\Delta'_c = \frac{2N_cH^2}{3EA_cB} \qquad (7.15a)$$

The Total Building Sway

The approximate total deflection for a rigid frame building consists of the summation of deformations due to shear wracking and cantilever action.

$$\Delta_{max} = \Delta_c + \Delta_g + \Delta'_c$$

$$\Delta_{max} = \frac{HV_ch^2}{12EI_c} + \frac{HV_gL^2}{12EI_g} + \frac{2N_cH^2}{3EA_cB} \qquad (7.16)$$

where N_c = axial wind force in the exterior column at the base
V_c/I_c = column wind shear/inertia of column about bending axis; take the ratio above third floor level
E = modulus of elasticity
A_c = area of exterior column at building base
V_g/I_g = girder wind shear/inertia of beam about x-axis; take ratio at same level as V_c/I_c
H = height of building frame
h = typical story height
B = base width of frame
L = girder span

PROBLEM 7.6

Determine the approximate lateral sway of the rigid frame building of Problem 7.5 with following known values:

$V_c = 11.50$ k $V_g = 13.2$ k $N_c = 126.15$ k $I_c = 1480$ in.^{4}
$I_g = 843$ in.^{4} $A_c = 46.5$ in.^{2} $h = 12$ ft $H = 180$ ft
$L = 20$ ft $B = 60$ ft $E = 29,000$ ksi

According to equation 7.16 the maximum building sway is

$$\Delta_{max} = 180\left[\frac{11.5(12 \times 12)^2}{12(29,000)1480} + \frac{13.2(20 \times 12)^2}{12(29,000)843}\right.$$

$$+ \frac{2(126.15)180}{3(29,000)46.5(60)} \Bigg]$$

$$= 180[0.463 \times 10^{-3} + 2.60 \times 10^{-3} + 0.187 \times 10^{-3}]$$

$$\Delta_{max} = 180(3.25)10^{-3} = 0.585 \text{ ft} = 7.02 \text{ in.}$$

The recommended maximum sway is

$$\Delta_{max \ all} = 0.002H = 0.002(180)12 = 4.32 \text{ in.} < 7.02 \text{ in.}$$

The frame sways too much; the bending stiffness of the girders in the lower portion of the building should be increased!

The percentages of total sway as caused by the individual components of deflection are as follows:

bending of columns:
  $[(0.463 \times 10^{-3})/(3.250 \times 10^{-3})]100 = 14.25\%$
bending of girders:
  $[(2.6 \times 10^{-3})/(3.250 \times 10^{-3})]100 \quad = 80.00\%$

      total for SHEAR wracking   94.25%

axial deformation
of columns: $[(0.187 \times 10^{-3})/(3.250 \times 10^{-3})]100 = 5.75\%$

Thus the lateral sway of the building is caused primarily by frame wracking. Furthermore, it is clearly indicated that the stiffness of the frame girders controls to a large extent the lateral deformation of the rigid frame building!

THE RIGID FRAME–SHEAR WALL STRUCTURE

The interaction of the rigid frame and shear wall structure is investigated in the following problem. The individual modes of behavior of the two structural systems (Fig. 5.17) are used for finding the portion of lateral pressure absorbed by each of the systems.

PROBLEM 7.7

The 15-story rigid frame building of Problem 7.5 is stiffened by two concrete core walls, 12-in. thick (Fig. 7.54). The concrete strength is $f'_c = 4000$ psi and the modulus of elasticity is $E = 3600$ ksi. Determine the percentage of wind load carried by each of the structural systems.

Assuming that the wind is resisted only by the rigid frames, the following load is carried by one frame:

$$W = 25(180)(0.02) = 90 \text{ k}$$

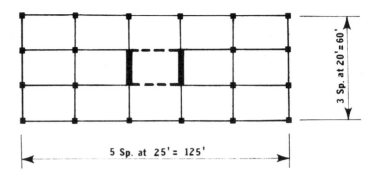

Fig. 7.54

The maximum deflection of the rigid frame at the top of the building according to Problem 7.6 is

$$\Delta_f = 7.02 \text{ in.}$$

Hence the flexural stiffness (Fig. 4.7) of the frame is

$$k_f = \frac{P}{\Delta_f} = \frac{90}{7.02} = 12.82 \text{ k/in.}$$

Assuming that the wind is carried by the concrete walls only, one wall resists the following load:

$$W = \frac{180(125)0.02}{2} = 225 \text{ k}$$

Considering the wall to behave as a cantilever (Fig. 5.17b) and not to change its shape as it bends, the maximum deflection is

$$\Delta_w = \frac{WH^3}{8EI} = \frac{225(180 \times 12)^3}{8(3600)[12(20 \times 12)^3/12]} = 5.70 \text{ in.}$$

The flexural stiffness of the wall is

$$k_w = \frac{P}{\Delta_w} = \frac{225}{5.70} = 39.47 \text{ k/in.}$$

The stiffness factors for the frame and the wall are constants, since the load and deflection are assumed proportional to each other, thus are independent of the actual load action on the frame and wall.

The total stiffness of the building, provided by the two walls and four frames, is

$$\sum k_w + \sum k_f = 2(39.47) + 4(12.82)$$
$$= 78.94 + 51.28 = 130.22 \text{ k/in.}$$

Hence the percentage of the load carried by the walls, assuming rigid diaphragm action of the floor structure, is

$$\frac{\sum k_w}{\sum k_w + \sum k_f}(100) = \frac{78.94}{130.22}(100) = 60.62\%$$

Thus 60.62% of the total wind load is carried by the core shear walls and only 39.38% by the four frames. In general, the shear walls are much stiffer than the rigid frames and resist a much larger portion of the lateral loads, as this problem demonstrates.

THE VIERENDEEL STRUCTURE

The cantilever building resisting constant horizontal pressure (Fig. 7.55*b*) behaves much like a beam carrying equally distributed vertical loads (Fig. 7.55*a*).

Fixing the cantilever beam (Fig. 7.55*b*) at the point of zero slope (i.e., $L/2$) of the deflected simply supported beam (Fig. 7.55*a*) yields a cantilever deformation equal to the maximum field deflection of the simply supported beam.

$$\Delta_{\max} = \Delta_2 - \Delta_1$$

$$\Delta_{\max} = \frac{(wL/2)(L/2)^3}{3EI} - \frac{w(L/2)^4}{8EI}$$

$$\Delta_{\max} = \frac{8wL^4}{384EI} - \frac{3wL^4}{384EI}$$

$$\Delta_{\max} = \frac{5wL^4}{384EI}$$

Hence the Vierendeel beam symmetrically loaded by gravity

Fig. 7.55

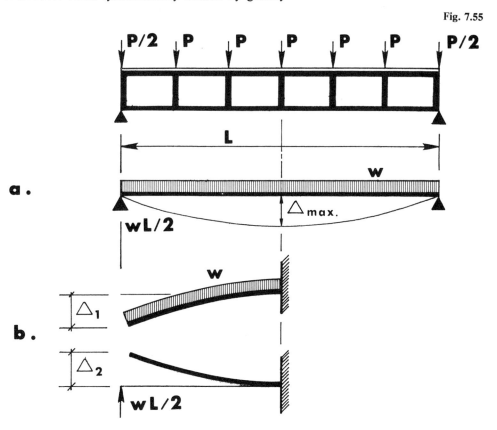

forces behaves analogously to a cantilevering rigid frame carrying lateral forces. Thus the portal method can be applied by assuming hinges to form at midheight of the columns and midspan of the beams in each bay of the Vierendeel truss.

PROBLEM 7.8

A three-story building is supported by two parallel facade trusses, as in Fig. 7.56. Determine the shear, axial, and moment diagrams for the truss and find approximate member sizes. The loads are assumed to act at the top chord joints only. Only gravity loads are considered.

Using the portal method, zero moment points (i.e., hinges) are assumed at midspan and midheight of each bay, as indicated in Fig. 7.56. Because of the symmetry of loading and geometry, only half the truss has to be considered.

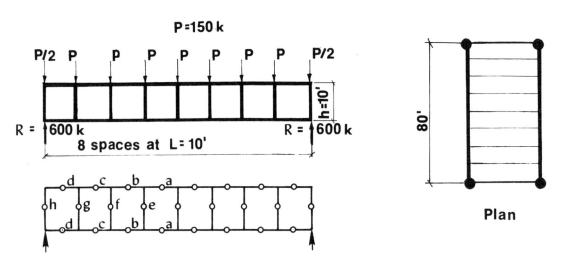

Fig. 7.56

A. Analysis of Shear and Axial Forces for Top and Bottom Chord Members

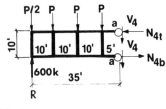

Fig. 7.57

Free bodies are taken by cutting the truss at midspan of the chords (i.e., zero moment points), ensuring that only internal shear and axial chord forces will occur.

Rotational equilibrium about the hinge yields the axial chord force (Fig. 7.57):

$$\sum M_a = 0 = 600(35) - 75(35) - 150(25)$$
$$- 150(15) - 150(5) - 10N_{4t}$$

$$N_{4t} = 1162.5 \text{ k (C)}$$

Horizontal equilibrium yields the axial force in the bottom chord

$$\sum H = 0 = N_{4b} - 1162.5 \qquad N_{4b} = 1162.5 \text{ k (T)}$$

Vertical equilibrium yields the chord shear forces

$$\sum V = 0 = 600 - 75 - 3(150) - 2V_4 \qquad V_4 = 37.5 \text{ k}$$

The same process is used for determining the shear and axial forces in the other chord members (Fig. 7.58).

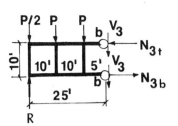

$$\sum M_b = 0 = 600(25) - 75(25) - 150(15) - 150(5) - 10N_{3t}$$

$$N_{3t} = 1012 \text{ k (C)}$$

$$\sum H = 0 = N_{3b} - 1012 \qquad N_{3b} = 1012 \text{ k (T)}$$

$$\sum V = 0 = 600 - 75 - 2(150) - 2V_3 \qquad V_3 = 112.5 \text{ k}$$

$$\sum M_c = 0 = 600(15) - 75(15) - 150(5) - 10N_{2t}$$

$$N_{2t} = 712.5 \text{ k (C)}$$

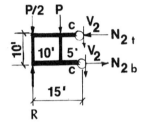

$$\sum H = 0 = N_{2b} - 712.5 \qquad N_{2b} = 712.5 \text{ k (T)}$$

$$\sum V = 0 = 600 - 75 - 150 - 2V_2 \qquad V_2 = 187.5 \text{ k}$$

$$\sum M_d = 0 = 600(5) - 75(5) - 10N_{1t} \qquad N_{1t} = 262.5 \text{ k (C)}$$

$$\sum H = 0 = N_{1b} - 262.5 \qquad N_{1b} = 262.5 \text{ k (T)}$$

$$\sum V = 0 = 600 - 75 - 2V_1 \qquad V_1 = 262.5 \text{ k}$$

B. Analysis of Shear and Axial Forces in Columns and Bending Moments in Chords and Columns

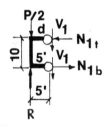

The truss is subdivided into free bodies, as in Fig. 7.59, to obtain the internal forces not yet known. Each member is cut at the assumed hinge location.

The unknown internal forces, shown in the free body of Fig. 7.60, are solved by using the known internal chord forces found before.

Horizontal equilibrium yields the column shear

$$\sum H = 0 = 262.5 - V_1' \qquad V_1' = 262.5 \text{ k}$$

Fig. 7.58

Fig. 7.59

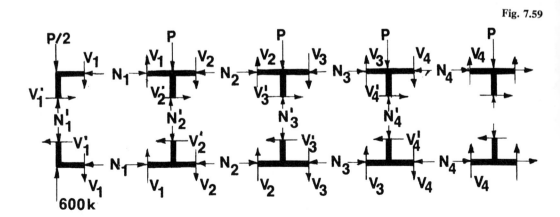

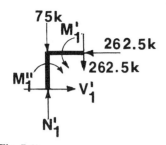

Fig. 7.60

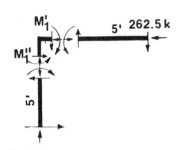

Fig. 7.61

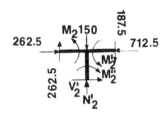

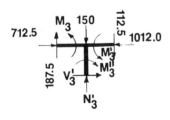

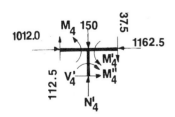

Fig. 7.62

Vertical equilibrium yields the axial column force

$$\sum V = 0 = 75 + 262.5 - N_1' \qquad N_1' = 337.5 \text{ k}$$

The maximum moments, at the intersection of chord and column, are found by rotational equilibrium about that point; or, in other words, by rotating the shear forces about that point (Fig. 7.61).

$$M_1' = V_1(5) = 262.5(5) = 1312.5 \text{ ft-k}$$
$$M_1'' = V_1'(5) = 262.5(5) = 1312.5 \text{ ft-k}$$

As an independent check, use the rotational equilibrium of the joint.

$$\sum M = 0 = 1312.5 - 1312.5 = 0 \qquad \text{OK}$$

The same procedure is used for the remaining free-bodies. The direction of forces is indicated on the free bodies (Fig. 7.62).

$$\sum H = 0 = 712.5 - 262.5 - V_2' \qquad V_2' = 450 \text{ k}$$
$$\sum V = 0 = 150 + 187.5 - 262.5 - N_2' \qquad N_2' = 75 \text{ k}$$
$$M_2 = 262.5(5) = 1312.5 \text{ ft-k}$$
$$M_2' = 187.5(5) = 937.5 \text{ ft-k}$$
$$M_2'' = 450(5) = 2250 \text{ ft-k}$$

Check: $\sum M = -937.5 - 1312.5 + 2250 = 0$ OK

$$\sum H = 0 = 1012 - 712.5 - V_3' \qquad V_3' = 300 \text{ k}$$
$$\sum V = 0 = 150 + 112.5 - 187.5 - N_3' \qquad N_3' = 75 \text{ k}$$
$$M_3 = 187.5(5) = 937.5 \text{ ft-k}$$
$$M_3' = 112.5(5) = 562.5 \text{ ft-k}$$
$$M_3'' = 300(5) = 1500 \text{ ft-k}$$

Check: $\sum M = 1500 - 562.5 - 937.5 = 0$ OK

$$\sum H = 0 = 1162.5 - 1012 - V_4' \qquad V_4' = 150 \text{ k}$$
$$\sum V = 0 = 150 + 37.5 - 112.5 - N_4' \qquad N_4' = 75 \text{ k}$$
$$M_4 = 112.5(5) = 562.5 \text{ ft-k}$$
$$M_4' = 37.5(5) = 187.5 \text{ ft-k}$$
$$M_4'' = 150(5) = 750 \text{ ft-k}$$

Check: $\sum M = 750 - 562.5 - 187.5 = 0$ OK

The force flow through the Vierendeel frame is shown in Fig. 7.63.

C. Approximate Design of Critical Members

A36 steel is selected with an allowable bending stress of $F_b = 24$ ksi and no stress reduction due to noncompactness or lack

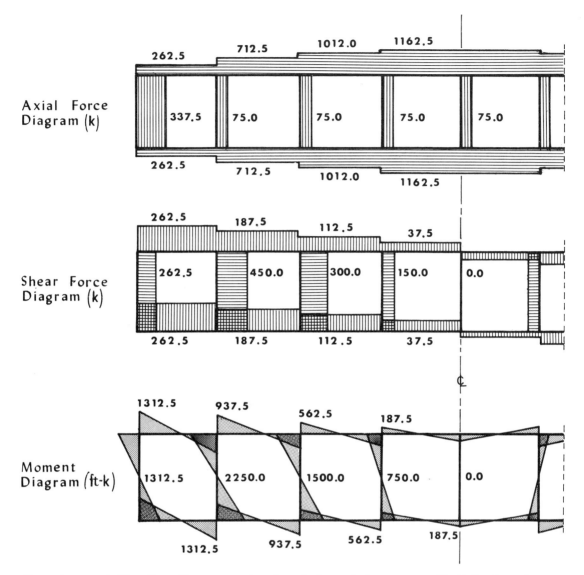

Axial Force
Diagram (k)

Shear Force
Diagram (k)

Moment
Diagram (ft-k)

Fig. 7.63. Force diagrams.

of lateral support. The allowable compressive stress is dependent on the slenderness ratio of the column having a maximum allowable stress $F_a = 22$ ksi. Because of high rotational rigidity of the boundaries, with a negligible sway effect of the medium long columns, an allowable stress of $F_a = 20$ ksi is used for the approximate design of the members. The approximate design formula for beam columns is

$$A = \frac{1}{F_a}(P + 2M/d) \qquad (7.11)$$

Check the top chord first—note that the top chord is more critical than the bottom chord, since it is in compression instead of tension.

A W14 section is assumed with a depth $d = 18$ in.

at midspan:

$$A = \frac{1}{20}(1162.5 + 187.5(12)2/18) = 70.6 \text{ in.}^2$$

at support:

$$A = \frac{1}{20}(712.5 + 1312.5(12)2/18) = 123 \text{ in.}^2 > 70.6 \text{ in.}^2$$

A W14 $\times$ 426 provides the necessary area; a deeper built-up section would weigh much less!

Note that the imbalance of stresses can be corrected by increasing the central bay sizes as illustrated in Fig. 7.64. This ensures that the central chord stresses are increased and the end chord stresses decreased.

Check the critical truss columns assuming a depth of $d = 18$ in.

end column:

$$A = \frac{1}{20}(337.5 + 1312.5(12)2/18) = 105 \text{ in.}^2$$

next to end column:

$$A = \frac{1}{20}(75 + 2250(12)2/18) = 154 \text{ in.}^2 > 105 \text{ in.}^2$$

Note that the column sizes are much more balanced if the bay geometry decreases toward the support; that is, the moment impact upon the columns is decreased (Fig. 7.64).

Figure 7.64 illustrates that for constant bay spacing, top chord and column members increase in size as they approach the support, whereas for decreasing bay spacing the top chord and column members tend to keep their size.

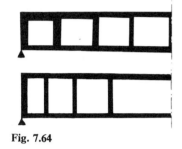

Fig. 7.64

PROBLEM 7.9

Design approximately the top chord for one Vierendeel truss of the interspatial building system of Fig. 7.65. The trusses are spaced 20 ft apart. A typical truss carries an equally distributed gravity load of 10 k/ft (the loading includes both top and bottom chords). The truss height is 10 ft. The truss is subdivided into 10 bays, each 10 ft wide.

It is assumed that the critical top chord stresses appear at midspan of the truss. Restraint provided by the heavy continu-

Fig. 7.65

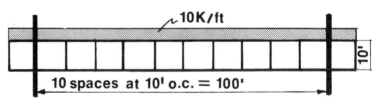

10K/ft

10'

10 spaces at 10' o.c. = 100'

ous building column and the cantilever will cause tension to occur in the top chords and compression in the bottom chords adjacent to the support, in contrast to Problem 7.8. This will be beneficial with respect to the design of the end top chords. On the other hand, because of the restraint, the hinge location is no longer at midspan of the first bay and moves further away from the support. Because of the change of hinge location, the moment in the end chords is increased, again in contrast to Problem 7.8.

For the sake of a fast approximation, a simply supported truss is assumed, with maximum chord stresses at midspan.

The maximum moment for a simply supported beam with an equally distributed load is

$$M_{max} = \frac{wL^2}{8} = \frac{10(100)^2}{8} = 12{,}500 \text{ ft-k}$$

Assuming that the moment to be resisted by an internal couple is equivalent to the axial forces in the top and bottom chords, we have

$$12{,}500 = N(10) \qquad N = 1250 \text{ k}$$

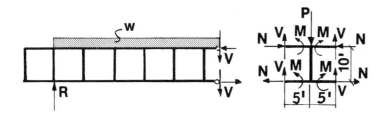

Fig. 7.66

This approach is conservative, since the moment was taken at midspan, not at assumed hinge location. The equally distributed load is replaced by its resultant P, as in Fig. 7.66.

$$P = 10(10) = 100 \text{ k}$$

Vertical equilibrium yields the shear forces

$$\sum V = 0 = 100 - 4V \qquad V = \frac{100}{4} = 25 \text{ k}$$

The moment generated by shear in the central chord is

$$M = 25(5) = 125 \text{ ft-k}$$

The top chord must be designed for an axial force of $N = 1250$ k and a moment of $M = 125$ ft-k. For the approximate design of a beam column, refer to Problem 7.8. Assuming A36 steel and a W14 section with a depth of 16 in. yields

$$A = \frac{1}{F_a}(P + 2M/d) = \frac{1}{20}(1250 + 2(125)12/16) = 72 \text{ in.}^2$$

Try a *W14 × 246.*

An increase in beam depth does not yield a much lighter section in this case, since the magnitude of the moment is relatively small.

PROBLEM 7.10

Determine the forces due to wind in the facade columns of a single span interspacial building.

The story-high Vierendeel trusses can be considered to be infinitely rigid for approximation purposes. In contrast to the behavior of a rigid frame, the deep beams do not wrack; only the columns at midheight of the open stories do so (Fig. 5.14a).

The forces in the columns are found in the same manner employed for the rigid frame (e.g., Problem 7.4); forces for a typical story appear in Fig. 7.67. If the staggered truss principle is applied to the building in Fig. 7.67, the columns will not wrack, hence do not have to resist any moments; they need to carry only axial forces indicated in the figure.

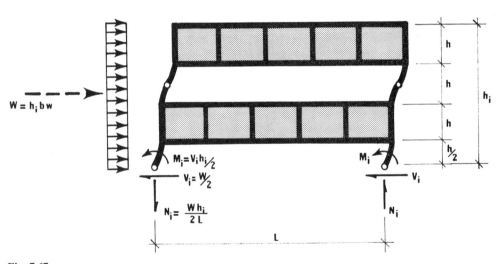

Fig. 7.67

THE HOLLOW TUBE STRUCTURE

The 110-story World Trade Center in New York City is selected in the following problem to exemplify the behavior of a tubular building structure under lateral load action.

PROBLEM 7.11

One of the World Trade Center towers (208 × 208 ft) can be visualized as a huge box beam, cantilevering 1350 ft out of the ground. The facade wall envelope is laterally braced by the composite floor structure serving as a rigid diaphragm tying the exterior wall to the central core. The Vierendeel walls are rigidly connected to each other at the corners which, in turn, are stiffened by continuous two-way floor truss systems. Thus any shear lag in the corner areas is reduced to a minimum.

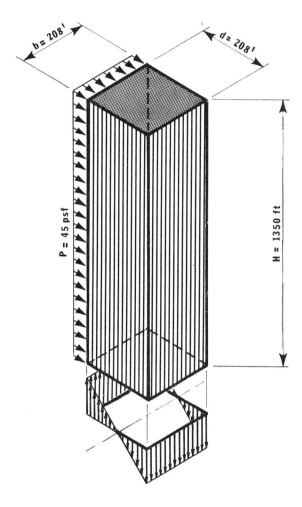

Fig. 7.68

It is assumed in the following analysis that only the exterior column envelope resists the lateral forces. Furthermore, we neglect any shear lag at the intersection of the web walls absorbing the shear and the flange walls resisting the axial forces (Fig. 7.68).

The columns at street level are spaced 10 ft apart. The cross-sectional area of a typical box column (27 × 32 in.) is assumed as $A_c = 408$ in.^{2}. There are $n = 19$ columns in the walls located perpendicular to the wind action (i.e., box flanges in Fig. 7.69).

For the actual design of the building, wind pressures of 55 psf for the upper 100 ft and 45 psf for the remaining portion were used.

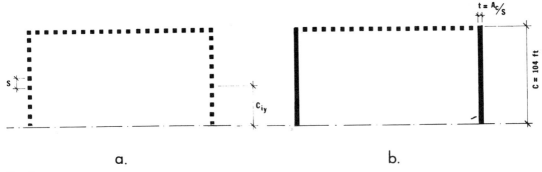

Fig. 7.69

Considering only 45 psf for the entire building height yields a maximum moment in the cantilevered tube at the street level of

$$M = \frac{0.045(208)1350^2}{2} = 8,529,300 \text{ ft-k}$$

The inertia of the column envelope about the neutral axis of the building is

$$I = \sum A_{ic} c_{iy}^2 \tag{a}$$

where A_{ic} = cross-sectional area of column i
$\qquad c_{iy}$ = distance of column i to the neutral axis

If all columns are assumed to have the same cross-sectional area at one floor level (i.e., actually not true for corner columns), then from equation (a) we have

$$I = A_c \sum c_{iy}^2 \tag{b}$$

Equation (b) is awkward for finding the inertia of the web columns, therefore an equivalent web wall area is assumed. The column area A_c is distributed between adjacent columns spaced at s distance across an equivalent wall width t (Fig. 7.69b):

$$A_c = s(t) \quad \text{or} \quad t = \frac{A_c}{s}$$

Thus the inertia for the web walls of the building is

$$I_w = 2\left(\frac{t(2c)^3}{12}\right) = 2\left(\frac{2c^3 A_c}{3s}\right) \tag{c}$$

The inertia of the building tube according to equations (b) and (c) is

$$I = 2(A_c)nc^2 + 2\left(\frac{2c^3 A_c}{3s}\right) \quad \text{or} \quad I = 2A_c c^2\left(n + \frac{d}{3s}\right) \tag{7.17}$$

where n is the number of columns on the windward side, not counting the corner columns (Fig. 7.69b).
For this example $A_c = 408 \text{ in.}^2 = 2.83 \text{ ft}^2$, $c = d/2 = 104 \text{ ft}$, $n = 19$, and $s = 10 \text{ ft}$.
Hence the inertia of the building is

$$I = 2(2.83)104^2 \left(19 + \frac{208}{3(10)}\right) = 1,587,601 \ \text{ft}^4$$

The maximum compressive stress in the columns on the leeward side is

$$f_{max} = \frac{Mc}{I} = \frac{8,529,300(104)}{1,587,601(12)^2} = 3.88 \ \text{ksi}$$

This yields an axial force for a typical column at street level of

$$N_c = f(A_c) = 3.88(408) = 1583 \ \text{k}$$

Neglecting the resistance of the web walls and assuming the flange walls to carry all the wind rotation obviously yields much higher axial forces.

$$N_c = \frac{M}{(n+2) \, d} = \frac{8,529,300}{(19+2)208} = 1953 \ \text{k}$$

This indicates that about 20% of the moment is carried by the web diaphragm parallel to the wind action.

The maximum deformation of a cantilever beam carrying an equally distributed load is $\Delta = wl^4/8EI$. However the inertia of the building tube is not constant; it decreases with the decrease of column area (A_c in equation 7.17). For purposes of approximation it is assumed that the column areas increase from zero at the top to a maximum at the base of the building; then the maximum sway of the building is

$$\Delta = \frac{wH^4}{2EI} = \frac{0.045(208)1350^4}{2(29,000)12^2(1,587,601)} = 2.35 \ \text{ft}$$

This lateral displacement is less than the recommended maximum value

$$0.002H = 0.002(1350) = 2.70 \ \text{ft}$$

It may be more realistic to find the lateral displacement of the tube by using equation 7.15, where the maximum column stress f_{max} at the base of the building is assumed to be initiated by the resultant wind force positioned at the top of the building. Hence the hypothetical moment is twice as large as the real one; that is

$$f_{max} = 2(3.88) = 7.76 \ \text{ksi}$$

$$= \frac{2f_{max}H^2}{3EB} = \frac{2(7.76)1350^2}{3(29,000)208} = 1.56 \ \text{ft}$$

This value is exactly two-thirds the result obtained from the more conservative approach.

The analysis of the building drift can be no more than a rough approximation: shear lag was neglected, and the wind pressure was considered a constant force only; that is, the vibration about the deflected position was neglected though this aspect was somehow taken care of by assuming a rather high, constant wind pressure.

CHAPTER EIGHT

The Floor Structure or Horizontal Building Plane

Floor structures form horizontal rigid planes. They stiffen and join the vertical building structure, allowing the building to respond to forces as a closed unit. The floor framing transmits gravity and lateral forces to the columns and/or walls.

The layout of the floor framing depends on the shape and structural system of the building. Typical layouts are discussed in the following sections.

The correct selection of a floor structure is of great importance because this determines the direction of flow of wind and gravity forces, thus influencing the geometry of the building skeleton; its depth also determines the overall building height, assuming the floor-to-ceiling height to be fixed. The floor depth must be optimized, since any increase in building height will cause an increase in overall architectural, mechanical, and structural costs. The floor depth is obviously related to the duct work, which may be accommodated within (e.g., open web joists or trusses) or below the structural framework.

In this chapter the discussion of floor structures is approached from the following points of view:

- The floor framing as related to common structural building systems and as a distributor of gravity forces.

- The floor framing as a distributor of lateral forces.

- The composite action of floor framing and concrete slab. Only composite floor systems are treated, since from a structural point of view they lead to optimum construction for high-rise buildings. Slab systems for low- and medium-rise buildings are not covered.

FLOOR FRAMING SYSTEMS

Gravity loads are carried by the concrete slab either directly or through the floor framing to the columns or walls. The concrete slab may distribute the gravity forces in

- Two-way action: two-way slabs, flat slabs (flat plates), waffle slabs.

- One-way action: solid slabs, pan joists.

Typical span-to-depth ratios for floor framing as based on strength and stiffness considerations generally range from 20 to 24. Rules of thumb often used in practice by designers as a rough, first approximation for floor member depth d (in.) as related to the respective span L (ft) are as follows:

$d = L/1.5$ for closely spaced open web steel joists and steel girders

$d = L/2$ for steel beams and continuous concrete beams and simple one-way concrete slabs (i.e., $L/d = 24$)

$d = L/3$ for continuous concrete slabs, hollow core slabs, pan joists, and flat slabs

This section deals primarily with typical floor framing systems and their relationship to the overall building structure. These systems are subdivided into typical floor systems as related to rigid frame skeletons (Fig. 5.10) arranged on a horizontal modular grid and typical floor systems as related to core-envelope structures.

In skeleton structures the column layout defines the horizontal structural building module. The primary beams form this module, while also acting as part of the vertical building frame. Depending on the scale, the module can be subdivided by filler beams, which form a subsystem. These filler beams or beam stringers have span ranges from 20 to 40 ft and are spaced at 8 to 10 ft centers. The typical floor framing systems for medium-high skeleton buildings in Fig. 8.2 are organized according to the direction of force flow (Fig. 8.1):

- Transverse or cross frames.

- Longitudinal frames.

- Two-way frames.

In transverse frame systems the gravity forces are distributed to the internal frames spanning the width of the building. Thus those frames must resist not only gravity but also the primary lateral forces. The slabs may span directly to the frame girders (Fig. 8.1a) if they are closely spaced and the loads are small.

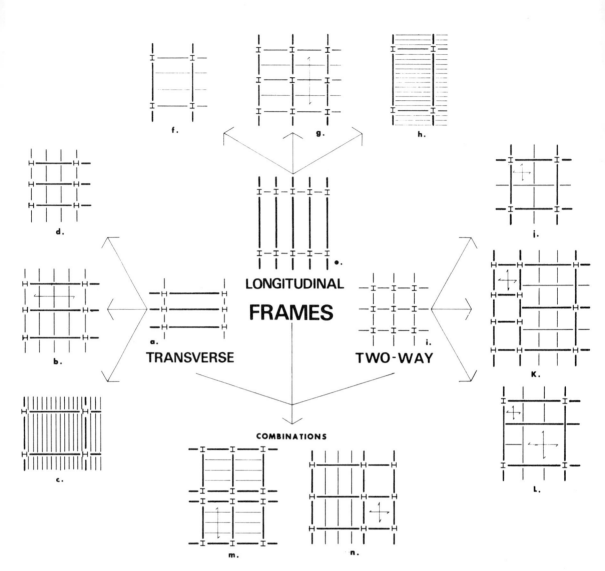

Fig. 8.1. Typical floor framing.

In the 20-story building in Fig. 8.2 *a*, a concrete slab spans 9 ft between 42 in. deep I-shaped concrete girders supported on load-bearing window mullions. In this building the lateral forces are resisted by the end cores. A similar principle is used for the seven-story staggered truss structure (Fig. 8.2*c*). Here 16 in. steel bar joists set on $2\frac{1}{2}$ ft centers with a $2\frac{1}{2}$ in. concrete slab are supported by the 9 ft 8 in. deep Pratt trusses spaced 56 ft apart at each floor level.

As the spacing of the frames increases, beam stringers or closely spaced joists (Figs. 8.1*b–d*) are needed to transfer the gravity loads to the frame girders. This approach is typical for rigid frame structures. The 18-story building (Fig. 8.2*d*) uses floor filler beams placed at midspan of the structural bay. The floor system consists of a 3 in. deep composite steel floor deck with a $3\frac{1}{4}$ in. topping of lightweight concrete.

The filler beams may be spaced at third or quarter points of

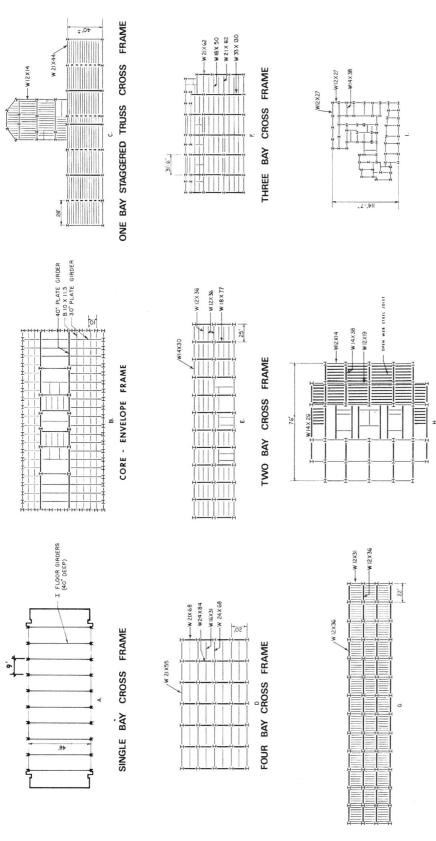

Fig. 8.2. Rectangular floor framing systems.

the structural bay as employed in the 9- and 10-story buildings in Figs. 8.2e, and f. Both buildings use steel cellular deck with $2\frac{1}{2}$ in. lightweight concrete fill as floor systems. The 11-story rigid frame (Fig. 8.2h) uses closely spaced open web steel joists with a $2\frac{1}{2}$ in. reinforced concrete slab.

In a longitudinal framing system (Figs. 8.1e–h) gravity loads are distributed to the frames parallel to the length of the building. In this case the transverse frames primarily resist the lateral forces. Again, as in the transverse framing systems, the concrete slab may span directly to the girders if their spacing and the loading are small, or it may be supported by filler beams. In the eight-story rigid frame structure (Fig. 8.2g) open web steel joists frame the width of the building and span $15\frac{1}{2}$ ft between the longitudinal girders. The transverse wind bents are spaced 22 ft 1 in. apart.

If the structural module of a building is almost square, two-way framing systems are often used (Fig. 8.1i–l). Concrete slabs with crosswise reinforcement disperse the loads in both directions. A similar effect is achieved by spanning the floor joists on one floor in one direction and those on the next floor in the opposite direction. This staggering of filler beams also distributes the gravity loads equally in both directions.

Possible combinations of framing systems appear in Figs. 8.1m, and n. For instance, in an apartment building the central corridor loads are directed to the longitudinal girders, and the apartment loads are carried by the transverse girders.

The distribution of loads is not always obvious from the layout of the floor framing. The 21-story building (Fig. 8.2i) with its irregular column layout is such an example.

A unique structural arrangement of floor beams was employed for the 15-story building in Fig. 8.3j. The diagonal floor framing required only eight columns in the interior space, thus providing virtually column-free spaces. The composite floor system, $3\frac{1}{2}$ in. lightweight concrete topping over $1\frac{1}{2}$ in. composite steel deck, acts as a natural diaphragm in transferring horizontal forces to the building's skewed corners, which are cross-braced in the vertical plane.

A seven-story rigid frame structure of truncated elliptical shape (Fig. 8.3d) necessitated unusual floor framing because the equal column spacing along the facade is not transversely parallel to the equal column spacing in the center of the building. The floor framing had to be arranged as braced bents to distribute wind forces to the respective columns (see Fig. 8.4).

Most of the examples in Fig. 8.3 employ a central core and an exterior perimeter structure. In general, beams run the shortest distance from the internal core to the external structural envelope.

In circular buildings there is a natural tendency for the floor framing to be composed of beams radiating from the central core and beams tying the layout together in a circular manner (Figs. 8.3a, e, i).

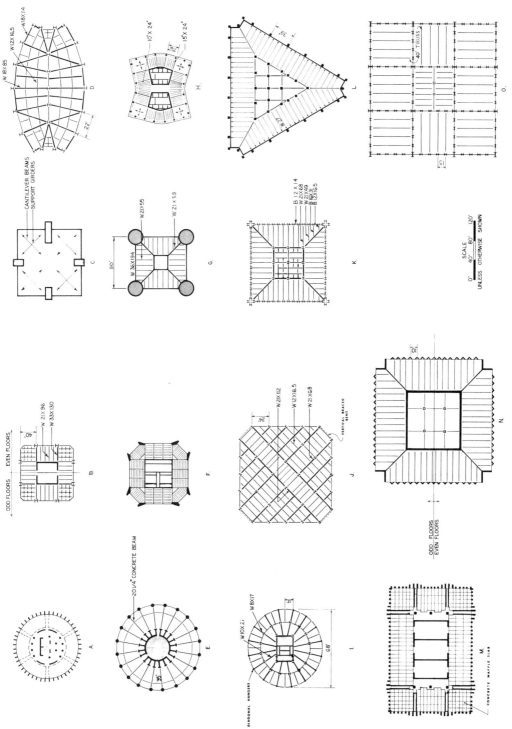

Fig. 8.3. General floor framing

Floor Framing Systems 193

The plan of Fig. 8.3a required only six radiating deep concrete beams, supported on the interior core and exterior column ring, because a prestressed concrete slab system was used. The building in Fig. 8.3e is wider and taller (600 ft vs. 182 ft high) and is tubular. Concrete beams ($20\frac{1}{4}$ in. deep) radiate 35 ft from the central concrete core to the perimeter columns. A $4\frac{1}{2}$ in. deep slab spans between the beams.

Because of the relatively small height (11 stories) of the building in Fig. 8.3i, the rigid frame principle was applied to the structure. Again, the beams radiate, but this time from a rectangular interior frame. Floor height limitations (i.e., shallow beams were required) made it impossible to cantilever the beams. They had to be supported at the perimeter by diagonal tension bars, which were attached to the outer columns. A 4 in. deep concrete slab spans between the radial beams.

In rectangular core-envelope structures, the perimeter structure may consist of corner cores or of large columns interconnected with girders or trusses, or it may consist of an equally spaced column envelope. Again, as for the circular buildings, beams span from the core to the facade the span range is 45 to 65 ft except for Fig. 8.3o. However a framing problem exists in the corner region. Either a diagonal girder can connect the corner of the core with the corner of the facade, thus increasing the load on the corner columns, or heavier beams parallel to the core walls can attract the corner loads, transferred preferably in two-way action, and placing more load on the envelope columns to which they are connected. The two-way distribution of the corner loads can also be achieved by using a one-way system and reversing the direction on alternate floors.

The primary structural subdivision in the 27-story building (Fig. 8.2b) consists of the central core and the peripheral envelope frames. Plate girders 30 in. deep span 45 ft between core and exterior columns. In the corner region these girders are supported by 40 in. deep plate girders linking the core to the cross facade frame. The floors are constructed of cellular steel decking 3 in. deep, and lightweight concrete.

A 52-story tube in tube structure (Figs. 8.3m and 5.20c), one-way concrete framing spans between the facade grid bearing wall and the interior core. In the corner area it merges into a two-way waffle slab that increases the floor load on the beam strips spanning from the corner of the core to the external columns, thus requiring larger column sizes. The increased column size may be expressed on the outside as shown or hidden inside the building to give a coherent wall grid pattern.

The principle of the floor framing in Fig. 8.3h (34-story shear core–hinged frame building) is similar to that of Fig. 8.3m. A composite concrete joist floor system spans from core to facade. A $7\frac{1}{2}$ in. two-way hollow tile floor slab was chosen for the corner region.

Instead of utilizing a column envelope as in the previous example, Fig. 8.3b (19-story core-frame structure) employs two main columns (W14 × 426) on each facade as exterior framing. Here the corner problem is solved by cantilevering the perimeter beams. To reduce deflection and allow for the imbalanced loading on any one floor, the cantilevered edge beams were vertically strutted with 4 in. diameter steel pipes. The direction of the floor beams in the corner region was altered on every floor to distribute the loads equally, as indicated by the broken lines.

Figure 8.3f, a 65-story core-frame structure, employs a similar column support system except that the cantilevered portion at the corner is removed.

The 10-story building in Fig. 8.3c is carried by four core towers located midway along each facade. The floor structure is a 30 in. diagonal grid waffle slab supported on girders spanning diagonally between the towers. Since the 55 ft corner cantilevers caused severe deflection problems, the grid slab had to be posttensioned.

The corner framing of core-facade envelope buildings may be solved by placing a girder diagonally from the core corner to the exterior building corner (Figs. 8.3n, k, g, l).

Figure 8.3g (23-story shear core structure) consists of four cylindrical concrete corner towers, connected by deep steel girders, and a central elevator core. The five hollow tubular columns support the steel floor framing and the concrete slab (see also Fig. 4.12g).

The 41-story building in Fig. 8.3k is wind braced across each facade with K-frames (Fig. 4.12b). The diagonals receive the lateral forces and transmit them to the four corner columns. The built-up corner columns also carry the additional corner loads because of gravity action from the diagonally placed floor girders.

The 83-story building (Fig. 8.3n), a tube-in-tube structure with closely spaced triangular shaped built-up column sections (Fig. 5.20f), employs a floor framing pattern similar to that in Fig. 8.3k. Trusses 38 in. deep and spaced 10 ft apart span 45 ft between facade and core. They are simply supported (i.e., only simple shear connections) and are staggered on each floor to frame into alternate sides of the exterior column, thus eliminating any eccentric load action. Diagonal beams span from the reentrant corner columns to the interior core corner columns. The floor consists of $1\frac{1}{2}$ in. cellular deck acting compositely with the $4\frac{5}{8}$ in. thick lightweight concrete topping (Fig. 8.5a). The floor framing not only carries gravity loads but also acts as a diaphragm in stabilizing the exterior wall and distributes the lateral forces to the interior tube.

The 78-story triangular building in Fig. 8.3l consists of exposed exterior box columns 39 ft apart, connected by box girders on every third floor and a triangular service core (see also Fig. 4.12j). The core is braced diagonally across three floors, and a hat space frame ties the exterior columns to the core at the top. The building is composed of a series of three-story buildings with every third floor—the primary floor only—

framing into the exterior columns. The secondary floors are supported by the core and by the primary floor framing at the exterior face.

The bundled tube principle is illustrated in Fig. 8.3o (see also Fig. 5.20h). The perforated wall of each tube is composed of columns 15 ft on center and deep beams at each floor. Two adjacent tubes share one set of columns and beams. Each tube is framed by one-way, simply supported, 40 in. deep trusses spanning 75 ft. The trusses act compositely with the floor system, which consists of $2\frac{1}{2}$ in. lightweight concrete and steel deck. The direction of the trusses is alternated every six floors to equalize the gravity loading on the columns and to improve the stiffness of the vertical tube.

HORIZONTAL BRACING

The floor framing not only distributes gravity loads to columns or walls but also acts as a diaphragm with respect to lateral forces. It may be visualized as a horizontal deep beam (i.e., rigid plate) transmitting transverse loads into the frame and/or shear wall system. Diaphragm action in a monolithic floor system seldom proves critical. If the stiffness of the floor diaphragm must be increased, however, horizontal bracing may have to be added, especially for widely spaced, simply connected beam systems using steel members or prefabricated reinforced concrete sections.

Figures 8.4a to c exemplify different types of horizontal bracing that stiffen the floor structure and transfer the lateral loads proportionally to the vertical braced bents (identified by heavy lines). The floor trussing generates composite action of the vertical shear wall system.

When facade columns are not laterally supported by floor beams and when it is necessary to increase the torsional resistance of the spandrel beams (e.g., in tubular systems), floor bracing may be employed along the periphery of the building spanning between the cross girders (Figs. 8.4d, e).

The 25-story building (Fig. 8.4f) employs a unique floor bracing solution. The building structure consists of two sections: a 10-story tower on top of a 15-story base. The lateral forces are resisted by the entire rigid frame skeleton of the tower but only by the exterior envelope in the base section. The change in structural action from the tower to the base necessitated extensive horizontal bracing in the transition zone at the 15th and 16th floors. The floor trussing transmits the lateral forces from the tower columns to the peripheral columns of the base. Similarly, in the Sears Towers (Fig. 5.20h) two-story trusses are placed at the locations where the tubes drop off. The trusses distribute the wind and gravity loads to the greater number of tubes below.

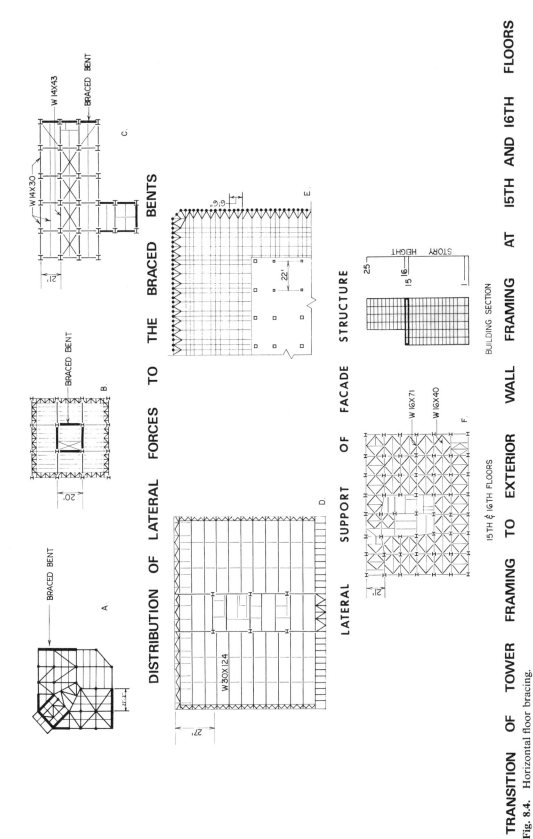

DISTRIBUTION OF LATERAL FORCES TO THE BRACED BENTS

LATERAL SUPPORT OF FACADE STRUCTURE

TRANSITION OF TOWER FRAMING TO EXTERIOR WALL FRAMING AT 15TH AND 16TH FLOORS

Fig. 8.4. Horizontal floor bracing.

COMPOSITE FLOOR SYSTEMS

In general, the strength and rigidity of an assemblage of structural elements is greatly improved if the elements can act together as one unit. In other words, the strength of the composite structural unit is much higher than the sum of the strengths of the individual components. In the hybrid action, moreover, the weakness of one element can be balanced by the strength of another.

Composite floor systems lead to an optimum solution for high-rise steel frame buildings. Cellular steel decks acting compositely with concrete slabs have been commonly used since about 1960. The number of applications of composite beam design in high-rise steel buildings is rapidly growing.

Composite Floor Decks

Most cellular steel deck systems are covered with little embossments and depressions to bond the deck to the concrete slab. Most corrugated steel forms are either $1\frac{1}{2}$ or 3 in. deep. The 3 in. deep deck is obviously stronger, spanning between 12 and 15 ft in composite action. The $1\frac{1}{2}$ in. deck, on the other hand, provides less depth for deck and slab, thus reduces the overall height of the building. Because of the variety of metal deck profiles and shear connection devices, a general composite deck design procedure has not yet been developed. The design is based on load tables provided by the manufacturer.

Some of the reasons for the use of cellular steel deck, acting compositely with the concrete slab, are as follows:

• An increase of lateral and vertical floor stiffness.

• An increase of beam span and beam spacing, a reduction of the number of beams, a decrease of floor weight, resulting in a reduction of framing and foundation costs.

• Faster construction process, elimination of formwork and shoring for concrete slabs, immediate storage area for construction materials.

• Wire-carrying capacity, flexible distribution of electrical systems.

An example of a composite floor deck is the floor system of the Standard Oil of Indiana Building in Chicago (Fig. 8.5a). The materials selected were panels 3 ft wide of 1 to $1\frac{1}{2}$ in. 18-gauge composite deck, alternating with 2 ft wide panels of 1 to $1\frac{1}{2}$ in. composite 18/20-gauge cellular deck for the electrical and communication distribution systems. A 4 in. lightweight concrete

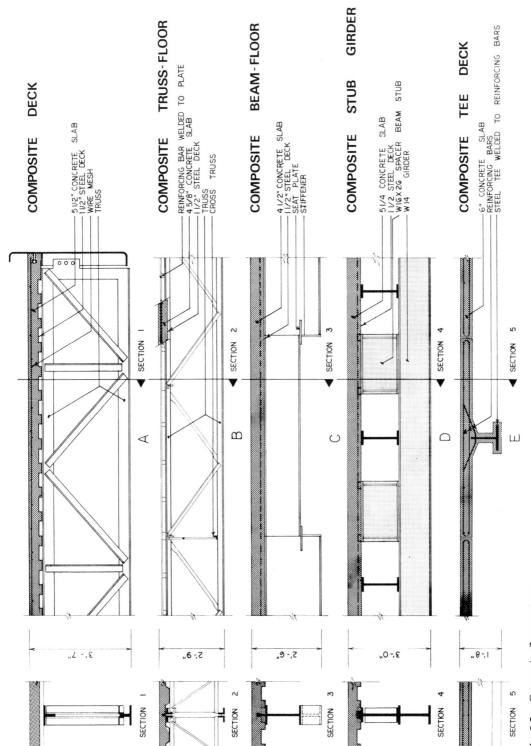

Fig. 8.5. Composite floor systems.

COMPOSITE DECK

5 1/2" CONCRETE SLAB
1 1/2" STEEL DECK
WIRE MESH
TRUSS

SECTION 1
A

COMPOSITE TRUSS-FLOOR

REINFORCING BAR WELDED TO PLATE
4 5/8" CONCRETE SLAB
1 1/2" STEEL DECK
TRUSS
CROSS TRUSS

SECTION 2
B

COMPOSITE BEAM-FLOOR

4 1/2" CONCRETE SLAB
1 1/2" STEEL DECK
SEAT PLATE
STIFFENER

SECTION 3
C

COMPOSITE STUB GIRDER

5 1/4 CONCRETE SLAB
1 1/2 STEEL DECK
W16 x 2G SPACER BEAM STUB
W14 GIRDER

SECTION 4
D

COMPOSITE TEE DECK

6" CONCRETE SLAB
REINFORCING BARS
STEEL TEE WELDED TO REINFORCING BARS

SECTION 5
E

3'-7"

2'-9"

2'-6"

3'-0"

1'-8"

SECTION 1

SECTION 2

SECTION 3

SECTION 4

SECTION 5

slab of 5000 psi over the top of the deck was used. To eliminate fireproofing on the underside of the deck, wire mesh was placed in the concrete slab to provide the necessary tensile capacity. Here reasons of economy prevented the use of the composite capacity of the floor deck in the structural design.

Composite Beams

In high-rise building construction many types of beams (rolled sections, girders, trusses, and open web steel joists, etc.) have been designed to act compositely with the concrete slab or the composite deck. For composite action of slab and beam, some type of shear connector is needed to transfer the longitudinal shear between the two elements. This eliminates slippage between the slab and beam flange. Generally, round steel studs welded to the flanges of the beam are used as shear connectors. Other types of shear connectors are spiral bars, angles, and channels.

In the noncomposite floor system (Fig. 8.6a) slab and beam respond separately to the loading. Each element is stressed in tension in the bottom fibers and in compression in the top fibers. This approach neglects the frictional interaction between slab and beam flange; free slippage is assumed at the interface of the two elements. If the floor system acts as a composite unit (Fig. 8.6c), no slippage between slab and beam is assumed to occur. There will be only one neutral axis. A portion of the concrete slab will act as the compression flange of the hybrid system. The effective width of the compression flange is defined by ACI and AISC specifications (see Problem 8.1). Through the composite action, the rigidity and strength of the floor system may be improved by 15 to 30% in comparison to noncomposite action. Several types of composite beam floor systems, presented in Fig. 8.5, are briefly discussed below.

Composite Beams with Composite Floors

Shear-stud connectors are field welded through the metal decking to the top flange of the beam, thus generating composite action of the concrete slab with the steel deck and beam. The steel deck corrugations can be parallel or perpendicular to the beam. The structural behavior of each of those composite systems is quite different. The response of a system having its corrugations parallel to its supporting beam is similar to the action of a solid slab. In the example of Fig. 8.5c a $1\frac{1}{2}$ in. deep corrugated steel deck is acting compositely with a $4\frac{1}{2}$ in. 3000 psi concrete slab and the beam. The unique feature of this design solution lies in the reduction of the beam depth at midspan, allowing the ductwork to pass through. This approach saved story height and about 30 ft of building height.

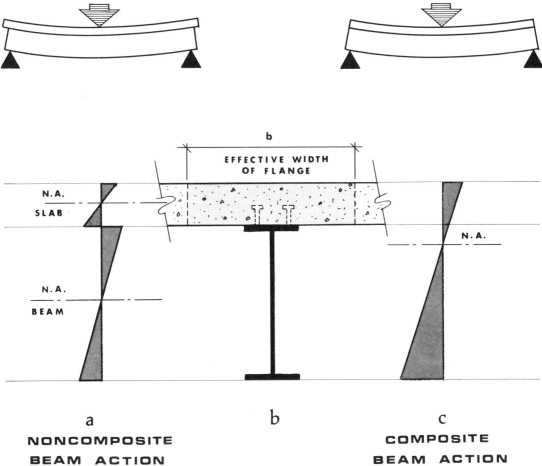

a

NONCOMPOSITE

BEAM ACTION

b

c

COMPOSITE

BEAM ACTION

Fig. 8.6

Composite Truss Systems

The floor trusses of the World Trade Center (Fig. 8.5b) used a unique shear connector, consisting of a continuous single number 4 bar attached at each panel point to the truss and centered on the $4\frac{5}{8}$ in. thick floor slab. The $1\frac{1}{2}$ in. deep 22-gauge corrugated steel deck has no structural function. It served only as formwork and working platform.

The stub-girder system (Fig. 8.5d), together with the slab, form a modified Vierendeel truss. The $5\frac{1}{4}$ in. deep composite floor deck acts compositely with the stub beams welded to the main girder.

Composite T-Deck

The prefabricated T-unit of Fig. 8.5e consists of a wide concrete top flange and an inverted steel T-section, fireproofed with a concrete cover. The concrete slab reinforcing, which is welded to the top of the T-web, enables composite interaction of the system.

Approximate Design of Composite Beams

The ultimate strength behavior of the composite section is used in the derivation of formulas for the approximation of beam size and number of shear connectors. In general, the neutral axis appears close to the top of the beam; its location may be within the slab or within the beam (Figs. 8.7b, c). Here we assume that the concrete slab is adequate in resisting compression— that is, the neutral axis is assumed to be within the slab. The tensile strength of the concrete below the neutral axis is neglected (Fig. 8.7c).

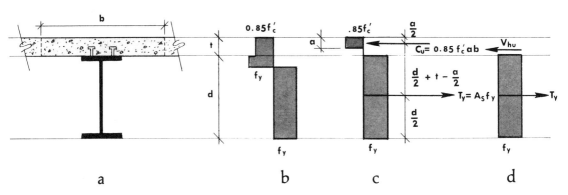

Fig. 8.7

The resultant ultimate compressive (C) and tensile (T) forces as based on rectangular stress distribution are given in Fig. 8.7c, where

$$A_s = \text{area of steel beam}$$
$$0.85\,f_c' = \text{average stress of concrete at compression failure}$$
$$f_y = \text{yield strength of steel}$$
$$b = \text{effective width of concrete flange}$$

The ultimate moment in terms of steel force is

$$M_u = A_s f_y \left(\frac{d}{2} + t - \frac{a}{2} \right)$$

The depth a of the stress block is obtained from the horizontal equilibrium of compression and tension forces.

$$T_y = C_u$$

$$A_s f_y = 0.85 f_c' a b$$

$$a = \frac{A_s f_y}{0.85 f_c' b} \tag{8.1}$$

As rough approximation, the stress block depth may be assumed to be equal to the slab depth. This yields an ultimate moment of

$$M_u = \frac{A_s f_y}{2}(d + t)$$

or a required steel beam area of

$$A_s = \frac{2M_u}{f_y(d + t)}$$

A load factor of 2 yields the required steel beam area as related to the service moment M: $M_u = 2M$

$$A_s = \frac{4M}{f_y(d + t)} \tag{8.2}$$

The connectors must resist the shear at the interface of slab and beam. The ultimate horizontal shear to cause slippage, as based on horizontal equilibrium (Fig. 8.7d), is

$$T_y = A_s f_y = V_{hu} = 2V_h$$

For a load factor of 2, the total horizontal shear as based on service loads for each *half-span* of beam (assuming equally distributed loads) is

$$V_h = \frac{A_s f_y}{2} \tag{8.3}$$

The number of connectors is obtained by dividing the shear V_h by the strength of one connector.

PROBLEM 8.1

Estimate the size of filler beams BM 1 in Fig. 8.8. The beam acts compositely with a 4 in. slab of 4000 psi concrete. Assume A-36 steel and a live load of 100 psf.

Since shored construction is to be used, temporary shoring will carry the floor structure during the construction process. After the curing of the concrete, the shores will be removed and the system will act as a composite unit. In unshored construction, on the other hand, the beam has to carry formwork, wet concrete, and some live load in noncomposite action.

LOADING

$$
\begin{aligned}
LL: &\quad 100 \text{ psf} \\
\text{4 in. slab } DL: &\quad 50 \text{ psf} \\
\text{ceiling, flooring, and beam weight:} &\quad \underline{25 \text{ psf}} \\
&\quad 175 \text{ psf}
\end{aligned}
$$

Loading acting on beam is

$$w = 175(8) = 1400 \text{ lb/ft} = 1.4 \text{ k/ft}$$

Assuming a simply supported beam yields a maximum moment

$$M = \frac{wL^2}{8} = \frac{1.4(30)^2(12)}{8} = 1890 \text{ k-in.}$$

The approximate beam size as based on equation 8.2 assuming a beam depth of 16 in. is

$$A_s = \frac{4M}{f_y(d + t)} = \frac{4(1890)}{36(16 + 4)} = 10.52 \text{ in.}^2$$

Try a W 16 × 36.

$$A_s = 10.6 \text{ in.}^2, \qquad S_x = 56.5 \text{ in.}^3, \qquad b_f = 6.992 \text{ in.}$$

The effective flange width, as based on AISC Specifications (1969, Section 1.11.1) is

$$b \leq \frac{L}{4} = \frac{30}{4} = 7.5 \text{ ft}$$

$$b \leq b_0 = 8 \text{ ft}$$

$$b \leq b_f + 16t = 6.992 + 16(4) = 71 \text{ in., which controls!}$$

Check if the slab is adequate as based on equation 8.1:

$$a = \frac{A_s f_y}{0.85 f'_c b} = \frac{10.6(36)}{0.85(4)71} = 1.58 < t = 4 \text{ in.}$$

The slab is adequate; only about 40% of the concrete flange area is used. A slightly smaller beam will be satisfactory because $a < a_{\text{assumed}} = t$.

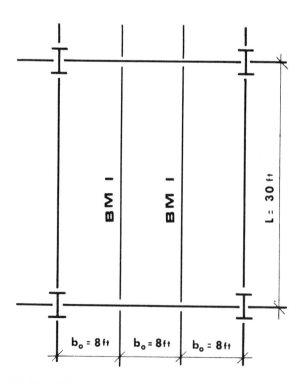

Fig. 8.8

The total horizontal shear to be transferred at the interface of flange and beam, as based on equation 8.3, is

$$V_h = \frac{A_s f_y}{2} = \frac{10.6(36)}{2} = 191 \text{ k}$$

Shear capacity of a $\frac{1}{2}$ in. $\phi \times 2$ in. headed stud (AISC Specifications, 1969, Table 1.11.4) is

$$q = 5.9 \text{ k}$$

The number of connectors required is

$$N = \frac{191}{5.9} = 32.4$$

Use 34 studs, $\frac{1}{2}$ in. $\phi \times 2$ in., equally spaced on each side of the beam's midspan. For beams carrying single loads, the uniform connector spacing would have to be modified.

The required beam size, as based on noncomposite action for a maximum depth of 16 in. is

$$f = \frac{M}{S}$$

$$S = \frac{1890}{24} = 78.8 \text{ in.}^3$$

Try W 16 × 50.

$$S = 80.8 \text{ in.}^3$$

$$= 56.5 + 30\% \quad (80.8)$$

The composite action has increased the effective strength of the beam by about 30%. As an approximation, beam sizes are often determined on the basis of noncomposite action, then reduced by 30% for composite action.

CHAPTER NINE

The High–Rise Building as Related to Assemblage Kits

The concept of mass producing building components and assembling them into a building unit was introduced on a large scale by Joseph Paxton (Crystal Palace, London, 1851). American trade catalogs were offering standardized mass-produced building components by the middle of the nineteenth century. Finished building products available included warehouses, iron roof systems, and entire building fronts involving structural and mechanical systems and the decorative finish. The development of the balloon frame at about the same time reflected the transition from the art of craftmanship to the trade approach, emphasizing the assemblage of standardized components within a relatively short time by less skilled workmen. Walter Gropius talked as early as 1910 about industrialization of housing through machine-produced, standardized building parts.

The prefabrication of building elements is only a small step toward the industrialized building approach, which encompasses the coordination of design, production and site operations, marketing, financing and administration of the final building. It is beyond the scope of this book even to touch the complexity of systems building, but the structural prefab element in its own physical context is briefly discussed.

Some of the advantages of producing building elements and assembling them on the site are as follows:

• Volume production.

• Maximum quality control.

- Reduction of construction time.

- Relatively weather-independent assembly.

- Need for only few skilled laborers on site.

The structural prefab component has the following identifying characteristics:

- *Shape:* linear, two-dimensional, spatial.

- *Weight:* lightweight (e.g., the weight one or two men can carry); heavyweight (e.g., necessity for special equipment).

- *Area:* size of panel.

- *Material:* conventional materials, paper, plastic and composites.

- *Internal structure:* solid, hollow, or ribbed.

- *Function within assemblage* beam, slab, column, wall, stair.

- *Degree of finishing:* from the simple structural building component (e.g., slab panel) to finished unit (e.g., mobile unit).

The size and dimensions of the components are dependent on the dimensional organization of the building. The modular coordinate system facilitates standardized elements. The goal of prefabrication is to use a minimum number of different components repeatable in a maximum number of variations.

The element must fit within the space allocated to it. Since it is impossible in the production and erection process to have exact dimensions, permissible tolerances must be taken into account. The joint is the critical element; it must be capable of adjusting to job conditions in the field to assure the fit of the building components. The linking techniques of the prefab elements constitute the most difficult part of the design of a building system. The design of connections entails many considerations. Table 9.1 indicates some of the criteria that become a designer's concern. As a rule field joints should be kept to a minimum and should be so located that the weather has a minimum effect on them.

The designer is obliged to keep in mind the erection sequence as an important design determinant. The linked prefab elements have to be laterally braced during the construction process. This can be done, for example, by using the central rigid core (i.e., elevator shaft) as a stabilizer. The capacity and location (i.e., liftoff radius) of the crane determine the maximum weight of the

Table 9.1

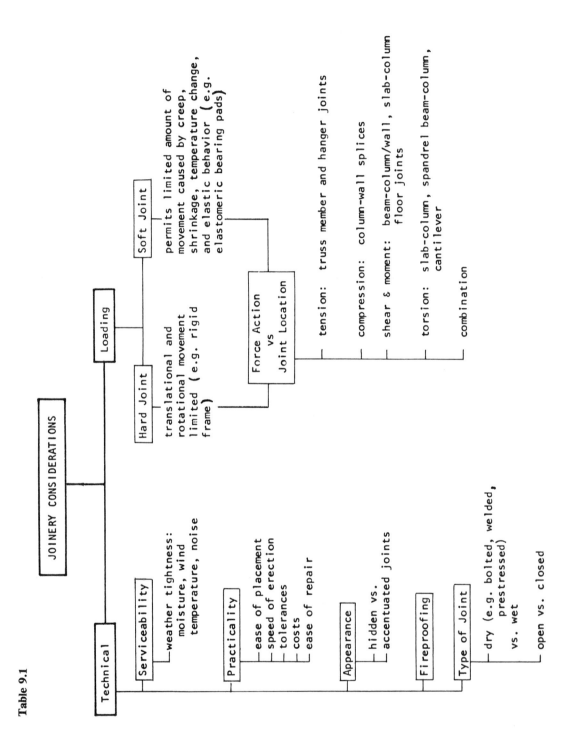

prefab component. The capacity of cranes is rated relative to the shortest boom (i.e., steepest possible angle), but this cannot be considered to be a normal working situation. The lifting of vertical building components presents a problem, since the pieces have to be moved from a flat position to a vertical one. The building component has to be designed not only for the service loads it must carry after installation but also for loads during handling. The stresses generated during erection may very well control the design of a prefab unit. Figure 9.1 contains shear and moment diagrams of a solid panel for a specific rigging situation.

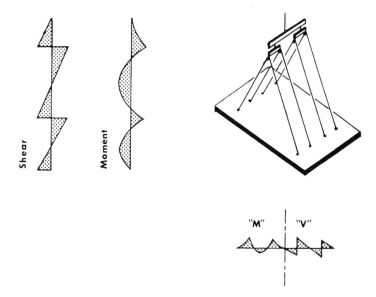

Fig. 9.1

The weight, size, and shape of the prefab component determine the number of trucks needed for transportation. A typical overall trucking volume is 8 ft wide, 8 ft high, and 40 ft long, with a load capacity of 40 k.

The following sections discuss the major high-rise structure systems as related to the structural assemblage kits; Table 9.2 presents the organization of these sections.

Table 9.2

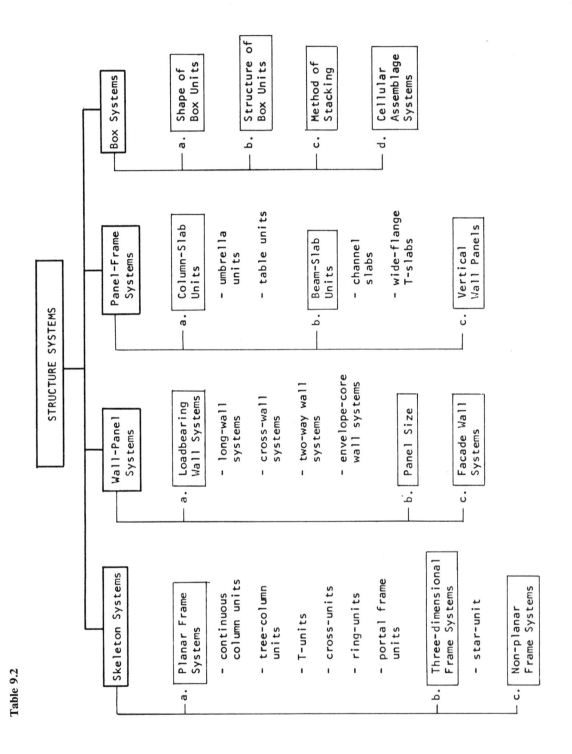

STRUCTURE SYSTEMS

Skeleton Systems

a. Planar Frame Systems
- continuous column units
- tree-column units
- T-units
- cross-units
- ring-units
- portal frame units

b. Three-dimensional Frame Systems
- star-unit

c. Non-planar Frame Systems

Wall-Panel Systems

a. Loadbearing Wall Systems
- long-wall systems
- cross-wall systems
- two-way wall systems
- envelope-core wall systems

b. Panel Size

c. Facade Wall Systems

Panel-Frame Systems

a. Column-Slab Units
- umbrella units
- table units

b. Beam-Slab Units
- channel slabs
- wide-flange T-slabs

c. Vertical Wall Panels

Box Systems

a. Shape of Box Units

b. Structure of Box Units

c. Method of Stacking

d. Cellular Assemblage Systems

SKELETON FRAME SYSTEMS

In the skeleton frame approach the load-bearing functions of the building are separated from the weather protection function. The use of lightweight curtains and partitions yields a relatively light building structure as compared to the bearing wall panel approach discussed in the next section.

The skeleton frame systems are made of elements that are horizontal (i.e., beams) and vertical (i.e., columns). A simple bent frame (i.e., a beam connecting two columns) is called a portal frame. A high-rise building frame may be visualized geometrically as a summation of portal frames. Some basic portal units appear in Fig. 9.2. They, in turn, may consist of different kit forms assembled on the site, assuming hinged joints equivalent to field connections.

Fig. 9.3 gives examples of skeleton frame buildings as related to their basic kit components. The first group in the outer circle of the illustration deals with beam column kits. In other words, the frame is formed by single prefabricated line elements. The columns may be either spliced at every floor level (Fig. 9.3b), they may be continuous over two stories and arranged in a staggered manner (Fig. 9.3c), or they may be continuous over several stories. Beams and columns are connected to each other rigidly, thus forming a continuous moment-resisting frame. The beams may also be pin connected to continuous columns (Fig. 9.3d), thus acting as struts with respect to the distribution of lateral forces to the fixed columns cantilevering out of the ground.

The next group involves preassembled beam-column kits. The multistory tree kit (Fig. 9.3e) consists of a continuous column and short cantilever beams, which in turn support simple beam elements. The hinge is located approximately at the point of zero moment, caused by equally distributed gravity loads. Another basic structural unit is the T- and L-shaped kit. The T-units may be jointed at midspan of the beams (Fig. 9.3f), at the zero moment location due to lateral loads, or they may be linked at the next column line (Fig. 9.3g).

Other kit units may form a cross or an H-shape (Fig. 9.3i). The column splices for the H-shaped unit may be located either at midheight or at one-third of the story height.

The last group in the outer circle of the illustration (Fig. 9.3j–l) uses portal frame units as basic building kits. One-story rigid frame units are superimposed on each other and hinged together, thus transmitting only horizontal and vertical forces from floor to floor.

Hinged frames must be stabilized against lateral and un-symmetrical vertical loading. The three cases represented in Figs. 9.3m, n, and o, respectively, indicate possible lateral stiffening of the frame by using a wall truss, a vertical Vierendeel frame, or a solid shear wall.

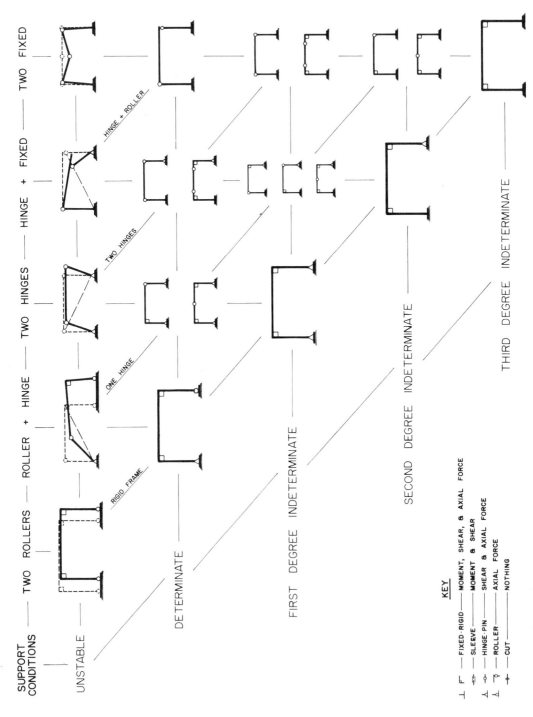

Fig. 9.2. Basic portal frames.

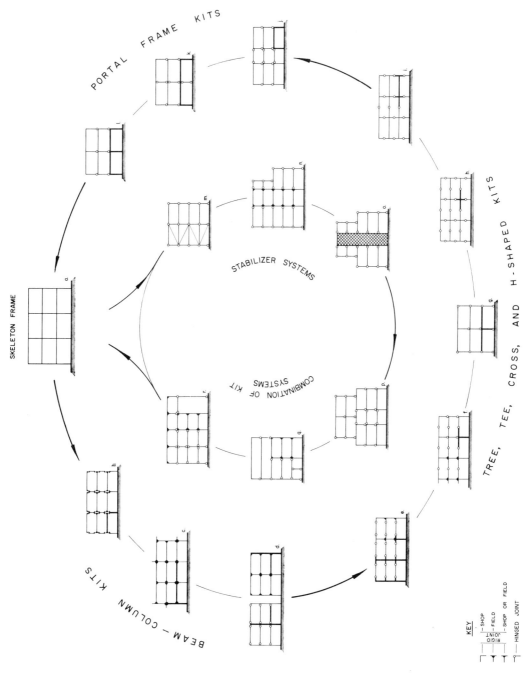

PORTAL FRAME KITS

SKELETON FRAME

STABILIZER SYSTEMS

COMBINATION OF KIT SYSTEMS

BEAM - COLUMN KITS

TREE, TEE, CROSS, AND H-SHAPED KITS

KEY
SHOP
FIELD
SHOP OR FIELD
RIGID JOINT
HINGED JOINT

Fig. 9.3. Kit systems for skeleton frames.

Skeleton Frame Systems 213

Of course any of the kit systems discussed may be combined if the spatial layout of the building requires it. Examples are given in Figs. 9.3p, q, and r.

Although only systems forming a planar frame have been discussed as typical examples of the skeleton approach, there are many other ways of applying the post-beam principle. For instance, the column tree in Fig. 9.4a supports on its branchlike beam projections beams that span across the building. In this case no beams are filling the space between the tree branches to form a planar frame.

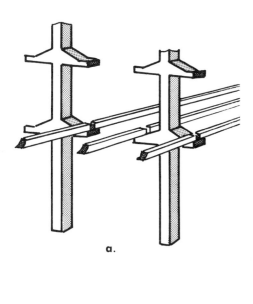

a.

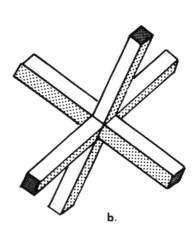

b.

Fig. 9.4

The star-shaped column-beam component in Fig. 9.4b is prefabricated as a three-dimensional unit. The jointing is at the location of minimum stress; hence it is separated from the point of convergence of vertical and horizontal members, the location of maximum stresses.

The shape of the basic building kit and the method of jointing (i.e., hinged vs. continuous) has an obvious influence on the behavior of the skeleton frame. In general, the components are prefabricated in the shop as rigid units; that is, the beam-column intersection is continuous and moment resistant. Then they are assembled in the field and simply connected, so that only shear must be resisted. Thus a physical hinge is formed that cannot transmit any moments.

The frame in Fig. 9.5c consists of star-shaped units simply connected to each other at midheight of columns and midspan of beams. The physical hinge locations approximately coincide

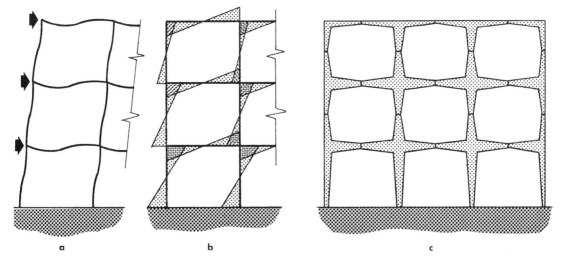

Fig. 9.5

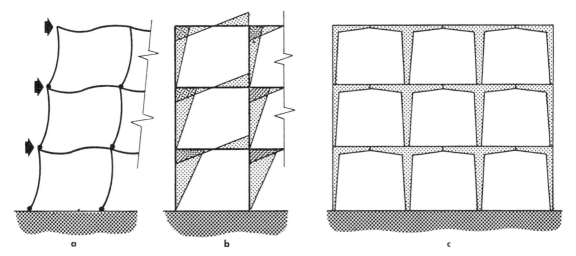

Fig. 9.6

with the inflection points in continuous rigid frames stressed by lateral loads (Figs. 9.5a, b; 5.12; 7.31). The member sizes respond to the magnitude of force flow; thus they are larger at the intersection of colunms and beams where maximum bending and shear stresses are located, and smaller at midheight and midspan, since at these points only shear stresses must be resisted.

In Fig. 9.6c the T- and L-shaped units are hinged to each other to form a high-rise skeleton frame. The frame deforms under lateral loads similar to a frame system composed of a series of two-hinged portal frames placed aside and on top of each other (Figs. 9.6a, b). Again, member sizes are directly related to the magnitude of force flow they have to carry.

LOAD–BEARING WALL PANEL SYSTEMS

This section emphasizes the facade wall, since here the designer must deal not only with structural and environmental control qualities but also with appearance.

Structural bearing wall building systems were introduced in Chapters 4 and 5. This section is confined to a brief consideration of typical load-bearing panels.

In general, external wall panels can be divided into three groups as based on their structural action:

- Curtain wall panels, supported by the facade framing and required to carry local wind forces only.

- Self-supporting wall panels, which carry their own height down to the foundations, hence are not supported by the building frame; they are not carrying any floor loads.

- Load-bearing wall panels, which are an integral part of the building structure (Chapter 5).

Any of the prefab panel systems listed may incorporate insulation, interior finishes, and windows. They may even include the utilities such as lighting, air conditioning, and heating.

A wall can be made of blocks or panels. A block is a small panel yielding joints within the room wall, whereas large panels have no joints within the room. The block approach requires many elements, hence many joints. For this reason the system is not widely used in the United States; block panels are more often employed in countries where heavy equipment is not available.

The large panel may span horizontally and be jointed at every floor level (e.g., multiple window-wall unit), or it may span vertically over several floors (Fig. 9.7). The wall panel may be a closed unit such as the window box in Fig. 9.7*j* or an open unit like the X-shaped kit in Fig. 9.7*k*. A closed unit offers more rigidity, hence allows easier handling.

Prefabricated wall panels can be made of a variety of materials such as reinforced normal or lightweight concrete, masonry, metals, timber, plastics, as well as any combination. Some wall panel systems are mentioned in the following section.

Concrete Wall Panels

Concrete panels may be axially prestressed for handling and control of cracks caused by temperature change and control of lateral deformation.

Precast concrete is available in various shapes that function both structurally and aesthetically. Some standard-shaped precast panels are shown in Fig. 9.7.

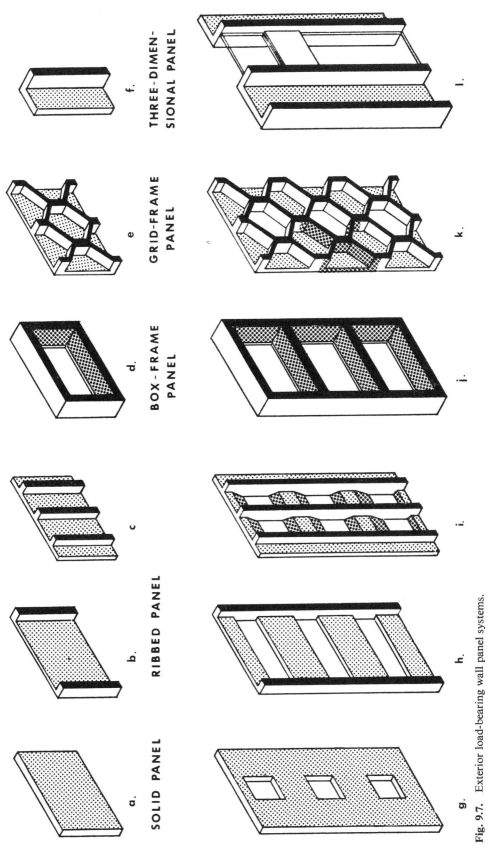

Fig. 9.7. Exterior load-bearing wall panel systems.

a. SOLID PANEL

b. RIBBED PANEL

c.

d. BOX-FRAME PANEL

e. GRID-FRAME PANEL

f. THREE-DIMEN-SIONAL PANEL

g.

h.

i.

j.

k.

l.

Slab Systems Used as Wall Components

Solid Panels

They can be built as single layer or as a sandwich element incorporating insulation. For instance, a 2 in. insulation at the center of a 6 in. sandwich component could be protected by 2 in. of nonstructural concrete. To reduce thermal stresses, the structural concrete should be on the inside, and the nonstructural concrete on the outside should be allowed to move.

Hollow Panels

The cores in the panels have insulation value; they may include pipes and wiring.

T-Panels

Single- and double-T wall units are standard precast panels. They provide excellent support for joist floor systems. The concentrated stresses applied by the joists on the wall are carried directly to the T-stems (i.e., columns), while the T-flanges act as enclosure.

Undulating and Corrugated Panels

Folded or shell-type plates are exposed to the outside of the building. Attached to them are flat insulation panels facing the inside of the building. The wall, however, could be a sandwich panel incorporating the insulation.

Ribbed Panels (Figs. 9.7b, c, h, i)

The thickness of the wall is reduced and requires strengthening and stabilization against buckling by vertical ribs. Depending on the continuity of the panels and the number of window openings, a stressed skin type of action may be achieved that is similar to an aircraft fuselage.

Box-Frame Panels (Figs. 9.7d, j)

Boxlike window frames form the structural wall. The units may be tied together horizontally to form a Vierendeel type truss with respect to horizontal loads for one or several floor levels, depending on the story height of the panel. The vertical loads are resisted by the columns in the trusslike wall.

Grid-Frame Panels (Figs. 9.7e, k)

Here the Vierendeel frame is replaced by some type of latticed truss. The inherent strength of the geometry is obvious.

Three-dimensional Panel (Figs. 9.7f, l)

The panel systems discussed thus far were of two-dimensional or surface character. If, however, a plate is bent into a channel shape, for example, with relative deep webs, the three-dimensional form greatly improves the rigidity of the wall. This heightened rigidity in turn may allow the use of nonstructural spandrels to span between the bearing units.

Masonry Wall Panels

Traditionally, the low tensile, shear, and bond strengths of nonreinforced masonry have forced the designer to use the gravity-type masonry structures. The search for lightweight construction techniques in masonry construction resulted in the development of mortar additives, which increase the bond and tensile strength of the cement/mortar so that the material approaches the capacity of the masonry units. Because of the improvement in strength, masonry panels can now be prefabricated without using any steel reinforcement.

Bearing wall panel systems other than concrete and masonry are only applied in low-rise construction.

Metal Wall Panels

Metal wall panels may use either steel or aluminum. There are two types of wall systems: sandwich wall panels and stud-framed walls.

Single or Double Sheet Sandwich Wall Panels

The typical sandwich panel consists of weather-resisting thin sheet metal that is either flat or corrugated and stiffened by vertical ribs. To achieve a higher load-carrying capacity and to eliminate the need for horizontal support, a structural skin may also be applied to the inner face. Polyurethane foam or glass fiber may comprise the insulation layer between the two metal skins.

Stud-framed Walls

The stud-framed system is based on the conventional timber stud wall principle. The plates and studs are produced from cold-rolled metal sheets. The studs are welded to the exterior or interior face of the outer metal plate.

Composite Wall Systems

Many composite load-bearing wall systems have been proposed, including polyurethane foam poured between cement asbestos board and surrounded by an aluminum extrusion. The exterior may be covered with an epoxy coating and stone aggregate. Further discussion of composite wall systems is beyond the scope of this text, since these systems are not used in high-rise construction at present.

PANEL–FRAME SYSTEMS

From a purely geometrical point of view, there are an infinite number of ways of combining different types of surface panels with linear elements. Only the typical applications of this approach in the building construction field are touched on here.

The panel–frame systems may be subdivided into the following groups:

- Column-slab units: umbrella and table units.

- Beam-column units: channel- and wide-flange T-slabs.

- Vertical wall panels: the panels are used to stabilize the hinged skeleton frame building type.

Examples of different types of column-slab systems appear in Fig. 9.8. The layout grid is approximately 20 × 20 ft, which is typical of many building applications. However the principles discussed in this section apply to other grid patterns.

The inner circle of Fig. 9.8 indicates the interrelationship of the slab components to the basic column grid.

- In case 1 the slab unit is identical with the column grid, thus forming a four-leg table unit.

- In case 2 the slab unit is horizontally translated with respect to the grid, forming a two-leg table unit.

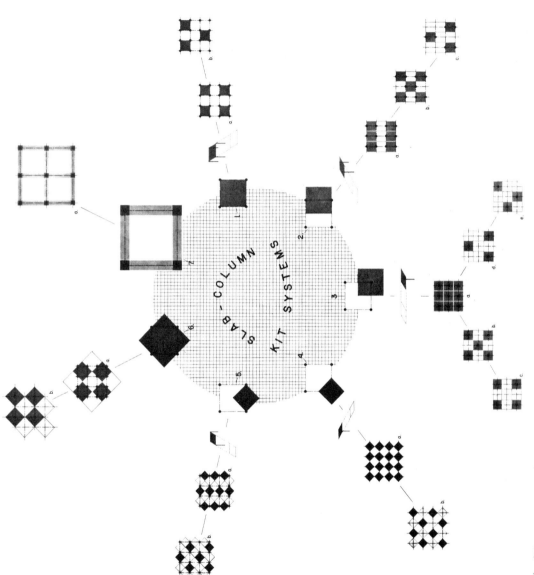

Fig. 9.8

- In case 3 the slab unit is horizontally and vertically translated with respect to the column grid, forming a one-leg table or umbrella unit.

- In cases 4, 5, and 6 the same types of table units just discussed are generated. However a new structural grid is formed by subdividing the basic grid diagonally.

- Case 7 represents a composite system caused by larger spans. A two-way floor slab is supported on girder slabs, which in turn are carried by capital slabs rigidly connected, to the columns.

Each of the cases is further subdivided, based on the location of the table unit within the structural grid. The spaces between the table units are bridged with intermediate floor slabs.

All cases presented in Fig. 9.8 will have the appearance of flat slab–plate construction in their final, assembled stage. However the arrangement of the units, together with the type of jointing, will cause a stress distribution (i.e., force flow) quite different from the continuous, cast-in-place or lift slab. The magnitude of stresses and the type of slab component used dictate the internal structure of the slab unit. It may be solid, waffle type, or radially ribbed as for an umbrella unit.

Of the many types of beam-slab systems, only two are mentioned, to indicate the principles of this kind of prefab approach from a geometric point of view.

A channel slab supported by continuous columns is shown in Fig. 9.9a. One may visualize the slab to fit the grid in case 1 of Fig. 9.8. The spaces between the channel slabs are filled with poured-in-place reinforced concrete, thus tying the columns to the slabs and generating continuous frame action. In steel construction, the prefab floor frame may consist of bar-joists, open web perimeter girders, and gypsum floor planks for flooring.

Another example of the beam-slab principle is the wide-flange T-slab unit in Fig. 9.9b. Visualize the web of the wide-flange unit forming a T-slab and the flanges forming the spandrel beams. Most of the floor loads are directly transferred through the T-beam and the continuous columns.

The advantages of the beam-slab systems just discussed lie in the minimum number of floor elements and the continuity of the columns, providing both stability and ease of erection.

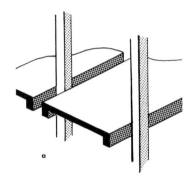

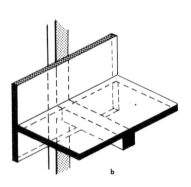

Fig. 9.9

MULTISTORY BOX SYSTEMS

Simple three-dimensional rectangular units, or spatial kits forming a box, are the subject of this section. This is a special case of the infinite number of space-filling or non-space-filling cellular systems.

Basic kits forming a rectangular space unit are illustrated in Fig. 9.10. The kit characteristics, from a formal point of view, are given below, with the appropriate section of Fig. 9.10 in parentheses:

- Tubular units   long-narrow shapes   upright (2a)
                                                horizontal (2b)

- Closed-wall units   short-wide shapes   upright (3a)
                                                horizontal (3b)

- Wall-floor shapes   long-narrow (4a, c)
                                short-wide (5a, c)
                                tilted: upright (4b)
                                        sideways (4d, 5b)

- H-shaped units (6a, b)

- Sliced units: for all shape forms (e.g., 2c, 3c)

There are three basic forms from a spatial point of view:

- Long, horizontal, closed shapes forming sequential spaces, thereby generating a tunnel effect.

- Vertical, closed shapes forming two-story space interaction.

- Wide, narrow, sectional, or sliced units allowing more freedom in subdividing space.

The kit units are produced either in a factory (i.e., off site) or on site. The size of the factory-made module is restricted by transportation requirements over the highways to 14 ft wide and 60 ft long; there are alternative means of transportation, however, such as helicopters. To overcome some of the geometrical or size limitations, the kit unit could be foldable, sectionalized (4c), or sliced (2c, 3c).

Three structural principles are applied in the construction of box units. In addition to economic considerations, the selection of the structure depends on the shape of the basic building kit, the amount of load the unit supports, and the linkage conditions. The structure of the cell can be one of three types.

- SKELETON TYPE: Rigid or trussed frame are made of steel, aluminum, or concrete, enclosed by nonstructural material. The system offers planning flexibility because of the application of nonstructural filler material, which can be omitted.

- STRESSED-SKIN TYPE. There is composite action of frame and skin such as steel plates enclosing steel studs, plywood skin

Fig. 9.10. Basic box kits.

over wood studs, concrete skin over a frame, or such other components as sandwich panels using wood on cellular honeycomb made of high-strength paper. This system offers less planning flexibility, since the structural skin should have a minimum of perforations.

- MONOLITHIC SHELL TYPE. The skin is the structure. It is continuous across floor and wall and as such is similar to a hollow tube. Concrete (e.g., self-stressing) and plastics (e.g., filament-wound fiberglass) lend themselves to this type of cell structure.

The box units can be combined in endless geometrical ways. The few examples given show the potential of the stacking principle with only one kit type, and they exclude the possibilities offered by shifting the units back and forth. Three methods of stacking a single unit are illustrated in Fig. 9.10:

- Direct stacking (2d, 4e, 6c).

- Alternate stacking (2f, 4g).

- Cross stacking (2e, 4f).

Tube boxes can also be used as hollow beams. There are infinite possibilities of combining different sized box units, or box units with other kits that happen to be linear (e.g., columns, beams), surface (e.g., plates, slabs), or spatial.

Three basic approaches are used for supporting cellular assemblages.

- SELF-SUPPORTING CLUSTERS. The modules are packed (i.e., stacked) requiring larger units at the base because of the increase of gravity loads. Lateral support is provided by simple local connections and/or by posttensioning the cellular assemblage together.

- STACKED MODULES WITH A STABILIZING STRUCTURAL SYSTEM. The packed units may be self-supporting with respect to gravity, but lateral loads may have to be carried by independent structural systems such as towers (i.e., vertical transportation systems), stabilized by struts such as streets (i.e., horizontal flow connectives).

- CELLULAR UNITS SUPPORTED BY PRIMARY STRUCTURES SUCH AS SPACE FRAMES AND SPACE NETS. The units are plugged in or clipped on the skeleton. Thus the units are identical, since they support only themselves.

CHAPTER TEN

Other High–Rise
Building Structures

This chapter introduces unconventional ways of constructing high-rise buildings. Although none of the specific principles is new, the application of each as the primary structural or constructional system is just beginning to be explored.

DEEP BEAM SYSTEMS

Figure 10.1 presents some of the many possible arrangements using the deep beam principle.

The whole facade can be built as one entire wall beam, which is supported by columns and bridges the ground level. These facade beams may be parallel to the longitudinal axis of the building (Fig. 10.1a); they may form a facade envelope if the building plan approximates a square (Fig. 10.1b); or they may cross the building in both directions forming a stiff, three-dimensional cage (Fig. 10.1c).

Deep beams that are only one story high can be arranged to generate free spaces of one or more stories. These beams may be used along two parallel or all four facades (Figs. 10.1d, e) or in a three-dimensional cage (Fig. 10.1f). Additional floors can be constructed on top of or suspended from the floor truss system (Fig. 10.1i).

Parallel, story-high trusses may span the width of the building in a staggered manner (Fig. 10.1g), or the trusses may be layered perpendicular to each other (Fig. 10.1h).

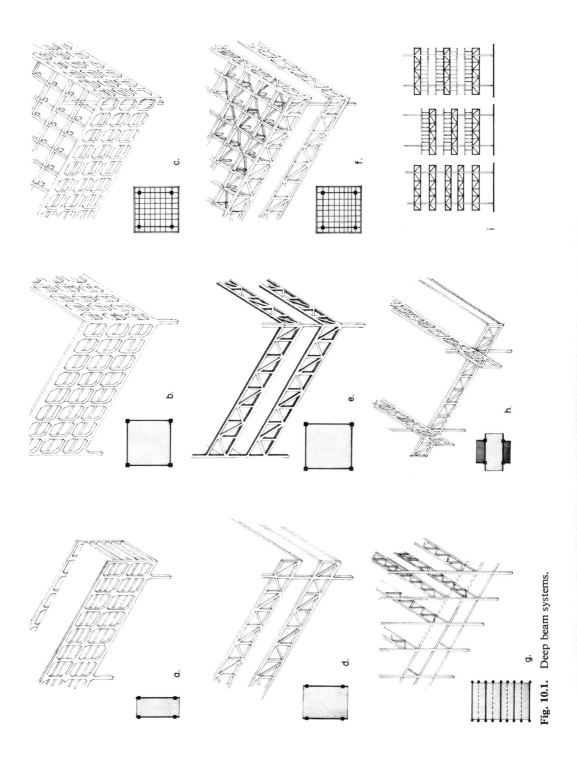

Fig. 10.1. Deep beam systems.

HIGH–RISE SUSPENSION SYSTEMS

Suspension systems are appealing because of their highly efficient use of materials and their potential for long spans. In suspension, all loads can only be carried in direct tension, therefore eliminating the need for a decrease in allowable stresses because of instability due to bending and buckling. For this reason, cross-sectional areas of tensile members can be reduced to a minimum. The economy of the material is further increased because of the high yield strength capacity of the cable steel, which can be more than 6 times higher than the same capacity for common structural steels. However the lack of flexural rigidity of the cables causes suspension structures to move as the loads change. This inherent instability of cable systems (e.g., aerodynamic instability or flutter) complicates the design and construction process; the stabilization of the overall building structure is a governing design factor. Furthermore, the high stress concentration in the tensile elements causes problems at the boundaries at which they are anchored.

Over the past four or five decades, several high-rise buildings and numerous proposals have employed the principles of suspension as their primary structural system. These suspension systems use a variety of geometrical forms, depending on desired erection methods, cost, time, and spatial requirements.

In the following pages an attempt has been made to organize high-rise suspension buildings. The overall organization is given in Table 10.1. The major subdivision is based on differences in structural behavior:

- The rigid core principle.

- The guyed mast principle.

- The tensegrity principle.

Each of these topics is further subdivided in relation to the following:

- Type of cable support system.

- Type of cable system.

- Geometrical form.

Most suspension buildings today use the principle of the rigid core. The core or cores carry the entire weight of the building and resist wind in cantilever bending. Figures 10.2 to 10.5 represent different types of supporting core systems, from which

Table 10.1

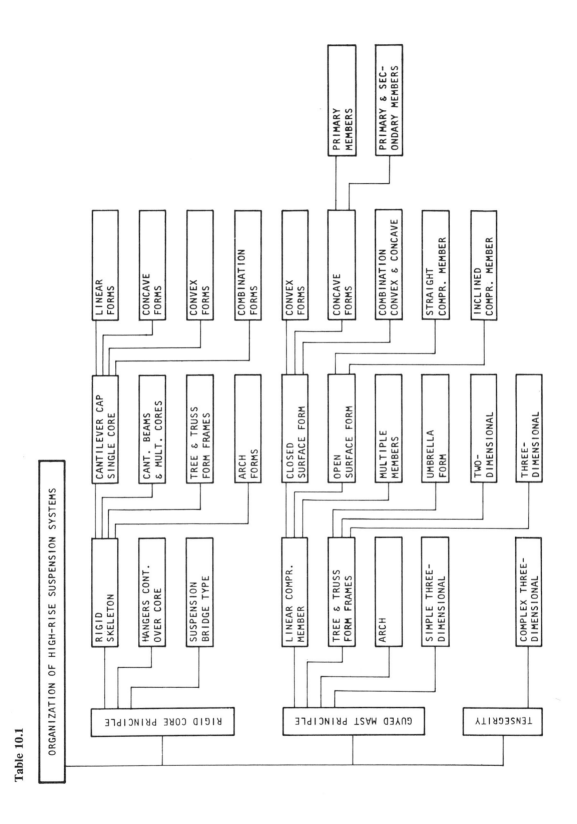

ORGANIZATION OF HIGH-RISE SUSPENSION SYSTEMS

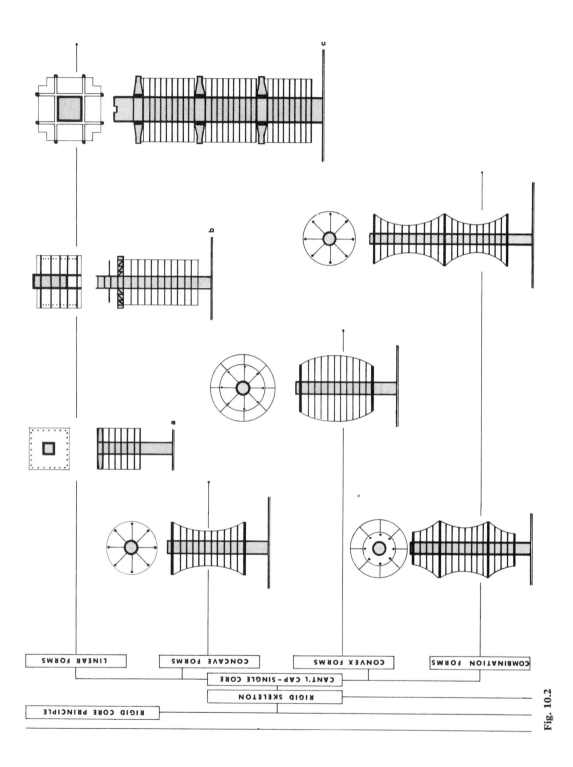

RIGID CORE PRINCIPLE

RIGID SKELETON

CANT'L CAP-SINGLE CORE

COMBINATION FORMS   CONVEX FORMS   CONCAVE FORMS   LINEAR FORMS

Fig. 10.2

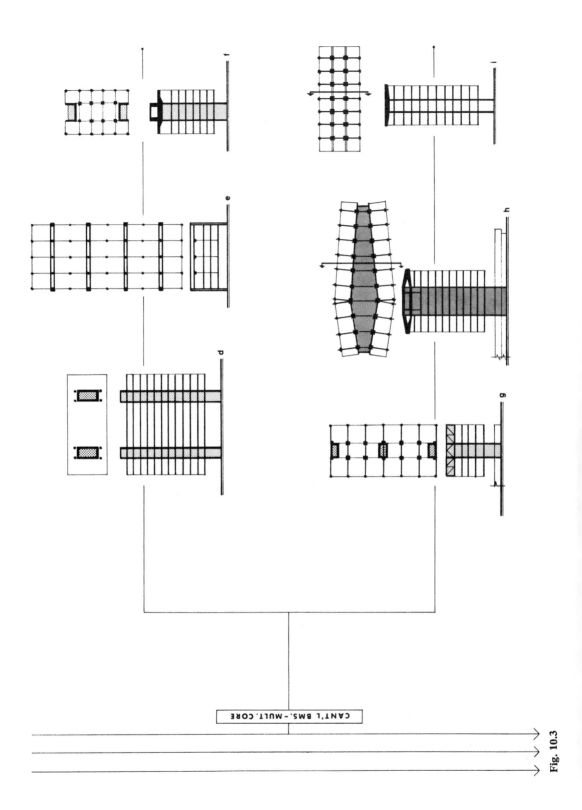

CANT'L BMS.-MULT.CORE

Fig. 10.3

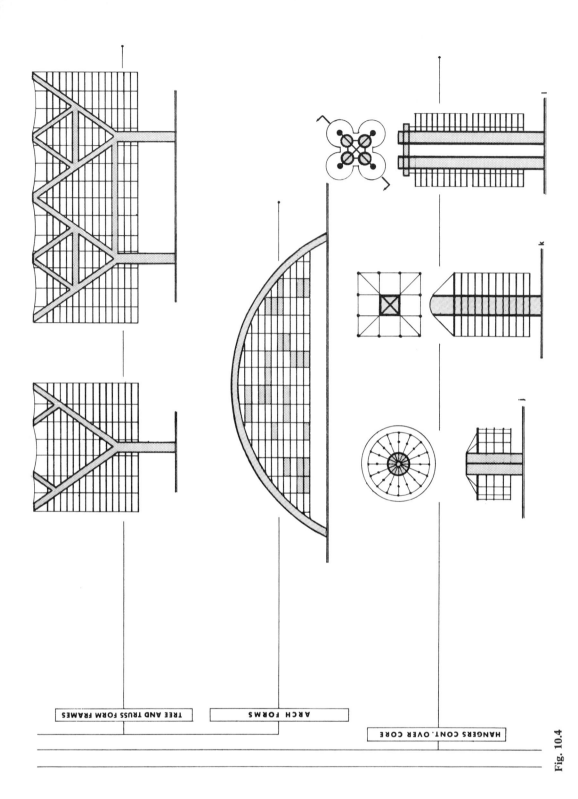

TREE AND TRUSS FORM FRAMES

ARCH FORMS

HANGERS CONT. OVER CORE

Fig. 10.4

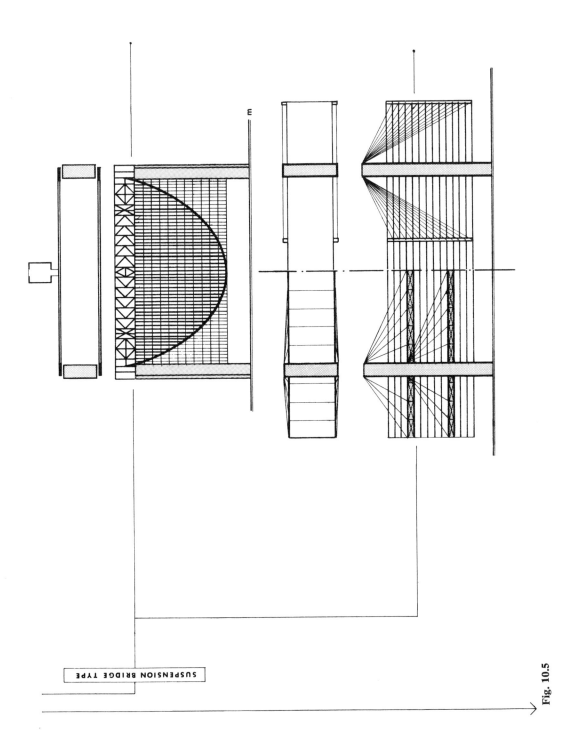

Fig. 10.5

SUSPENSION BRIDGE TYPE

the floors are suspended. Some of the disadvantages of the system are as follows:

- The lateral forces must be resisted entirely by the core.

- The relative movement between hangers and core must be taken into account.

- The vertical loads have to travel much further to get to the ground.

- Very substantial foundations are required for the core.

The second major category of high-rise suspension buildings applies the guyed mast principle (Figs. 10.6–10.10). The guyed cables are prestressed and directly anchored to the ground or supported by another structural system. The mast responds to the tension cables in compression and stabilizes the space; the entire building structure is prestressed. Since the guy cables are pretensioned; they absorb lateral forces and support floors suspended from them while basically retaining their shape.

The third category, the tensegrity structure, is a closed system consisting of continuous tensile elements and individual (noncontinuous) compression members. The entire system must be prestressed to ensure stability. Until now the principle has been applied by artists (Fig. 10.11) or has been investigated in models by researchers. Although tensegrity yields an optimum solution with respect to a minimum weight of material and consists of repetitive elements, its complex spatial configuration frightens the designer and the builder. Not only does antigravity challenge the traditional perception of a building as gravitational, but the building process, the interpretation of structural behavior, and the methods of detailing must be completely revised, as well.

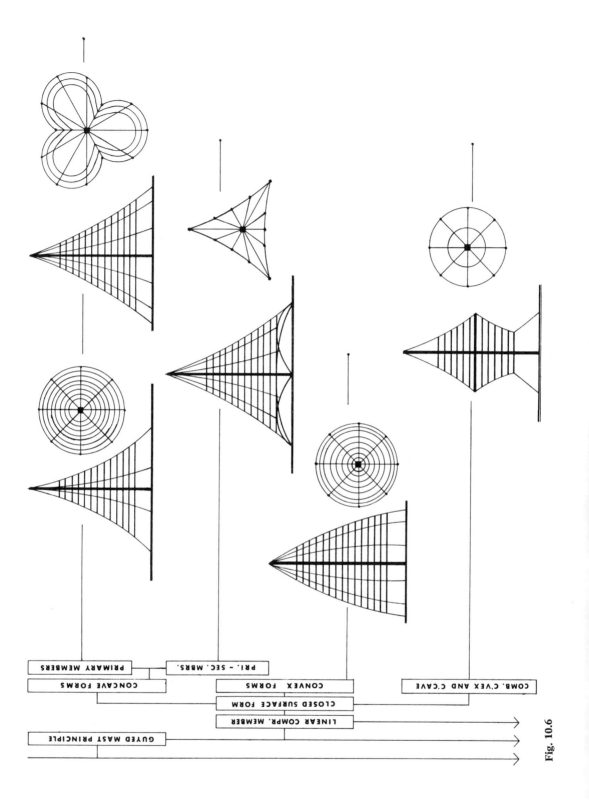

GUYED MAST PRINCIPLE

LINEAR COMPR. MEMBER

CLOSED SURFACE FORM

CONCAVE FORMS   CONVEX FORMS   COMB. C'VEX AND C'CAVE

PRI.- SEC. MBRS.

PRIMARY MEMBERS

Fig. 10.6

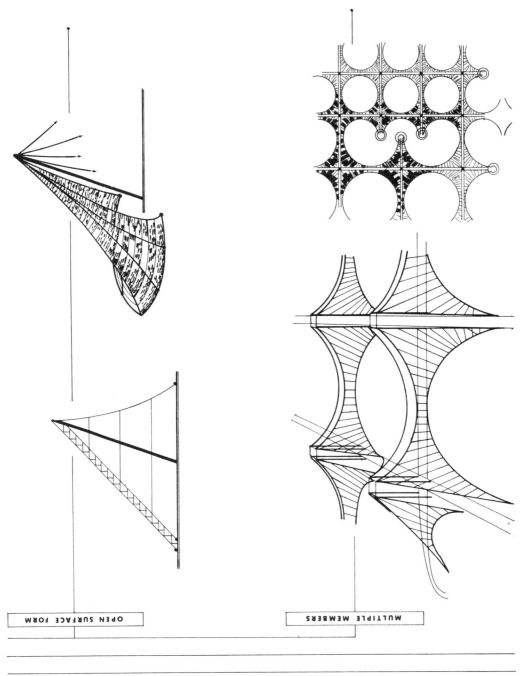

OPEN SURFACE FORM

MULTIPLE MEMBERS

Fig. 10.7

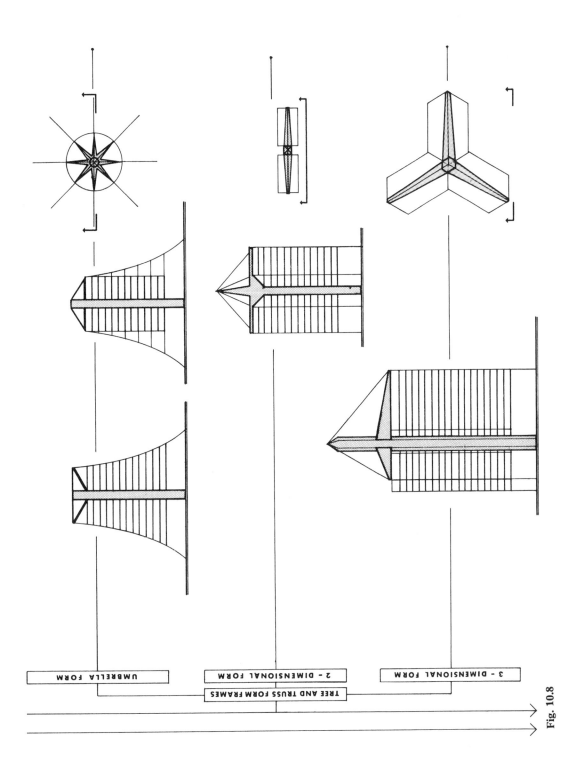

UMBRELLA FORM

2 - DIMENSIONAL FORM

3 - DIMENSIONAL FORM

TREE AND TRUSS FORM FRAMES

Fig. 10.8

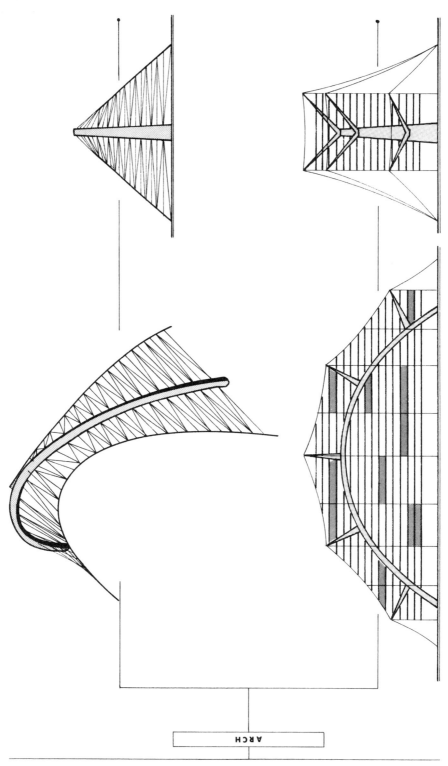

ARCH

Fig. 10.9

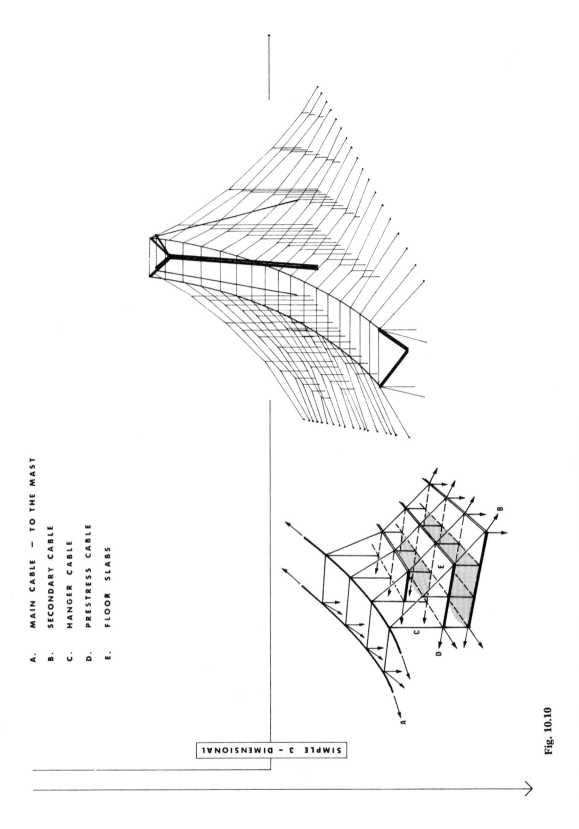

A. MAIN CABLE – TO THE MAST
B. SECONDARY CABLE
C. HANGER CABLE
D. PRESTRESS CABLE
E. FLOOR SLABS

SIMPLE 3 – DIMENSIONAL

Fig. 10.10

High–Rise Suspension Systems   239

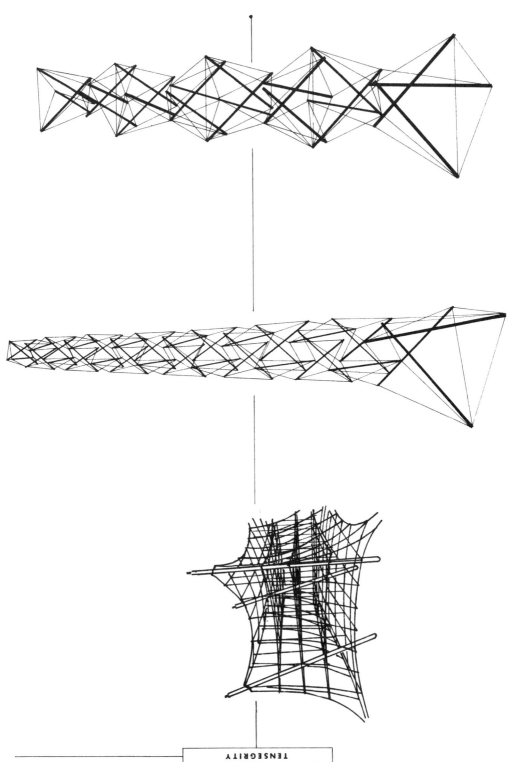

TENSEGRITY

Fig. 10.11

PNEUMATIC HIGH–RISE BUILDINGS

Awareness of pneumatics dates back about 200 years (observation balloons), yet the application to shelter of these principles has only recently begun to be explored. Over the past decade or so, exhibition halls and stadiums have made use of low-rise, low pressure pneumatic structures for spans of up to 722 ft (stadium in Pontiac, Mich., 1975). However these structures are mainly solutions to problems related to multifunctional spaces where a great many people will be accommodated at one level. Frequently, when more than one level is required, the space is divided vertically by means of conventional construction. In no case is the conventional structure ever attached to the pneumatic one.

The principle of pneumatic structures lies in the relatively thin membrane supported by a pressure difference. In other words, the pressure of the enclosed space is higher than the atmospheric pressure. This pressure difference generates tension in the membrane. The membrane can be stable only under tension. Any compression induced by external forces must be overcome by an increase in internal pressure or by the membrane adjusting its shape, if it is sufficiently flexible. Any stresses generated in the membrane must be below the allowable limit for that particular membrane.

There are two types of pneumatic structures: air supported and air inflated.

The air-supported structure uses a low positive pressure (3–6 psf) to support a membrane over a given area. Air must be supplied constantly because of the continuous leakage, primarily through the building's entries. Figure 10.12 illustrates this type of pneumatic structure.

The air-inflated structure forms conventional structural elements (walls, beams, columns, arches, etc.). Rigidity of the members is generated through high air pressure contained in the membrane form (30–40 psf, auto tire pressure is about 4300 psf). Two types of air-inflated structures presently exist: the dual wall (Fig. 10.13b) and the inflated rib systems (Fig. 10.13a).

To date, the air-supported structures have been used most often because of their relatively low cost, their simplicity of design and fabrication, and the availability of a suitable membrane. These structures have the greatest potential for high-rise building application, however, because they have not only the ability for self-support but the potential to support an attached structure.

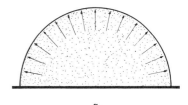

a.

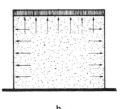

b.

Fig. 10.12

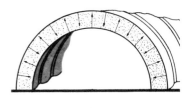

a.

b.

Fig. 10.13

In the past few years several people have begun to investigate high-rise pneumatics. J. P. Jungmann, approaching the inflated high-rise as a designer, has developed an organization of forms capable of multilevel habitation with an organic growth potential (Fig. 10.14).

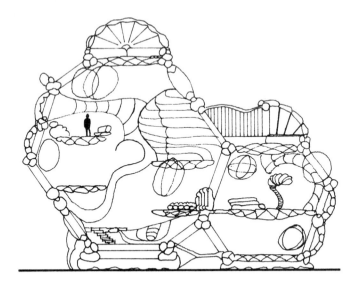

Fig. 10.14. Experimental pneumatic house.

Prof. Jens G. Pohl, of California Polytechnic State University at San Luis Obispo, has developed a technological approach to pneumatic high-rises that is new both in theory and application.

Pohl's basic premise can be explained with the example of an inflated tube closed at both ends, as in Fig. 10.15. When air is pumped into it, internal pressure causes the skin of the tube to accept tensile stresses, while the two capped ends are pushed apart. Under this pressurized condition, the upper capped end can support a load either from above or suspended from below.

Fig. 10.15. Pohl's basic premise.

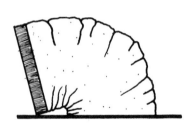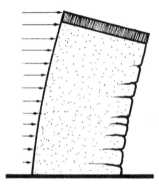

The inflated tube's (column's) resistance to failure by bending, buckling, or torsion stresses is directly dependent on the slenderness ratio of the "column" and the ratio of the load to the internal pressure. In most cases the flexible column fails when axial compression and deflection moment cancel out the tensile stresses present in the column skin or membrane. Subsequently the load-bearing capacity decreases rapidly because an ever-increasing moment arm has been caused by the lateral sway of the building. This further increases the bending moment. Pohl has suggested several solutions to this specific problem in conjunction with other technical problems of the pneumatic high-rise.

One major problem that has not been thoroughly investigated involves the physiological effects of a compressed air environment. Little is known about this subject except for case histories of persons engaged in deep caisson work beneath the earth or water. It now seems feasible to work within the pressure of 1 to 2 atm, (i.e., 0–14 psi internal pressure) and still generate enough pressure to stabilize a pneumatic high-rise building.

The typical floor load for a high-rise may be assumed to be $w = 140$ psf. Hence an internal pressure of 1 psi $= 144$ psf above atmospheric pressure would be required for supporting each floor in a building. This pressure would then have to be increased because of the reduction in strength of the membrane attributable to the slenderness ratio. Pohl showed that for an eight-story building, 100 ft high and 50 ft wide, the pressure would have to be 8.85 psi (Reference 10.10).

Assuming 1 psi per floor, then for 8 floors, $8(1) = 8$ psi would be needed. But because of the slenderness ratio effect, 8.85 psi was proposed, resulting in an increase of pressure by about 10%. This internal pressure is still well below the 14 psi presently considered safe to work in.

A flexible membrane skin in a pneumatic high-rise is both the structure and the enclosure of the building. As a structure, it must be capable of taking loads like any conventional building. However technology has not yet produced an economical flexible skin that is strong enough to do this by itself.

For the eight-story building just mentioned (Fig. 10.16), the hoop force will be

$$T = pr = 8.85(25 \times 12) = 2650 \text{ lb/in. of height}$$

For a membrane thickness of 0.13 in., the tensile stresses in the skin will be

$$f = \frac{T}{A} = \frac{2.650}{1(0.13)} = 20.4 \text{ ksi}$$

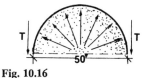

Fig. 10.16

For an assumed safety factor S.F. = 2, the material capacity must be

$$f_{ult} = 2(20.4) = 40.8 \text{ ksi}$$

This high tensile stress is the main reason for the use of a cable net system having a much higher strength. The net works with the membrane to allow larger pressures where needed. Figure 10.16 illustrates a possible cable net system.

As the enclosure of a building, the skin must shield heat gain and heat loss, transmit light, and, most important for a pneumatic structure, it must be able to localize a rupture of the surface to prevent pressure loss.

Several other unsolved problems are directly related to the pressure factor, including the mechanical difficulties associated with entry and exit; safety, with respect to maintenance of design pressures and fire hazard; and the nature and performance of suitable membrane materials, some of which have been mentioned.

Pohl has developed several design solutions for a 10-story pneumatic structure. Realizing that there are still many questions concerning human habitation in a pressurized environment, he has devised several schemes for a pneumatic high-rise that do not incorporate a pressurized work environment. For the cases of a nonpressurized working environment, the upper bearing cap is supported either by a high pressure column at the center of the structure (Fig. 10.17a) or by a high pressure cylinder on the periphery of the building (Fig. 10.17b). Buildings that do have a pressurized work environment may use either a flexible membrane and cable net system around the

Fig. 10.17

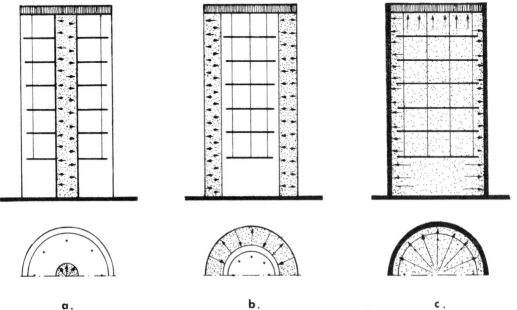

a.   b.   c.

building perimeter, or a rigid self-supporting wall, as in Fig. 10.17c. In each of these cases the pressurized environment serves mainly to support the top cap of the building, from which all the floors are suspended (Reference 10.11).

SPACE FRAMES APPLIED TO HIGH–RISE BUILDINGS

The space frame consists of a three-dimensional framework of straight members. These members or bars may be either rigidly or pin connected, or they may be a combination of both. In a pin-connected system, loads applied from any direction to the joints will be resisted axially. Bending is generated only by secondary effects. Space frames are the most rigid structures using the least amount of material because the members respond directly to the loads.

Space frames can be assembled from a minimum number of standardized prefabricated elements. Therefore they can be dismantled (depending on joint type) and reused without wasting material. Another major advantage lies in the potential for subdividing space.

Space frames have mainly been applied as long span systems for horizontal roofs where column-free space is needed (com-

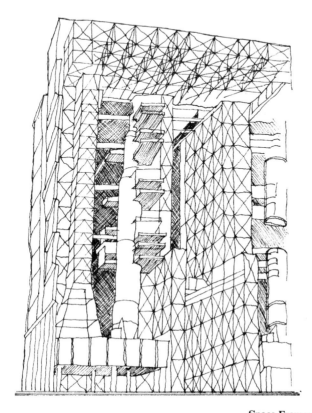

Fig. 10.18. Vehicle Assembly Building, Cape Kennedy, Fla.

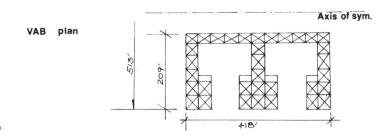

VAB plan

Fig. 10.19

munity swimming pools, factories, convention halls, etc.). They have also been used for the construction of electric transmission towers and double surfaced geodesic domes.

A space frame seems to be able to function in high rise building applications: the frame may replace conventional structural members such as walls and floors (i.e., beams) or it may subdivide the enclosed living space in a polyhedral, close packing manner. The Vehicle Assembly Building at Cape Kennedy, Florida, designed by architect Max O. Urbahn, uses the first type of construction (Fig. 10.18). It is the largest building in the world in terms of enclosed volume: it is as tall as a 50-story skyscraper and so large that clouds sometimes form indoors and it rains. The building consists of three towers acting as vertical cantilevers against lateral forces. They are arranged in plan as two E's placed back to back. The two building blocks are braced by horizontal diaphragms (Fig. 10.19).

Fig. 10.20. Swenson's proposed tower.

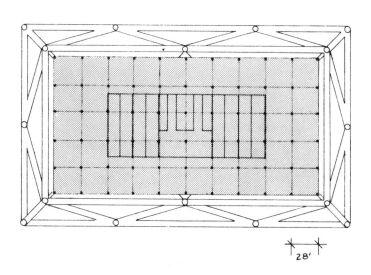

Along the same lines, Alfred T. Swenson has proposed a 150-story office-apartment tower (Fig. 10.20). His external space frame brings 100% of the gravity load and 65% of the structural steel to the perimeter of the building, a necessary step to counter wind overturning problems in such a tall structure. The steel tubes at the bottom of the building are 7 ft in diameter, with a 4 in. wall thickness; at the top of the building the tubes are 4 ft in diameter with a $1\frac{1}{2}$ in. wall thickness. The hollow tubes are filled with water, which circulates on the gravity principle during a fire, thus controls the temperature within the structural space frame.

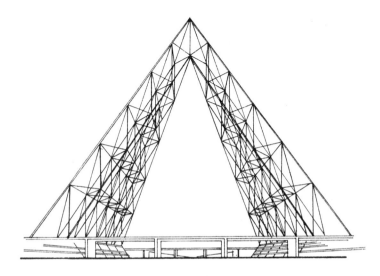

Fig. 10.21. Tigerman's A-frame space frame.

Stanley Tigerman's proposed tetrahedral megastructure, an example of the second type (Fig. 10.21), uses a giant three-hinged A-frame space frame to house an urban environment. It is hoped that the inherent strength of the form and its subdivision will overcome the shortcomings of the cantilevering vertical skyscraper.

Louis Kahn proposed a 616 ft high building truly subdivided by space frames (Fig. 10.22). The floors are supported by tetrahedrons 66 ft high. At the intersection nodes he provided spaces 11 ft deep to house mechanical services. Floors at the nodal levels are part of the space frame, but intermediate floors are allowed to vary in height.

Another system, proposed by architect Günter Günschel, uses clusters of three-dimensional space frames attached to central core columns (Fig. 10.23).

The usage of space frames is not only applicable to individual buildings but to a whole urban macro environment. Eckhard Schulze-Fielitz, Yona Friedman, and the Metabolists in Japan have proposed large-scale space frames covering entire portions

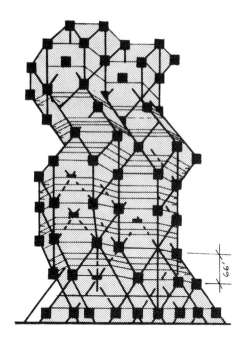

Fig. 10.22. Kahn's proposed tower.

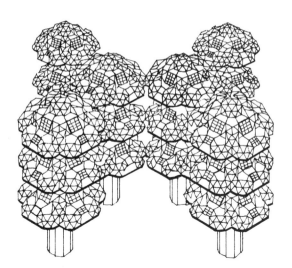

Fig. 10.23. Günschel's proposed towers.

of a city. The subdivided space is considered extremely adaptable to change; it permits a free flow and exchange of living components and working units.

CAPSULE ARCHITECTURE

Capsule architecture is a rather new development in high-rise construction. Since there are only a few examples, one specific case is discussed: Kurokawa's Nakagin Tower in Tokyo, Japan (Reference 10.7).

In Kurokawa's own words, one of the aims of capsule architecture is 100% mass production of individual rooms, and he has come close to achieving this on a limited scale. In the recently completed Nakagin Capsule Tower (Fig. 10.24), Kurokawa used two central core towers to which 140 capsules are attached. The capsules cantilever from the two separate cores (Fig. 10.25) and do not support one another. The vertical and horizontal clearances between them are 12 and 8 in., respectively. Each capsule is 8 ft high, 8 ft wide, and 13 ft long and weighs nearly 4 tons without furnishings.

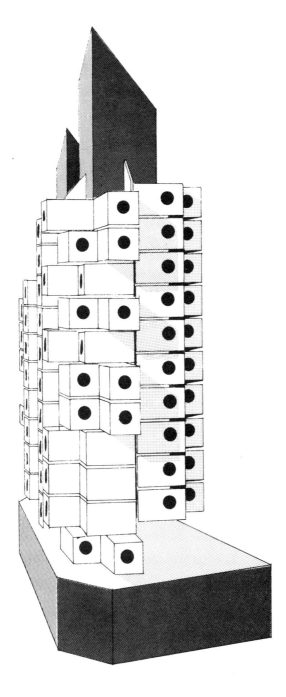

Fig. 10.24

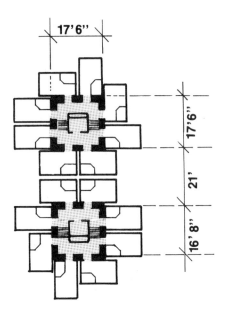

Fig. 10.25

The capsules are welded, lightweight steel truss boxes. The assembling of the truss box (Fig. 10.26) is similar to the process used for the manufacturing of large shipping containers. A renovated and improved container jig becomes the basis for all welding and truss surface assemblage. Exterior surface treatment consists of galvanized, rib-reinforced steel panels treated with a rust preventive paint. To comply with fire code requirements, an additional coat of asbestos was applied to the main structural and exterior panel parts. All the prefabricated capsules were manufactured with over-the-road shipping in mind, since the factory is 280 miles way from the construction site.

The capsules are nested, around two steel-framed concrete towers, 21 ft apart, containing elevators, stairways, and water tanks in each tower's upper portion. The towers act as cores to support lateral loads and capsule weight. One of the towers rises 175 ft, and the other, 150 ft.

Each capsule is connected to the core at its four corners. At the lower corners 4 in. steel boxes and at the top corners 8 in. I-beams are cantilevered 6 in. out of the concrete wall. The capsule is bolted to these four seats.

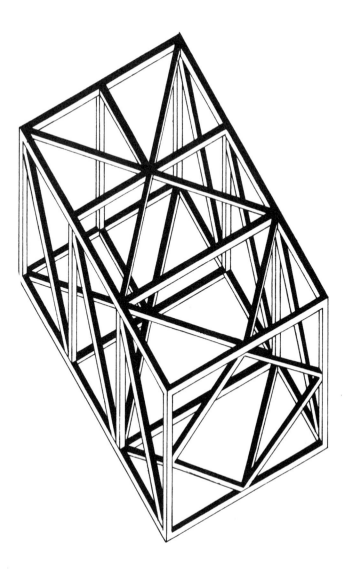

Fig. 10.26

List of Building Illustrations

Figure 4.9

D. South Central Bell Telephone Co. Building (30 stories), Birmingham, Ala., *Design of Steel Structures*, 2nd ed., by Edwin E. H. Gaylord and Charles N. Gaylord, McGraw-Hill, New York, 1972.

E. High-rise office building (28 stories), Moscow, Russia, Reference 5.4.

F. Chase Manhattan Bank (60 stories), New York, Skidmore, Owings, and Merrill (S.O.M.), *Forum*, July 1961; see also *K*.

G. Federal Reserve Bank Building (165 ft pylons and 43 stories), New York, Roche-Dinkeloo Architects, *Forum*, March 1974.

H. U.S. Steel Building (64 stories), Pittsburgh, Harrison, Abramowitz and Abbe, Architects, "Pittsburgh Skyscraper Achieves Breakthrough in Steel Fireproofing," *Architectural Record*, April 1967; "Big Steel Spike," *Forum*, December 1971.

K. Chase Manhattan Bank (60 stories), New York (S.O.M.), *Forum*, July 1961; see also *F*.

Figure 4.12

A. Liberty Plaza Proposal, New York, S.O.M., *Architecture and Engineering News*, October 1972.

B. Boston Company Building, Boston, Pietro Belluschi and Emery Roth & Sons, *Building Case History 1*, Bethlehem Steel Corp., August 1970.

C. First Wisconsin Center, Milwaukee, Wis., S.O.M., *Progressive Architecture*, October 1972.

D. Alcoa Building, San Francisco, S.O.M., *Engineering News Record*, 1965.

G. Knights of Columbus Building (23 stories), New Haven, Conn., Kevin Roche, John Dinkeloo and Associates, *Progressive Architecture*, September 1970.

H. Place Victoria (47 stories), Montreal, Canada, Moretti and Nervi, *Canadian Architecture*, July 1965.

I. Liberty Plaza, New York, S.O.M., *Architecture and Engineering News*, October 1972.

J. U.S. Steel Headquarters, Pittsburgh, Harrison, Abramowitz and Abbe, Architects, *Architectural Record*, April 1967.

Figure 5.1

A. Pennley Park Apartment Building (8 stories), Pittsburgh, *Technical Notes on Brick and Tile Construction*, *Case Study 24*, Structural Clay Products Institute, February 1966.

B. High-rise dormitory (8 stories), Augustana College, Sioux Falls, S.D., The Spitznagel Partners, Inc., *Contemporary Brick Bearing Wall*, *Case Study 22*, Structural Clay Products Institute, October–November, 1969.

C. Apartment building (3 stories), Budapest, Hungary, Olgyay and Olgyay, *New Structures* by R. Fisher, ed., McGraw-Hill, New York, 1964; see also *O*.

D. Housing for the elderly (11 stories), Rock Island, Ill., E. W. Angerer and I. J. Milani, *ASCE Journal*, September 1966.

E. Low-rent high-rise for the elderly (11 stories), Macon, Ga., W. P. Thompson, Jr., *Contemporary Brick Bearing Wall*, *Case Study 33*, Brick Institute of America, January 1973.

F. Oakcrest Towers (8 stories), Prince Georges County, Md., Bucher-Meyers and Associates, *Contemporary Brick Bearing Wall*, *Case Study*, Structural Clay Products Institute, December 1966–January 1967.

G. High-rise dormitory (9 stories), Highlands University, Las Vegas, N.M., Register, Ross and Brunet, *Contemporary Brick Bearing Wall*, *Case Study 21*, Structural Clay Products Institute, August–September, 1969.

H. Housing for the elderly, Heritage House (8 stories), Canton, Ohio, Lawrence, Dykes, Goodenberger and Associates, *Contemporary Brick Bearing Wall*, *Case Study*, Structural Clay Products Institute, June 1966.

I. Apartment building (18 stories), Zurich, Switzerland, *Technical Notes on Brick and Tile Construction*, *Case Study 24*, Structural Clay Products Institute, February 1966.

J. Apartment building (13 stories), Basel, Switzerland, Clarence B. Monk, Jr. and James G. Gross, "Swiss Set Pace in Brick Bearing Wall Structures," *Progressive Architecture*, February 1966.

L. Holiday Inn (13 stories), Austin, Tex., Lundgren-Maurer, *Contemporary Brick Bearing Wall*, *Case Study*, Structural Clay Products Institute, May 1966.

M. High-rise apartment (16 stories), Biel, Switzerland, *Technical Notes on Brick and Tile Construction*, *Case Study 24*, Structural Clay Products Institute, February 1966.

N. Hatfield Towers (12 stories), London, England, Messers, Buchanan, and Coulter, Reference 5.5b.

O. Apartment building (3 stories), Budapest, Hungary, Olgyay and Olgyay, *New Structures* by R. Fischer, ed., McGraw-Hill, New York; see also *C*.

Figure 5.7

A. Bayview Terrace Apartment (25 stories), Milwaukee, Wis., Rasche, Shroeder and Spansy, *Architectural Record*, August 1964.

B. Knights of Columbus building (23 stories), New Haven, Conn., Kevin Roche, John Dinkeloo and Associates, *Progressive Architecture*, September 1970.

C. Ohio State University dormitory (24 stories), Columbus, Schooley, Cornelius and Schooley, *Forum*, November 1967.

D. University of Montreal dormitory (17 stories), Montreal, Canada, Papineau, Gerin-Lajoie and LaBlanc, *The Canadian Architect*, July 1966.

E. Pirelli Building (34 stories), Milan, Italy, Gio Ponti, Antonio Fornaroli, and Alberto Rosselli, *Architectural Design*, November 1970.

F. Office tower (50 stories), Singapore, Architects of Team 3, *Engineering News Record*, February 1974.

G. Shrine of the Missionaries (210 ft), Sault Ste. Marie, Mich., Design Associates, Inc., *Architectural and Engineering News*, January 1968.

H. Proposed tower (27 stories), Milan, Italy, Alberto Rosselli, *Architectural Digest*, November 1964.

I. Apartment building (22 stories), Bremen, Germany, Alvar Aalto, *Architectural Record*, March 1963.

J. First National Tower Building (12 stories), Fort Collins, Colo., Marvin E. Knedler, *Progressive Architecture*, March 1971.

K. Proposed tower (1200 ft), Milan, Italy, Alberto Rosselli, *Art and Architecture*, November 1964.

L. House, Italy (4 stories), Paolo Portoghesi, Vittorio Gogliotti, *WERK*, February 1970.

M. Claredale Street building (15 stories), London, England, *Tall Buildings*, by A. Coull and B. Stafford Smith, eds., Pergamon Press, London, 1967.

N. Banco de Bilbao (25 stories), Madrid, Spain, *l'Architecture d'Aujourdhui*, December 1971.

O. Proposed St. Mark's Tower (20 stories), Frank Lloyd Wright, *Urban Space and Structures* by L. Martin and L. March, Cambridge University Press, London, 1972.

P. Las Torres Blancas (White Towers), (25 stories), Madrid, Spain, Javier Saenz de Oiza, *Forum*, August 1968; *Architectural Design*, September 1966.

Figure 5.10

A. Gas Building (28 stories), Detroit, Mich., Yamasaki and Associates, *Forum*, May 1963.

B. Osaka Kokussi Building (32 stories), Osaka, Japan, Takenaka Komuten Company, *Japan Architect*, June 1973.

C. Boston Company Building (41 stories), Boston, Pietro Belluschi and Emery Roth & Sons, *Building Case History 1*, Bethlehem Steel Corp., August 1970.

D. Royal Bank Building (41 stories), Montreal, Canada, I. M. Pei, *Planning and Design of Tall Buildings*, Vol. C, ASCE, IABSE, 1972.

E. Dresser Tower in Cullen Center (40 stories), Houston, Tex., Neuhaus and Taylor, *Building Case History 21*, Bethlehem Steel Corp., June 1972.

F. Chase Manhattan Bank Building (60 stories), New York, S.O.M., *Forum*, July 1961.

G. Washington Plaza Hotel (36 stories), Seattle, Wash., John Graham and Company, 1970.

H. One Chemung Canal Plaza (7 stories), Elmira, N.Y., Haskell and Conner and Frost, *Building Case History 23*, Bethlehem Steel Corp., August 1972.

I. Kaiser Center (27 stories), Oakland, Calif., Welton Becket and Associates.

J. Morningside House (20 stories), New York, Phillip Johnson and John Burgee, *L. Zetlin Publication*, Vol. 2, 1970.

Figure 5.15

A. Churchill Academic Tower (11 stories), Canisius College, Buffalo, N.Y., Leroy H. Welch, *Building Case History 18*, Bethlehem Steel Corp., March 1972.

B. Johnson Wax Building, Laboratory Tower (16 stories), Racine, Wis., Frank Lloyd Wright, *Contemporary Structure in Architecture* by Leonard Michaels, Reinhold, New York, 1950.

C. Highfield House (13 stories), Baltimore, Md., *Forum*, April 1968.

D. Nibelungen Building (393 ft), Frankfurt, Germany, Reference 5.3b.

E. Portland Plaza Condominium (25 stories), Portland, Ore., Daniel, Mann, Johnson and Mendenhall, *Architectural Record*, October 1973.

F. Building B, Santiago Central Development Program (24 stories), Santiago, Chile, Aguirre, Bolton, Prieto, Larrain, and Lorca, Reference 5.3.

G. Television Tower, Bratislava, Czechoslovakia, Reference 5.3c.

H. Tower 22, San Borja Residential Renewal Project (22 stories), Santiago, Chile, Sandoval and Vives, Reference 5.3.

I. Office Building G1, Olympic Village, Munich, Germany, Reference 5.3b.

J. Office Building of Deutsche Krankenversicherung, Cologne, Germany, Reference 5.3b.

K. Australia Square (45 stories), Sydney, Australia, Seidler and Associates, *Art and Architecture*, November 1965.

L. Tennessee Building (33 stories), Houston, Tex., S.O.M., *Forum*, September 1963.

M. Office Building of Continental Companies (23 stories), Chicago, C. F. Murphy and Associates, *Forum*, May 1963.

N. Point Royal (19 stories), Bracknell, England, S.O.M., *Canadian Architect*, September 1964.

O. U.S. Steel Building (64 stories), Pittsburgh, Harrison, Abramowitz, and Abbe, Architects, *Architectural Record*, April 1967.

P. Marina City Towers (60 stories), Chicago, Bertrand Goldberg and Associates, *Building Construction*, August 1961.

Q. Place Victoria (47 stories), Montreal, Canada, Nervi and Moretti, *Canadian Architecture*, July 1965.

R. EHG Enterprises (40 stories), Miami, Fla., James Chaplin, *Engineer*, July 1972.

S. I.D.S. Building (57 stories), Minneapolis, Minn., Phillip Johnson and John Burgee and John Baker Associates, *Architectural Record*, August 1970.

T. Lake Point Tower (70 stories), Chicago, Schipporeit and Heinrich, *Forum*, November 1967.

Figure 5.16

One Biscayne Tower (40 stories), Miami, Fla., Fraga Associates, *Archittural Record*, February 1974.

Figure 5.20

A. Brunswick Building (38 stories, 474 ft, concrete), Chicago, S.O.M., *Architectural and Engineering News*, October 1968.

B. Seattle First National Bank (50 stories, 620 ft, steel), Seattle, Wash., Naramore, Bain, Brady & Johnson, *Architectural Record*, June 1970.

C. One Shell Plaza (52 stories, 714 ft, concrete), S.O.M., *Forum*, April 1972.

D. Student project, I.I.T., "Optimizing the Structure of the Skyscraper," *Architectural Record*, October 1972.

E. Hancock Building (100 stories, 1100 ft, steel), S.O.M., *Forum*, July–August, 1970.

F. Standard Oil Building (83 stories, 1136 ft, steel), Chicago, Edward Durell Stone & Associates, *Engineering News Record*, November 1971.

G. World Trade Center (110 stories, 1350 ft, steel), New York, Minoru Yamasaki & Associates, *Civil Engineering Journal*, ASCE, June 1971.

H. Sears Building (109 stories, 1450 ft, steel), Chicago, S.O.M., *Civil Engineering Journal ASCE*, November 1972.

I.   Alcoa Building (26 stories), San Francisco, S.O.M., *AISC Contemporary Structures*, 1970.

J.   King County Administration Building (9 stories), Seattle, Wash., Harmon, Pray & Detrich, *Engineering News Record*, February 1970.

K.   IBM Building (13 stories), Pittsburgh, Curtis and Davis, *Progressive Architecture*, September 1962.

Figure 5.25

A.   Proposed apartment building (80 stories), Severud, Perrone, Sturm, Conlin, and Bandel, *Architectural Record*, August 1970.

B.   Proposed apartment building (92 stories), I.I.T. student project, *Architectural and Engineering News*, September 1966.

Figure 5.27

Office building (60 stories), Tokyo, Nikken Sekkei, *Engineering News Record*, April 1973.

Figure 5.28

Office building (40 stories), Charlotte, N.C., Thompson, Ventulett, & Stainback, *Engineering News Record*, October 1973.

Figure 5.29

Western Pennsylvania National Bank Building (32 stories), Pittsburgh, S.O.M., *Engineering News Record*, August 1973.

Figure 6.1

A.   American Broadcasting Company Building (576 ft, 55 stories), Los Angeles, Minoru Yamasaki & Associates, *Engineering News Record*, March 1974.

B.   Le France Building (44 stories), Paris, France, Jean de Mailly, *Engineering News Record*, May 1974; *Techniques & Architecture*, February 1973.

C.   Toronto City Hall (27 and 20 stories), Toronto, Canada, Viljo Revell, *Progressive Architecture*, March 1963; *Engineering News Record*, July 1965.

D.   First National Bank of Chicago (60 stories), Chicago, C. F. Murphy Associates, The Perkins & Will Partnership, *Architectural Record*, September 1970.

E.   Transamerica Building (50 stories, 853 ft), San Francisco, William L. Pereira & Associates, *Engineering News Record*, November 1971.

F.   Marina City Towers (60 stories), Chicago, Bertrand Goldberg, *Architectural Record*, September 1963.

Figure 8.2

A.   Earth Science Building (20 stories), M.I.T., Cambridge, Mass., I. M. Pei and Aldo Cossutta, *Building Skeletons*, Brian Shawcroft and students, Student Publication of the School of Design, Vol. 17, No. 1, North Carolina State University, 1967.

B.   Houston Lighting and Power Company Electric Tower (27 stories),

Houston, Tex., Wilson, Morris, Cain and Anderson, *Building Report*, Vol. 4, No. 1, American Iron and Steel Institute.

C. St. James Apartments (7 stories), Treasure Island, Fla., Edward Hanson, *Structural Report*, *United States Steel*, September 1972.

D. Two Turtle Creek Village (21 stories), Dallas, Tex., George L. Dahl, *Building Case History 20*, Bethlehem Steel Corp., May 1972.

E. Braniff Building (10 stories), Dallas, Tex., Lane, Gamble and Associates, *Save with Steel in Multi-Story Buildings*, AISC, December 1965.

F. Columbus and Southern Ohio Electric Building (9 stories), Columbus, Ohio, Edgar I. Williams, *Save with Steel in Multi-Story Buildings*, AISC, December 1965.

G. Wayne-Manchester Towers (8 stories), Silver Spring, Md., Cohen, Haft and Associates, *Save with Steel in Multi-Story Buildings*, AISC, December 1965.

H. Henry J. Pariseau Apartments (11 stories), Manchester, N.H., Isaak and Moyer, *Building Case History 30*, Bethlehem Steel Corp., July 1973.

I. 345 East 56th Street Building (21 stories), New York, Schuman and Lichtenstein, *Save with Steel in Multi-Story Buildings*, AISC, December 1965.

J. Parklane Towers (15 stories), Dearborn, Mich., Rossetti and Associates, *Building Case History 19*, Bethlehem Steel Corp., April 1972.

K. Boston Company Building (41 stories), Boston, Pietro Belluschi and Emery Roth & Sons, *Building Case History 1*, Bethlehem Steel Corp., August 1970.

L. U.S. Steel Office Building (64 stories), Pittsburgh, Harrison, Abramowitz and Abbe, Architects, *American Society of Civil Engineering Journal*, April 1970.

M. One Shell Plaza (52 stories), Houston, Tex., S.O.M., *Planning and Design of Tall Buildings*, Vol. C, ASCE, IABSE, 1972.

N. Standard Oil of Indiana Building (83 stories), Chicago Edward Durell Stone and the Perkins and Will Corp. *Journal of the Structural Division*, *ASCE*, April 1973.

O. Sears Tower (109 stories), Chicago, S.O.M., *The Engineering Journal*, *AISC*, Third Quarter, 1973.

Figure 8.3

A. Kingsway Development (15 stories), London, England, R. Seifer and Partners, *Planning and Design of Tall Buildings*, Vol. C, ASCE, IABSE, 1972.

B. CNA Regional Office Building (19 stories), Orlando, Fla., Reynolds, Smith and Hills, *Building Case History 13*, Bethlehem Steel Corp., October 1971.

C. Poudre Valley National Bank (10 stories including future additions), Fort Collins, Colo., James M. Hunter and Associates, *PCI Journal*, October 1967.

D. One Chemung Canal Plaza (7 stories), Elmira, N.Y., Haskell and Conner and Frost, *Building Case History 23*, Bethlehem Steel Corp., August 1972.

E. Tower Building in Australia Square (45 stories), Sydney, Australia, Seidler and Associates, *Planning and Design of Tall Buildings*, Vol. C, ASCE, IABSE, 1972.

F. M.L.C. Centre Proposal (65 stories), Sydney, Australia, Seidler and Associates, *Planning and Design of Tall Buildings*, Vol. C, ASCE, IABSE, 1972.

G. Knights of Columbus Building (23 stories), New Haven, Conn., Kevin Roche, John Dinkeloo Associates, *Progressive Architecture*, September 1970.

H. Millbanc Tower Block (34 stories), London, England, Ronald Ward and Partners, *Structural Engineer*, January 1962.

I. Churchill Academic Tower (11 stories), Canisius College, Buffalo, N.Y., Leroy H. Welch, *Building Case History 18*, Bethlehem Steel Corp., March 1972.

Figure 8.4

A. Life and Casualty Insurance Building (30 stories), Nashville, Tenn., *Engineering News Record*, September 1956.

B. Gensert, R. M., "High-Rise Apartment Structures of Steel," *Architectural and Engineering News*, November 1968; *Architectural Record*, November 1964.

C. Tower Building (18 stories), Little Rock, Ark., Harry A. Barry and Dallas and E. E. Withraw, *Save with Steel in Multi-Story Buildings*, AISC, December 1965.

D. IBM Building (13 stories), Pittsburgh, Curtis and Davis, United States Steel, August 1963.

E. World Trade Center (110 stories), New York, Minoru Yamasaki and Associates and Emery Roth & Sons, *Contemporary Steel Design*, AISI, Vol. 1, No. 4, 1965.

F. Equitable Life Building (25 stories), San Francisco, *Design of Steel Structures*, 2nd ed., by Boris Bresler, T. Y. Lin, and John B. Scalzi, Wiley, 1968.

Figure 8.5

A. Standard Oil of Indiana Building (83 stories), Chicago, Edward Durell Stone and The Perkins and Will Corp., *Structural System—Standard Oil of Indiana Building* by Alfred E. Picardi, *Journal of the Structural Division*, *ASCE*, Vol. 99, No. ST4, April 1973.

B. World Trade Center (110 stories), New York, Minoru Yamasaki and Associates and Emery Roth & Sons, *Contemporary Steel Design*, AISI, Vol. 1, No. 4, 1965.

C. Jacob Grossman and Robert Rosenwasser, "Composite Design Cuts Costs," *Modern Steel Construction*, AISC, Fourth Quarter, 1969.

D. Dresser Tower in Cullen Center (40 stories), Houston, Tex., Neuhas and Taylor, *Building Case History 21*, Bethlehem Steel Corp., June 1972.

E. Anthony F. Nassetta, "A New Look at Office Buildings: 3, Floor Systems, Wind Bracing, Fire Protection," *Architectural and Engineering News*, November 1968.

Figures 10.2 to 10.11

A. City Hall Center, Marl, Germany, J. H. van den Brock & J. B. Bakema, *Engineering News Record*, May 1965.

B. Lincoln Income Life Insurance Co., Louisville, Ky., Taliesin Associated Architects of the F.L.W. Associates, *Building Report*, AISI, Vol. 2, No. 2.

C. Standard Bank Building, Johannesburg, South Africa, A. Hentrick and Mallows, Stucke, Harrison, Riche & Partners, *Engineering News Record*, November 1968.

D. Holiday Inn, Huntington, W.Va., Cann-Termohlen, with International Environmental Dynamics, *Engineering News Record*, April 1973.

E. Security National Bank, Huntington, N.Y., The Eggars Partnership–Lev Zetlin Associates, *Building Design and Construction*, June 1971.

F. Lincoln Savings and Loan Association, Sherman Oaks, Calif., Deasy and Bolling, *Modern Steel Construction*, *AISI*, Fourth Quarter, 1966.

G. Armstrong Rubber Company, New Haven, Conn., Marcel Breuer and Robert Gatje, *Building Case History 4*, Bethlehem Steel Corp., August 1970.

H. Phillips Administration Building, Eindhoven, the Netherlands, Verhave, Luit and deJong.

I. British Petroleum Ltd., Antwerp, Belgium. Leon M. J. R. Stynen, Paul de Meyer and J. Reusens, Progressive Architecture, September 1961.

J. Ohio Presbyterian Homes, Rockynol, Ohio, Samborn, Steketee, Otis and Evans, *Engineering News Record*, December 1965.

K. Westcoast Office Building, Vancouver, B.C., Canada, Rhone and Iredale and B. Babicki and Associates, *Engineering News Record*, June 1969; *Progressive Architecture*, October 1969.

L. Bavarian Motor Works, Munich, West Germany, Karl Schwanzer, *Engineering News Record*, March 1972; *Architectural Record*, July 1973.

M. Federal Reserve Bank of Minneapolis, Minn., Gunnar Birkerts and Associates, *Architectural Record*, October 1971; *Architectural Record*, November 1973; *Engineering News Record*, November 1973.

References

Chapter 2

2.1. American Society of Civil Engineers, International Association for Bridge and Structural Engineering: Proceedings of the International Conference on Planning and Design of Tall Buildings, Vol. 1b, *Tall Building Criteria and Loading*, Lehigh University, Bethlehem, Pa., 1972.

a. Johnson, Sidney M.: "Dead, Live and Construction Loads," *State of Art Report*, No. 3.

b. Mainstone, Rowland J.: "Internal Blast," *State of Art Report*, No. 6.

c. Mitchell, G. R.: "Loadings on Buildings," *State of Art Report*, No. 2a.

d. Newmark, Nathan M.: "External Blast," *State of Art Report*, No. 7.

e. Reese, Raymond C.: "Gravity Loads and Temperature Effects," *Theme Report*.

2.2. Aynsley, Richard M.: "Wind Effects Around Buildings," *Architectural Science Review*, March 1972.

2.3. Aynsley, Richard M.: "Wind Effects on High and Lowrise Housing," *Architectural Science Review*, September 1973.

2.4. Berg, Glen V.: "Designing for Earthquakes," *Contemporary Steel Design*, Vol. 2, No. 3, American Iron and Steel Institute, New York.

2.5. Brisker, Sydney H.: "With Wind Tunnels, Design Is a Breeze," *Progressive Architecture*, March 1967.

2.6. Chang, Fu-kuei: "Human Response to Motions in Tall Buildings," *Journal of the Structural Division, ASCE*, Vol. 99, No. ST6, June 1973.

2.7. Coull, A. and Smith, B. Stafford, eds.: *Tall Buildings*, Pergamon Press, London, 1967.

a. Davenport, A. G.: "The Treatment of Wind Loading on Tall Buildings."

2.8. "Dampers Blunt the Wind's Force on Tall Buildings," *Architectural Record*, September 1971.

2.9. Degenkolb, Henry J.: "Earthquake Forces on Tall Structures," Bethlehem Steel, Booklet 2717, 1970.

2.10. Dym, Clive L. and Klabin, Don: "Architectural Implications of Structural Vibration," *Architectural Record*, September 1975.

2.11. Fintel, Mark and Khan, Fazlur R.: "Thermal Effects of Column Exposure in Highrise Structures," *Building Research*, September–October, 1967.

2.12. Hansen, Robert J., Reed, John W., and Vanmarcke, Erik H.: "Human Response to Wind-Induced Motion of Buildings," *Journal of the Structural Division*, *ASCE*, Vol. 99, No. ST7, July 1973.

2.13. International Conference of Building Officials: Uniform Building Code, Section 2312, 1967 edition.

2.14. O'Hare, Michael: "Designing with Wind Tunnels," *Forum*, April 1968.

2.15. O'Hare, Michael: "Wind Whistles Through M.I.T. Tower," *Progressive Architecture*, March 1967.

2.16. Rutes, W. A.: "A New Look at Office Buildings: 2," *Architectural and Engineering News*, October 1968.

2.17. State of New York, Housing and Building Code Bureau: *State Building Construction Code*, Albany, 1972.

2.18. Steinbrugge, Karl V.: "Earthquake Damage and Structural Performance in the United States," Robert L. Wigel, ed.: *Earthquake Engineering*, Prentice-Hall, Englewood Cliffs, N.J., 1970.

2.19. "Temperature Effects on Tall Steel Framed Buildings," *AISC Journal*, October 1973.

a. Khan, F. R., and Nasetta, A. F.: "Design Considerations," Part 3.

b. McLaughlin, E. R.: "Response of Steel Columns to Temperature Exposure," Part 1.

2.20. "Wind, Sun, Rain and the Exterior Wall," *Architectural Record*, Special Report No. 2, September 1967.

2.21. Yanev, Peter: *Peace of Mind in Earthquake Country*, Chronicle Books, San Francisco, 1974.

Chapter 3

3.1. American Society of Civil Engineers, International Association for Bridge and Structural Engineering: Proceedings of the International Conference on Planning and Design of Tall Buildings, Vol. 1a, *Tall Building Systems and Concepts*, Lehigh University, Bethlehem, Pa., 1972.

a. Daryanani, Sital: "Heating, Ventilating and Air Conditioning (HVAC)," *State of Art Report*, No. 2. Technical Committee No. 2

b. Fitzsimons, Neal: "The History and Philosophy of Tall Buildings," *State of Art Report*, No. 1.

c. Halpern, Richard C.: "Control of the Construction Process," *State of the Art Report*, No. 2. Technical Committee No. 4

d. Kozak, Jiri: "Structural Systems of Tall Buildings with Core Structures," *State of Art Report*, No. 8.

e. Steyert, Richard D.: "The Economics of Highrise Apartment Buildings," *State of Art Report*, No. 4A. Technical Committee No. 1

f. Thoma, Rudiger: "Service Systems in Relation to Architecture," *State of Art Report*, No. 1.

g. White, Edward E.: "Foundations," *State of Art Report*, No. 4A. Technical Committee No. 4

3.2. Farkas, Nicholas: "Selecting the Framing System," *Architectural and Engineering News*, September 1966.

3.3. Giedion, Sigfried: *Space, Time and Architecture*, 5th ed., Harvard University Press, Cambridge, Mass., 1967.

3.4. Ruderman, James: "Comparing Highrise Structural Systems," *Architectural and Engineering News*, September 1965.

3.5. Thomsen, Charles: "How High to Rise," *AIA Journal*, April 1965.

Chapter 4

4.1. American Society of Civil Engineers, International Association for Bridge and Structural Engineering: Proceedings of the International Conference on Planning and Design of Tall Buildings, Vol. III, *Structural Design of Tall Concrete and Masonry Buildings*, Lehigh University, Bethlehem, Pa., 1972.

   a. Brakel, J.: "List of Limit States," *State of the Art Report*, No. 2.

4.2. Coull, A. and Smith, Stafford, B., eds.: *Tall Buildings*, Pergamon Press, London, 1967.

   a. Frischmann, Wilem W. and Prabhu, Sudhakar A.: "Planning Concepts Using Shear Walls."
   b. Frischmann, Wilem W. and Prabhu, Sudhakar S.: "Shear Wall Structures—Design and Construction Problems."

4.3. Engel, Heinrich: *Structure Systems*, Praeger, New York, 1967.

4.4. Gaylord, Edwin H., Jr., and Gaylord, Charles N.: *Design of Steel Structures*, 2nd ed., McGraw-Hill, New York, 1972.

4.5. Henn, Walter: *Buildings for Industry*, Vol. 1, "Plans, Structures and Details," Iliffe Books, London, 1965.

4.6. *Precast and Prestressed Concrete*, *PCI Design Handbook*, Prestressed Concrete Institute, Chicago, 1971.

4.7. "Research Leads to a Bolder Expression of the Steel Frame," *Architectural Record*, July 1973.

4.8. Rutes, W. A.: "A New Look at Office Buildings: 2," *Architectural and Engineering News*, October 1968.

4.9. Salvadori, Mario and Levy, Matthys: *Structural Design in Architecture*, Prentice-Hall, Englewood Cliffs, N.J., 1967.

4.10. Siegel, Curt: *Structure and Form in Modern Architecture*, Reinhold, New York, 1962.

Chapter 5

5.1. American Concrete Institute Committee 442: "Response of Building to Lateral Forces," No. 68-11, American Concrete Institute Journal, February 1971.

5.2. American Institute of Steel Construction: "Less Steel per Square Foot," *Modern Steel Construction*, First Quarter, 1972.

5.3. American Society of Civil Engineers, International Association for Bridge and Structural Engineering: Proceedings of the International Conference on Planning and Design of Tall Buildings, Vol. 1a: *Tall Building Systems and Concepts*, Lehigh University, Bethlehem, Pa., 1972.

   a. Christiansen, John V.: "Cast in Place Reinforced Concrete Systems," *State of Art Report*, No. 2.
   b. Konig, Gert: "Cast in Place Reinforced Concrete Systems," *State of Art Report*, No. 7.
   c. Kozak, Jiri: "Structural Systems of Tall Buildings with Core Structures," *State of Art Report*, No. 8.
   d. Yorkdale, Alan: "Masonry Building Systems," *State of Art Report*, No. 9.

5.4. ASCE, IABSE: Proceedings of the International Conference on Planning and Design of Tall Buildings, Vol. II: *Structural Design of Tall Steel Buildings*, Lehigh University, Bethlehem, Pa., 1972.

a. Iyengar, S. Hal: "Preliminary Design and Optimization of Steel Building Systems," *State of Art Report*, No. 3.

b. Scalzi, John B. and Arndt, Arthur P.: "Plate Wall Cladding," *State of Art Report*, No. 3B.

5.5. ASCE, IABSE, Proceedings of the International Conference on Planning and Design of Tall Buildings, Vol. III: *Structural Design of Tall Concrete and Masonry Buildings*, Lehigh University, Bethlehem, Pa., 1972.

a. Smith, Bryan Stafford and Coull, Alex: "Elastic Analysis of Tall Concrete Buildings," *State of Art Report*, No. 1.

b. Sutherland, R. J. M.: "Structural Design of Masonry Buildings," *State of Art Report*, No. 4.

5.6. Belford, Don: "Composite Steel—Concrete Building Frame," *Civil Engineering Journal*, *ASCE*, Vol. 42, No. 7, July 1972.

5.7. Coull, A. and Smith, B. Stafford, eds.: *Tall Buildings*, Pergamon Press, London, 1967.

a. Khan, Fazlur R.: "Current Trends in Concrete Highrise Buildings," Appendix I.

b. Robertson, Leslie E.: "On Tall Buildings," Appendix II.

5.8. Dikkers, Robert D.: "Brick Bearing Walls for Multistory Structures," *Civil Engineering Journal*, *ASCE*, September 1966.

5.9. Friedlander, Gordon D.: "New Horizons in Structural Steel," *AIA Journal*, February 1972.

5.10. Gensert, Richard M.: "Apartment Framing to Resist Wind," *Architectural Record*, January 1963.

5.11. Gensert, Richard M.: "Highrise Apartment Structures of Masonry," *Architectural Record*, February 1965.

5.12. Gensert, Richard M.: "Versatile Structures for Apartment Framing," *Architectural Record*, July 1964.

5.13. Khan, Fazlur: "The Bearing Wall," *Architectural and Engineering News*, September 1966.

5.14. Khan, Fazlur: "The Bearing Wall Comes of Age," *Architectural and Engineering News*, October 1968.

5.15. Khan, Fazlur R.: "The Future of Highrise Structures," *Progressive Architecture*, November 1972.

5.16. Macsai, John: *Highrise Apartment Buildings—A Design Primer*, John Macsai Publisher, Chicago, 1972.

5.17. "Optimizing Structural Design in Very Tall Buildings," *Architectural Record*, August 1972.

5.18. "Optimizing the Structure of the Skyscraper," *Architectural Record*, October 1972.

5.19. Scalzi, John B.: "Drift in Highrise Steel Framing," *Progressive Architecture*, April 1972.

5.20. "Staggered Truss Framing Systems for Highrise Buildings," United States Steel Technical Report, May 1971.

5.21. Tarics, Alexander G.: "Concrete-Filled Steel Columns for Multistory Construction," *Modern Steel Construction*, *AISC*, Vol. 12, First Quarter, 1972.

5.22. Viest, Ivan, Chairman: "Composite Steel–Concrete Construction," Subcommittee on the State of the Art Survey, Task Committee on Composite Construction, of the Committee on Metal, Structural Division, *Journal of the Structural Division*, *ASCE*, Vol. 100, No. ST5, Proc. Paper 10561, May 1974.

Chapter 6

6.1. "Dampers Blunt the Wind's Force on Tall Buildings," *Architectural Record*, September 1971.

6.2. Khan, Fazlur: "The Future of Highrise Structures," *Progressive Architecture*, October 1972.

6.3. Robertson, Leslie: "Heights We Can Reach," *AIA Journal*, January 1973.

6.4. Scalzi, John B.: "Drift in Highrise Steel Framing," *Progressive Architecture*, April 1972.

6.5. Zuk, William: "Kinetic Structures," *Civil Engineering Journal*, *ASCE*, December 1968.

Chapter 7

7.1. Anderson, Paul and Nordby, Gene M.: *Introduction to Structural Mechanics*, Ronald Press, New York, 1960.

7.2. Ben-Arroyo, Abraham: "Preliminary Wind Analysis of Multistory Bents," *AISC Engineering Journal*, January 1970.

7.3. Fisher, R., ed.: *New Structures*, McGraw-Hill, New York, 1964.

a. Davidson, R. L. and Monk, C. B.: "Thin Brick Walls Are the Only Support in a Design for Multi-Story Buildings."

7.4. Gaylord, Edwin H., Jr. and Gaylord, Charles N.: *Design of Steel Structures*, 2nd ed., McGraw-Hill, New York, 1972.

7.5. Grogan, John C.: "Load Bearing Masonry Systems," *Architectural and Engineering News*, September 1965.

7.6. Gross, James G.: "Designing Load Bearing Brick Walls," *Architectural and Engineering News*, July 1966.

7.7. Hong, Morris L.: "Designing Steel Columns: A Simplified Method," *Architectural and Engineering News*, September 1966.

7.8. Howard, Seymour H., Jr.: *Structure: An Architect's Approach*, McGraw-Hill, New York, 1966.

7.9. McCormac, Jack C.: *Structural Analysis*, 2nd ed., Intext, Scranton, Pa., 1967.

7.10. McCormac, Jack C.: *Structural Steel Design*, 2nd ed., Intext, Scranton, Pa., 1971.

7.11. Morris, Charles Head and Benson, Wilbur: *Elementary Structural Analysis*, 2nd ed., McGraw-Hill, New York, 1960.

7.12. "Preliminary Design of the Contemporary Bearing Wall," *Technical Notes on Brick and Tile Construction*, *24A*, Structural Clay Products Institute, March–April, 1966.

7.13. *Recommended Practice for Engineered Brick Masonry*, Structural Clay Products Institute, 1969.

7.14. Richardson, Gordon and Associates: "Welded Tier Buildings," *United States Steel Structural Report*, May 1963.

7.15. Salvadori, Mario and Levy, Matthys: *Structural Design in Architecture*, Prentice-Hall, Englewood Cliffs, N.J., 1967.

7.16. *State Building Construction Code*, State of New York, Housing and Building Code Bureau, Albany, July 1972.

7.17. White, Richard N., Gergely, Peter, and Sexsmith, Robert G.: *Structural Engineering*, Vol. 1: *Introduction to Design Concepts and Analysis*, Wiley, New York, 1972.

Chapter 8

8.1. "Composite Structures: Definition and Types," *The Architects' Journal*, July 1973.

8.2. Dallaire, E. E.: "Cellular Steel Floors Mature," *Civil Engineering Journal, ASCE*, July 1971.

8.3. Henn, Walter: *Buildings for Industry*, Vol. 1, "Plans, Structures and Details," Iliffe Books, London, 1965.

8.4. Iyengar, Hal S.: "Bundled-tube Structure for Sears Tower," *Civil Engineering Journal, ASCE*, November 1972.

8.5. Khan, Fazlur: "The Bearing Wall Comes of Age," *Architectural and Engineering News*, October 1968.

8.6. Macsai, John: *Highrise Apartment Building—A Design Primer*, John Macsai Publisher, Chicago, 1972.

8.7. Nassetta, F. Anthony: "A New Look at Office Buildings: 3, Floor System, Wind Bracing, Fire Protection," *Architectural and Engineering News*, November 1968.

8.8. Salmon, G. C. and Johnson, J. E.: *Steel Structures Design and Behavior*, Intext, Scranton, Pa., 1971.

8.9. Subcommittee on the State of the Art Survey, of the Task Committee on Composite Construction: "Composite Steel–Concrete Construction," *Journal of the Structural Division, ASCE*, Vol. 100, No. ST5, Proc. Paper 10561, May 1974.

Chapter 9

9.1. *Architectural Precast Concrete*, Prestressed Concrete Institute, Chicago, 1973.

9.2. *Building Blocks: Design Potentials and Constraints*, Office of Regional Resources and Development Center for Urban Development Research, Cornell University, Ithaca, N.Y., 1971.

9.3. Cutler, S. Laurence and Cutler, S. Sherrie: *Handbook of Housing Systems for Designers and Developers*, Van Nostrand Reinhold, New York, 1974.

9.4. Henn, Walter: *Buildings for Industry*, Vol. 1, "Plans, Structures and Details," Iliffe Books, London, 1965.

9.5. Koncz, Tihamer: *Manual of Precast Concrete Construction*, Bauverlag GmBH, Wiesbaden, Germany.

a. Vol. 1: *Principles—Roof and Floor Units—Wall Panels*, 1968.

b. Vol. 2: *Industrial Shed-type and Lowrise Buildings—Special Structures*, 1971.

c. Vol. 3: *System Building with Large Panels*, 1970.

9.6. *The New Building Block: A Report on the Factory-Produced Dwelling Module*, Research Report No. 8, Center for Housing and Environmental Studies, Cornell University, Ithaca, N.Y., 1968.

9.7. "Pre-Fab Metal Walls," *American Metal Market–Metalworking News*, July 17, 1973.

9.8. Reidelbach, A. J., Jr.: *Modular Housing in the Real*, Modco, Annandale, Va., 1970.

9.9. Svec, J. J. and Jeffers, P. E., eds.: *Modern Masonry Panel Construction Systems*, Cahner, Boston, 1972.

9.10. "Systems Building," *Engineering News Record*, October 30, 1969.

9.11. "Toward More Effective Use of Aluminum: A Thin-Skin Load-bearing Wall," *Architectural Record*, January 1970.

Chapter 10

10.1. "Cape Kennedy," *Architectural Forum*, January–February, 1967.

10.2. Cook, Peter: *Experimental Architecture*, Universe Books, New York, 1970.

10.3. Dahinden, Justus: *Urban Structures of the Future*, Praeger, New York, 1972.

10.4. Engel, Heinrich: *Structure Systems*, Praeger, New York, 1968.

10.5. Günschel, Günter: "Systems Geodesiques Composites," *Techniques and Architecture*, February 1973.

10.6. Exhibition catalog of Kunstverein, Hannover: *Kenneth Snelson*, Hannover, Germany, 1971.

10.7. "Kurokawa and his Capsules," *Architectural Record*, February 1973.

10.8. Lehman, Conrad Roland: "Multi-Story Suspension Structures," *Architectural Design*, November 1963.

10.9. Minke, Gernot: "Hanging Flats," *Architectural Design*, April 1968.

10.10 Pohl, Jens G. and Cowan, J. H.: "Multi-story Air-Supported Building Construction," *Build International*, March–April, 1972.

10.11. Smith, Peter R. and Pohl, Jens G.: "Pneumatic Construction Applied to Multistory Buildings," *Progressive Architecture*, September 1970.

10.12. Swenson, Alfred: "The 150-Story Superframe Tower," *Architectural Forum*, September 1971.

10.13. Tigerman, Stanley: "Instant City," *Arts and Architecture*, June 1966.

Index

For location and names of most buildings and architects refer to the List of Building Illustrations.